Broadening and Deepening Democracy

Exploring the Political in South Asia

Series Editor: Mukulika Banerjee
                 Reader in Anthropology, University College
                 London.

Exploring the Political in South Asia is devoted to the publication of research on the political cultures of the region. The books in this Series will present qualitative and quantitative analyses grounded in field research, and will explore the cultures of democracies in their everyday local settings, specifically the workings of modern political institutions, practices of political mobilisation, manoeuvres of high politics, structures of popular beliefs, content of political ideologies and styles of political leadership, amongst others. Through fine-grained descriptions of particular settings in South Asia, the studies presented in this Series will inform, and have implications for, general discussions of democracy and politics elsewhere in the world.

Also in this Series

The Vernacularisation of Democracy: Politics, Caste and Religion in India
Lucia Michelutti
ISBN: 978-0-415-46732-2

Rise of the Plebeians? The Changing Face of Indian Legislative Assemblies
(Eds) Christophe Jaffrelot and Sanjay Kumar
ISBN: 978-0-415-46092-7

Broadening and Deepening Democracy

Political Innovation in Karnataka

E. Raghavan
James Manor

Routledge
Taylor & Francis Group

LONDON AND NEW YORK

First published 2009
by Routledge

2 Park Square, Milton Park, Abingdon, Oxfordshire OX14 4RN
711 Third Avenue, New York, NY 10017

Routledge is an imprint of the Taylor & Francis Group, an informa business

First issued in paperback 2018

Transferred to Digital Printing 2009

Typeset by
Star Compugraphics Private Limited
D–156, Second Floor
Sector 7, Noida 201 301

British Library Cataloguing-in-Publication Data
A catalogue record of this book is available from the British Library

ISBN: 978-0-415-54454-2 (hbk)
ISBN: 978-1-138-38422-4 (pbk)

To our families

Contents

List of Tables

List of Abbreviations

AIADMK	All India Anna Dravida Munnetra Kazhagam
BDO	Block Development Officer
BJP	Bharatiya Janata Party
BSP	Bahujan Samaj Party
CPI	Communist Party of India
CPI (M)	Communist Party of India (Marxist)
DMK	Dravida Munnetra Kazhagam
MP	Member of Parliament
RSS	Rashtriya Swayamsevak Sangh
TDP	Telugu Desam Party
UP	Uttar Pradesh

Glossary

Adivasis	Scheduled Tribes
boosa	Cattle-feed
chaku-churi	Knife and dagger
Dalits	Scheduled Castes
dharna	A sit-in strike; a protest
gherao	To take someone temporary prisoner, in order to register a point
goonda	A thug
jati	An endogamous caste group, that is, a group within which people find marriage partners for their children.
kurta	Shirt
Lok Sabha	The Lower House of the Indian Parliament
Lokayukta	The state's obudsman
math	Monastery
Mandal Panchayats	Elected councils at local levels
mela	A mass gathering
neeru	Kannada for water
Nyaya Panchayats	Village councils to settle petty disputes
panchayat	Village council
pooja	An act of worship; reverential observance
pradhan	Leader
ragi	A millet much grown in India
Raj Bhavan	The common name of the official residence of the state Governors in India
Rajya Sabha	The Upper House of the Indian Parliament
Rashtrapati Bhavan	The official residence of India's President.
sab	A corrupted variant of the Urdu word *saheb,* used as a form of address to people of rank
satyagraha	A campaign of non-violent civil disobedience.
swamiji	Often a form of address for a Hindu religious instructor
taluk	sub-district

Taluk Panchayat Samitis	Elected councils at the sub-district level
vanavas	Literally, living in a forest; figuratively, banishment
Veerasaivism	A religious reform movement within Hinduism
Vidhana Souda	The Karnataka state assembly building
Zilla Parishads	Elected councils at the district level

Foreword

This third book in the series *Exploring the Political in South Asia* is a truly unusual one in the field of Indian politics. Eschewing analysis at the level of generalities and national trends, the authors of this book turn their scholarly attention to a single state — Karnataka, in southern India — and its politics. This is one of the larger states in India, and Raghavan and Manor bring together their formidable knowledge, gathered during their parallel careers in journalism and academia, to provide an accessible and exciting text that provides an explanation for why the state has enjoyed an unusual stability and relative prosperity in a progressively democratising climate, compared to several other states within the Indian union.

Karnataka makes for an interesting case on account of an unusual political past. Despite being a predominantly rural state, the incidence of landlessness here has been amongst the lowest in the country, the ruling classes of the princely state of Mysore were not linked to dominant castes, franchise had been introduced remarkably early (in 1882), and the local rulers developed a distinct style of statecraft that involved anticipation and defusing of conflict. The authors demonstrate the notable persistence of this manner of statecraft into the post-independence period. They do this by looking in detail at the role of three men who have served as Chief Ministers of the state: Devaraj Urs, Ramakrishna Hegde and Gundu Rao, in the two decades of the 1970s and 1980s. The first two are the heroes of this story, men who had the political nous and vision to preserve and perpetuate the political traditions of their predecessors. The authors argue that on their watch, three major changes took place: the dominance of the Lingayats and Vokkaligas gave way to coalitions of greater diversity of social groups; voters gained a genuine choice after 1983 as the dominance of the Congress Party was broken; and the centralised and top-heavy bureaucratic system gave way to greater powers at local levels. The authors show how Urs and Hegde *broadened* and *deepened* democracy through a number of different strategies, all of which have stopped Karnataka going the way of some other Indian states where power has become over-centralised or where political parties have come to be associated with particular caste groups. Instead, the accommodative tradition of politics in Karnataka has forced leaders of all major political parties to cultivate support from all and the *same* social groups, thereby avoiding narrow sectional interests to a large extent. This study also provides another example of how the 'Congress system' worked after independence in this part of the country where, ironically, it was responsible for bringing in Brahmin dominance that was otherwise absent in colonial Mysore because of the prescient strategies of its ruling classes of including all caste groups into the state administration.

This book is therefore enjoyable for a number of reasons. It doesn't shy away from focusing on the role of individual leaders in shaping history, but does so within the context of a developing political tradition and without hiding any of the machinations of *realpolitik* they had, perforce, to have engineered. To not do so, they point out, is to write Hamlet without the Prince. In any other country, politicians such as Ramakrishna Hegde and Devaraj Urs would not be relegated to the role of 'regional' — and by implication 'minor' — politicians, and thereby ignored in scholarly writings. Their policies affected very large numbers of people and as this book demonstrates, their careers display the heady mix of vision, guile and charisma that makes for compelling political stories. Further, by taking the state as a unit of study, this book gives due recognition to the fact that Indian states are large and populous political units that merit individual attention. To put things in perspective, Karnataka's population is nearly the same as the combined population of Canada, Australia and New Zealand. In size, it is larger than all but two countries in Africa, and all but four amongst the countries of Asia and Latin America. It is therefore time that historians and social scientists pay more attention to the study of individual Indian states, and much-needed political biographies of politicians emerge. In this, we hope, this book will be a trendsetter. By focusing on one particular state, and by looking at the continuities and discontinuities between the colonial past and the democratic present, it is possible to identify, as Manor and Raghavan have done, the development of particular 'habits of statecraft' that are unique to particular settings.

Finally, this book provides an excellent example of how elusive social equality can be brought about in the context of a democracy that guarantees only political equality. The story of Karnataka's politics shows how political changes can generate social changes over time. While not directly linked, in the case of Karnataka it is now possible to see that the result of caste hierarchies being challenged, when combined with the spread of education and the weakening association of castes with occupations, can begin to change the status quo.

London   **Mukulika Banerjee**
June 2009

Preface

It is important to stress that most of this text has been written by E. Raghavan. James Manor has contributed numerous passages which seek to situate this story in the social science literature, in Karnataka's recent history, and in comparative context alongside other Indian states, and sometimes other countries. And since he has been a witness, intermittently, to many important events in this story, he has also contributed to the accounts of them. He has interviewed hundreds of political actors in the state over the last 35 years, and material from those encounters appears here.

But Raghavan has been no intermittent witness. As a journalist, he has been immersed in the political affairs of Karnataka day in and day out, since 1972, when the story that we tell here begins. When interviews conducted by Manor are used, he is named, to distinguish these from the more abundant material collected by Raghavan.

To tell this story properly, it is necessary to refer to certain people and things that are largely unknown to Indian readers outside Karnataka, and completely new to readers outside India. We have therefore provided detailed footnotes to clarify matters for both sets of readers.

The authors are grateful to the Institute of Development Studies, University of Sussex, for providing a visiting fellowship to Raghavan. It enabled him to spend an extended period in England, comparing notes with Manor as he wrote most of the text. We are also grateful to the Institute for Social and Economic Change, Bangalore, which provided Manor with a visiting professorship that enabled the authors to meet frequently during 2006 and 2007.

This book is in part the product of three decades of discussions between the two authors: a journalist who has sought to be analytical, and an academic who has tried not to be obscure. Readers may judge for themselves whether they have succeeded in these aspirations.

Bangalore   **E.R. and J.M.**
June 2009

Introduction

Democracy had come a long way in Karnataka during the first two decades after India's Constitution came into force in 1950. On four occasions, free and fair elections to the Indian Parliament and the state's own legislative assembly within this federal system had occurred, with high turnouts by international standards. A political awakening had occurred throughout society, so that low-status groups no longer allowed land-owning castes, who dominated village society in this predominantly rural state, to influence their votes, as they had done in earlier elections. The same could be said of elections to local bodies: city and town councils in urban centres, and village councils or *panchayats* in rural areas. (Indeed, the first election in India based on mass franchise had occurred in the Bangalore municipality in 1951, several months before the first general election in 1952.) Politicians in this state had also established their pre-eminence over civil servants, had become acutely aware of the need to respond to important interest groups, and had become quite sophisticated in the art of doing so.

But in 1970, democracy in Karnataka stopped short of full maturity in three important ways.

- Despite the political awakening, two clusters of land-owning castes — the Lingayats and the Vokkaligas — were still able to translate their dominance at the local level into control over state-level politics. They saw to it that the lion's share of the political spoils flowed to their own respective castes. The remaining three-quarters of the population had to make do with half measures or, often, mere tokenism.
- Meaningful competition between political parties had yet to occur. The Congress Party dominated politics, and was in turn dominated by the Lingayats and Vokkaligas. Its formidable political 'machine' distributed the spoils mainly to these two castes and depended on their (diminishing) influence among the rural majority to achieve majorities in the state assembly. Opposition parties had long existed and fought gamely, but had found it impossible to dent the Congress dominance.

- Democracy at the local level had withered. Local bodies, especially in rural areas, had never been given significant powers. And the state government had acquired the habit — common in most other Indian states as well — of failing to hold local elections so that, for long periods, affairs at the grassroots were managed by bureaucrats who were answerable only to higher levels. Power had thus become over-centralised.

This book examines how, between the early 1970s and the late 1980s, these three things changed, that is, how democracy in Karnataka achieved robust maturity on all these fronts. By 1989, three historic changes, which are also our main themes, had occurred.

- The control which the Lingayats and Vokkaligas had exercised over state politics had been broken, and was replaced by a system in which power was widely shared within very broad, rainbow coalitions of interest groups, broadening and deepening democracy.
- The dominance which the Congress Party had exercised over Karnataka's politics until 1983 had given way to a competitive party system, giving voters a genuine choice between plausible alternatives in each subsequent election.
- The highly centralised political system in which immense powers were concentrated at the state level had been brought to an end after 1983, as substantial powers were transferred to elected councils at lower levels, thereby deepening democracy further.

These three changes added up to a 'transformation' of politics in Karnataka. But it is important to stress that this was a political, and not a social, transformation. It did not produce marked changes in social relations within villages or urban centres. Significant social change occurred eventually, as the power of caste hierarchies waned. It was partly driven by these political changes, but other factors, especially the spread of education, and the breakdown of the old system in which various castes stuck to their traditional occupations played an even more important role. But even though this transformation was limited to political arrangements, it still made an important difference to the lives of many ordinary people, especially low-status groups. Moreover, it occurred in Karnataka earlier than in almost all other Indian states.

How did this transformation happen? Why here, in this comparatively quiet corner of south India? The explanation owes much to the imaginative machinations of two remarkable politicians who served as Chief Ministers of Karnataka for most of the period covered here: D. Devaraj Urs (1972–80), Ramakrishna Hegde (1983–88) and, ironically, to the hapless actions of a third Chief Minister, R. Gundu Rao, who held power between 1980 and 1983. But, in attributing the political transformation to the manoeuvres of these three politicians, we are not trying to revive the 'great man' theory of history. Other things also had an immense impact: the complex political processes and the interplay of social forces that evolved under these leaders, and not least, the political tradition that had developed in Karnataka before 1970, which we discuss in some detail in the following section.

A Tradition of Political Accommodation: Reforming to Anticipate Conflict

Since the 1880s, this part of India has mostly experienced reasonably enlightened government, first under princely rule (in the state known as 'Mysore', which is roughly the southern-half of present-day Karnataka) before independence, and thereafter under democratic regimes. The political tone of these regimes was strongly influenced by the traditions established in princely Mysore. Even during the Emergency (1975–77), which brought outrageous abuses to most of India, Karnataka was spared excesses by a canny, humane Chief Minister, as we shall see in Chapter 2.

Unlike their counterparts in many other parts of India, the former princely rulers here had no connections to the dominant castes on the land. They were thus unable to anchor their power in kinship ties to the rural elite. They needed a different strategy to establish their legitimacy. The one that they chose had three core elements. First, they tended to pursue political accommodation: bargains and understandings based on shared interests. They were especially careful to attend to the interests of the Lingayats and the Vokkaligas, but this accommodative approach embraced many other groups as well. It fostered a spirit of give and take, and avoided winner-takes-all attitudes that produce bitterness and politically dangerous alienation among losers. The second strand in the princely rulers' strategy was enlightened governance: greater political openness and inclusion than existed anywhere else in princely India (which accounted for about one-third of the subcontinent before independence) to counteract alienation, especially among the landed castes and the urban middle classes, but also among disadvantaged groups. Indeed, at times, they went further than the British did in the parts of India which they administered directly. Finally, the maharajas (princes) took anticipatory action to defuse potential conflicts before they became acute and damaging. These three principles — political accommodation, enlightened governance, and reform to anticipate and defuse conflict — lived on, as widely understood ideals, after independence.

What specific actions did the princes take in pursuit of these three strands in their strategy? To encourage accommodative politics, they took steps that are decidedly modest by today's standards, but even these limited initiatives were quite remarkable given the (often vile) autocracies in most other princely states. They created a Representative Assembly at the state level in 1882 — an astonishingly early date. It was elected on a very limited franchise and had only minimal powers, but it marked this princely state out as the most progressive in India. Thereafter, elected councils were created lower down at the district level, and these had greater substance than in any other princely state. These actions helped to establish the maharajas' reputation for accommodative, enlightened governance.

To entrench the spirit of accommodation still further, they made gradual (and thus non-disruptive) changes to ease resentments which might have led to conflict that could have damaged the social fabric and made politics uncivilised. The most notable of these occurred during the 1920s, which is, again, an astonishingly early date. Until that time, the upper tier of the state's civil service had been heavily dominated by south Indian Brahmins, who stood at the apex of the traditional caste hierarchy and who had been much quicker than other castes to obtain Western-style education. But this posed a political dilemma for the state's princely rulers (who were non-Brahmins), because Brahmins represented less than 4 per cent of the state's population. They faced a clamour from the educated elite among non-Brahmins for a greater role in the administration. After inviting a committee headed by a British judge to consider the issue, Maharaja Krishnaraja Wadiyar IV opened the public service to less exalted groups in the caste hierarchy, anticipating by decades similar actions elsewhere. This helped him combat politically dangerous feelings of alienation and exclusion, even as it promoted the other key element in the public life of the state — a sense of at least minimal political inclusion.

After independence in 1947, princely rule soon yielded to democracy, and to a rule by the Congress Party, which had led the struggle for self-rule in pre-independence India and which had established a strong presence in this comparatively liberal state. In this early phase, in Karnataka as in most other parts of India, the Congress was controlled by land-owning castes which dominated life in the villages, where the great majority of people lived. Neither the maharajas nor the prosperous groups that captured power after 1947 pursued accommodation and inclusion as energetically as they might have done. We see, then, that these political initiatives often seemed to be aspirations rather than realities. But the princes' democratic successors built upon this accommodative tradition, though only up to a point.

This is discussed in more detail in Chapter 1, but brief comments are in order here. During the first 25 years after independence, leaders of the ruling Congress Party carefully maintained accommodative arrangements, that is, political bargains among representatives of various powerful social groups *within* the party. They also distributed the spoils — goods, services and funds — *beyond* the party to an array of social groups from which they needed votes to be re-elected. The result was a 'Congress system'[1] that was inclusive, but within strict limits. Within the party and the state government, most important posts went to politicians from the two land-owning caste groups of the Lingayats and Vokkaligas, who dominated village life. Leaders from other, less powerful and prosperous groups had to make do mainly with minor roles. Beyond the party too, political spoils predominantly went to the Lingayats and the Vokkaligas. These arrangements were easily sustainable at first because Lingayats and Vokkaligas received considerable deference from others. But before long, a political awakening began to develop among the great majority of the population over which these landed castes exercised dominance at the village level. This made the 'limits' on inclusiveness and accommodation seem increasingly tight and frustrating to those largely left out; this political awakening among them created the possibility of change.[2]

---

[1] The classic studies of how the Congress maintained its dominance in this era are Kothari (1964), Weiner (1967), and Morris-Jones (1967).

[2] These themes are discussed in much greater detail in Manor (1977c).

Reform in a Society Congenial to Accommodative Politics

This opportunity was seized after 1972 by a shrewd and forceful innovator, Chief Minister Devaraj Urs. He rode to power in 1972 on a surge of popular support for Indira Gandhi's version of the Congress Party which promised action against poverty and inequality. He came from the same tiny caste as the former maharajas, and like them, had no links to the Lingayats and Vokkaligas on the land. Most leaders from these two castes had remained with the version of the Congress opposed to Mrs Gandhi after the party had split in 1969, so Urs's election victory in 1972 had broken, for the time being, their grip on state-level politics.

To sustain himself in power thereafter, and to resist predictable efforts by the landed castes to re-establish their control, Urs had to draw most of his backing from less prosperous groups. We explain in Part I of this book how he accomplished it. Two of his innovations were crucial. First, he implemented policies which delivered substantial concrete benefits, while offering important symbolic gestures to the disadvantaged groups. Second, at the cabinet level, he ensured that the state would be governed by rainbow coalitions in which leaders from disadvantaged groups were given important posts instead of mere tokenism. (This second step anticipated by two decades similar changes in north India.)

He proved adroit enough to institutionalise rainbow coalitions, by ensuring that any state government which wanted to endure had to adopt this approach. As a result, since 1972, political parties in Karnataka have competed to appeal to all sections of society, and not to narrow social bases, as their counterparts in some other states have done. They have thus avoided the divisive, spiteful politics that have sometimes emerged elsewhere.

Since major political parties in Karnataka seek votes from the same broad array of social groups, they have tended to pursue similar policies. As such, policy continuity is a strong feature of this state's politics when ruling parties change, as they have done in every state election since 1985. This is far more constructive than the practice that has prevailed in India's largest state — Uttar Pradesh — between the early 1990s and the present, where successive ruling parties, representing narrow social bases, uproot virtually all the policies of their predecessors and start from scratch. And, since rainbow coalitions require parties to sink roots deep into society (deeper than the landed elite), they face pressure from a broad array of social groups to govern responsively. This aspect of rainbow coalitions is yet another feature that is missing in some other Indian states.

As Table 1 shows, in pursuing his strategy, Urs had political arithmetic on his side.

Table 1: Caste-wise break-up (in percentage terms) of the population in Karnataka

Social groups	
Brahmins	3.5
Lingayats	15.3
Vokkaligas	10.8
Backward Classes	32.5
Scheduled Castes (or Dalits)	16.7
Scheduled Tribes (or Adivasis)	6.7
Muslims	11.6
Other minorities	2.9

Source: Survey by Sandeep Shastri, based on Reddy (1990) and *Census of India, 2001.*
Note: These figures are broadly consistent with an earlier caste census conducted by the Havanur Commission.

Urs extended the principle of accommodation to the three-quarters of the state's population which appears below Lingayats and Vokkaligas in Table 1. This table is arranged in rough conformity to the traditional caste hierarchy, although the Scheduled Tribes (Adivasis), Muslims and other minorities largely stand outside this hierarchy.

He was assisted in his pursuit of greater accommodation and inclusion by an important feature of the socio-economic landscape. The southern-half of present-day Karnataka (the former princely state of Mysore) has, for at least two centuries, had the lowest incidence of landlessness in South Asia. The relatively equitable distribution of land has given many members of groups of middling and low status in the old caste hierarchy at least a modest stake in the existing order. It has also helped to prevent people of low status (even those who lack land) from suffering the kind of gross abuses and deep alienation from the social and political order which low-status groups have experienced in many other states. Society is somewhat more cohesive here than in other regions of India, and political accommodation and inclusion are thus more feasible.[3]

People in other regions look with puzzlement, and sometimes scorn, upon the quiescence of the people of Karnataka, called Kannadigas

---

[3] This is discussed in greater detail in Manor (1989).

(speakers of the main regional language, Kannada). Unkind Tamils claim that Kannadigas 'eat mud' (a reference to the staple food — *ragi*, served in a grey wad — of people in the southern part of the state), and that this makes their passions and brains sluggish. But the real explanation for the quiescence and moderation of Kannadigas lies in the comparatively equitable agrarian social order that has long existed here, and in the accommodative and inclusive politics that have developed partly as a response to it.[4]

Before independence in 1947, most Kannadigas were scattered across several different but contiguous territories. They were ruled by different political dispensations, but shared a common culture that went beyond a common language. While the southern half of what is now Karnataka was a princely state (Mysore), the north-western portion was part of the British-ruled Bombay Presidency and the north-eastern section was ruled by an autocratic prince, the Nizam of Hyderabad. Unlike princely Mysore, which was in many ways a model state (both economically and socially), other Kannada-speaking regions in pre-independence India, including Bellary and South Kanara, which were within the British-ruled Madras Presidency, were economically less developed.[5]

In 1956, when the boundaries of many states were redrawn to conform to linguistic regions, all these territories were integrated into a single state, called Mysore until 1972, when it was officially renamed Karnataka. While integration sealed cultural cohesion, the disparities between former princely Mysore and the rest were severe and proved difficult to repair. Even today, disparities exist and occasionally cause groups in the under-developed sub-regions to articulate a sense of neglect. But successive governments since 1956 deserve credit for their consistent efforts to remove regional imbalances.

Nevertheless, while inequalities existed in Karnataka, the social order across most of the state was less oppressive than in other parts of India, so that discontents here were less marked. Thus, over many decades, we

---

[4] The politics of accommodation has made governments in this state particularly well equipped to adapt well to what is perhaps the most fundamental change to occur in India since independence — the declining power of caste hierarchies.

[5] The same can be said of the tiny princely state of Sandur in which still more Kannadigas lived.

have seen comparatively little emigration from Karnataka, otherwise a common feature among alienated, and often desperate, groups in many other states. Kannadigas have long been far less evident in other parts of India than Gujaratis, Bengalis, Tamils and others. And they are even less evident overseas. In Britain today, there are large numbers of Punjabi and Bengali restaurants, but only one calls itself 'Kannadiga' — and it is run by Tamils. Kannadigas prefer to stay at home.

Readers outside India, who may never have heard of Karnataka, may wonder if it is perhaps a rather small place. It is not one of India's most populous states, but by international standards it is sizeable. Its population in the *Census of India, 2001* was 52.85 million. It is just under twice the size of the whole of Scandinavia, and larger than Spain and Portugal put together. It is (for Americans) over three times larger than the whole of New England, and over twice the size of Indiana, Illinois and Iowa combined. Or, if you prefer, it nearly equals the combined populations of Canada, Australia and New Zealand. We know, then, that large numbers of people have been affected by the events examined in this book.

Three Chief Ministers

We focus primarily on three key leaders who stood at the apex of power in Karnataka during the period between 1972 and 1988, when the democratic process was broadened and deepened.[6] As the foregoing discussion of the socio-economic order indicates, we do not believe that these politicians utterly predominated in the political transformation that occurred. But they still deserve the attention they receive here because they were immensely important. Leading politicians across India (indeed, across Asia, Africa and Latin America) make most of the key decisions about the characters of their governments, public policy and state–society relations. But most of the literature on politics and development in these regions has, astonishingly, paid little or no heed to politicians. Instead, studies focus on technocratic blueprints, administrative processes, incentive systems, etc. They give us Hamlet without the prince. And far too many analysts assume that politicians

---

[6] We also believe that we provide greater detail and more 'inside information' on key episodes and themes than do other studies on state politics in India.

and politics have been consistently destructive. This is not true, as two of the three politicians who loom large in this story vividly demonstrated.[7] Not all three were heroic figures. The first, Devaraj Urs (Chief Minister, 1972–80) was, as we have noted, the architect of a new inclusive, accommodative politics. But the second, Gundu Rao (1980–83) was a man of severely limited ability who achieved office thanks to his close ties to Sanjay Gandhi and his extravagant expressions of loyalty to Indira Gandhi. He radically centralised power in his own incapable hands, and excluded his legislators from having any influence, imposing something close to civil servant 'raj'. The result was an insensitive, unresponsive and occasionally brutish government. But he ruled ineptly and relatively briefly, so that he did not reverse Urs's shift to politics that gave lower-status groups a genuine voice and stake. The third leader, Ramakrishna Hegde (1983–88), was as adroit as Gundu Rao had been incapable. He repaired the damage of the Gundu Rao years and consolidated the practices which Urs had introduced. He implemented imaginative policies to address the basic needs of the rural majority, and crucially, enabled them to begin governing themselves. He made democracy in the state stronger by devolving substantial powers and funds onto elected councils at local and district levels. This initiative anticipated and helped inspire a strong international trend of the 1990s — democratic decentralisation. And since Hegde headed the first government led by a *non*-Congress party, he and his colleagues ushered in a genuine multiparty democracy in Karnataka.

In other words, this book deals with extreme cases. Urs and Hegde were immensely imaginative, adept leaders. Their careers were not free of ambiguities, as we explain in subsequent chapters in great detail. But overall, they were as constructive as the best chief ministers that any Indian state has seen since independence. Gundu Rao was breathtakingly insensitive and incapable. He was more destructive than all but a tiny handful of Chief Ministers seen in this and other Indian states since 1947. And yet, ironically, his very ineptitude made an unwitting 'contribution' to the continuance of the political transformation examined here. It is

---

[7] This argument has been made in more detail in Melo, Ng'ethe and Manor (forthcoming), which deals with the presidents of Brazil and Uganda, and an Indian Chief Minister, Digvijay Singh (Madhya Pradesh, 1993–2003).

astonishing that one state should produce three such extraordinary leaders within a single generation, and in succession too.

Despite our preoccupation with the three Chief Ministers, and our patent admiration for two of them, we do not believe that they solved all of Karnataka's problems. Indeed, in broadening and deepening democracy, they made one important problem worse. When Urs drew less prosperous groups fully into the political game, he invited their demands and compounded his own difficulties, since the government was already suffering from an overload of demands from the landed castes. And when Hegde empowered elected councils at lower levels, he stimulated demands from below still further. Both of them were shrewd enough to recognise this problem, but both decided, nevertheless, to invite demands from previously excluded groups. They saw this as the right thing to do, and as a risk worth taking. In the process, both deepened democracy and advanced the cause of social justice. But the constructive policies they introduced, which encouraged many social groups to register their demands made governing more difficult, which partly explains why no ruling party has been re-elected in Karnataka since Hegde last achieved it in 1985.

The Need for Studies of Politics in India's States

Finally, we hope that this book will persuade those who analyse politics in the other states in India's federal system to produce similar studies. It is nearly impossible to find serious analyses of individual states. There are plenty of books containing articles on various states, but even the best papers cannot achieve adequate depth or detail.

India's states matter enormously and richly deserve such detailed attention. State governments have considerable power and room for manoeuvre within the Indian federal system. It is from the state level, and not New Delhi (the seat of the central government), that most of the actual governance of the various states occurs in India. Karnataka is not a particularly large state, but it is larger than all but two countries in Africa, all but four in Asia, and all but four in Latin America. It has, as international observers are beginning to see, also been the site of hugely important events. The remarkable boom in Bangalore has seized the imagination of a global audience, and its policies and politics have belatedly attracted the notice of international development agencies. Other states are similarly worthy of attention, although not always for the same reasons.

Until more books address other states, it will not be possible to develop a full understanding of India and its admirable, complex, ambiguous experiment with democracy. It is made complex, in part, by the remarkable contrasts between the recent political histories of various states.[8] Indian society is the most complex on earth, and striking differences among the states are a crucial part of this complexity. Indian states vary enormously in a multitude of other ways, and until we analyse that in detail, we cannot attempt to know this country. We seek to make a start here.

---

[8] For a recent demonstration of this, see Jenkins (2005).

Part I

D. Devaraj Urs, 1972–80

I

The Emergence of Urs: The Challenge to the Landed Castes' Dominance of State Politics

Urs, Chief Minister of Karnataka from 1972 to 1980, did more than any predecessor, and as much as any counterpart elsewhere in India, before or since, to make the democratic process more genuine for the disadvantaged groups who form a substantial majority of the state's population. By doing this, he initiated a process of broadening and deepening democracy that would be completed by a successor government led by Hegde from 1983 to 1988.

The magnitude of Urs's achievement becomes apparent only when we understand what he was up against. As we noted in the Introduction, he broke the control which the two land-owning caste-clusters of the Lingayats and the Vokkaligas had exercised on state-level politics since independence. There are two dimensions to this story, since Urs faced daunting challenges both at the 'local' level (which, in this predominantly rural state, mainly meant the village level) and at the 'state' level from which he governed.

In Urs's time, life in most Karnataka villages was dominated by Lingayats and Vokkaligas. They constituted a minority of the rural population, and just 26.1 per cent of the entire population of the state after its enlargement in 1956 (cf. Table 1, p. 7). But a little more than a quarter of the population still represents considerable numerical strength. Because they were mostly concentrated in geographically exclusive areas (Vokkaligas in southern Karnataka and Lingayats in the northern part of the state), their dominance was far greater than their percentage of the overall population would suggest. More crucially, they controlled most of the better land, a decisive resource. Lingayats and Vokkaligas at the village level provided support to politicians from their respective castes at the state level, and in return, they received material support (goods, services and funds) and helpful interventions from these politicians through networks of clients. If he was to survive at the head of the government, Urs had to change state-level politics, and the networks connecting the state level to the villages, in ways that would undermine their power. He could expect stiff resistance. To compound his problems, he belonged to neither landed caste, and politicians from both were determined to reassert their control over state politics, which they regarded as the natural order of things.

To accomplish this change at the state level, Urs also had to induce change at the lower levels. It was not necessary that he transform the rural socio-economic order to prevail at the apex of the system — which was just as well, since such a transformation was impossible at the time. Evidence of a significant decline in the power of the old caste hierarchies in villages did not emerge in Karnataka or other parts of India until the 1990s. But he had to induce a substantial change in the political dynamics between the apex and the base of the system, and in government policies, if he was to mobilise support from the majority of villagers who did not belong to the land-owning castes.

Once we understand what he was up against, we explain (as we do in this and the next two chapters) how he overcame these impediments. Here again, we must consider both the state and the local levels, and changes that occurred in between. Urs used the enticements that are available to any leader in power to attract support from a few Lingayat and Vokkaliga leaders. But he also concentrated on raising new leaders from less exalted social groups to serve as allies within his government, and as intermediaries between him and their caste fellows at the grassroots.

He proved to be a remarkably effective communicator and a gifted manipulator: charming and tough by turns, and consistently shrewd and imaginative. These qualities enabled him to secure his position at the state level. To ensure the support of villagers from lower-status groups, he made startling pledges and undertook initiatives — both symbolic and substantive — that were widely popular among them. So, far more than Indira Gandhi and most of her Chief Ministers in other states, Urs delivered concrete results to back his promises of help to disadvantaged groups.

To begin with, his party could not have been elected if a political awakening had not gained momentum among lower-status groups in the villages. This awakening entailed greater awareness, assertiveness, organisational strength, and discontent with dominant-caste rule at the state level. But on its own, the awakening was not enough. Support from these groups could be consolidated only by providing them with solid reasons to back him. He did so by implementing policies that brought tangible change (see Chapter 2). Whether we call this an 'enlightened conservative', a 'progressive' or even a 'radical' approach is not an issue that should detain us. In truth, it entailed some of all these things.

In pursuing these goals, Urs was conforming to the political tradition that had developed well before independence in princely Mysore, where he had spent his life as a member of the tiny caste of the state's maharajas. He, like the princes on several key occasions before him, recognised the need for change and took decisive action to achieve it. This way he could anticipate and defuse potentially serious conflict. The national election of 1971 and the state election of 1972 indicated that the rural majority was impatient with the dominance of state politics by the landed minority. Urs had no choice but to mobilise this majority, since it was the only way he could survive politically in the teeth of inevitable attempts by the Lingayats and Vokkaligas to dislodge him. But by including lower-status groups in a broadened political settlement at the state level, he removed the threat of their demands triggering destructive conflict of the kind which convulsed north India in 1990 and still afflicts it. And by establishing a tradition (which has endured) of rainbow coalitions within the state cabinet, in which leaders from lower-status groups held key posts alongside Lingayats and Vokkaligas, he served the cause of future political and social accommodation and stability.

Lingayat–Vokkaliga Dominance at Local and State Levels

Land was more equably distributed in Karnataka (especially in the state's southern half) than in any other region in South Asia. Partly as a consequence, caste hierarchies have long been less oppressive here for lower- status groups (for a detailed account, see Manor 1989). But during the first four decades or so after independence, the Lingayat–Vokkaliga dominance in most villages (where over two-thirds of the people lived) was still a patent, and sometimes painful, reality. It is worth noting that the fieldwork which led to the classic study of 'dominant castes' in India (Srinivas 1959) occurred in southern Karnataka.

Who are the Lingayats and Vokkaligas? They are not single castes, but clusters of castes, that is, of *jati*s.[1] The term 'Vokkaliga' refers to an occupation, since it literally means 'those who thresh', which is to say

---

[1] A *jati* is an endogamous caste group, that is, a group within which people find marriage partners for their children.

that they traditionally cultivate grain. There are six main Vokkaliga *jati*s or sub-castes which occupy distinct but over-lapping areas, nearly all of which are in southern Karnataka. As region-wide politics became important in the 20th century, they found it beneficial to band together to seek influence as a coherent 'caste' group.

The Lingayats form another cluster of sub-castes or *jati*s. They are occupationally more diverse than the Vokkaligas, since they trace their origins to a religious reform movement within Hinduism, Veerasaivism, which in the pre-modern era won followers from many occupational groups, mainly in northern Karnataka, but to some extent in the south as well. Several Lingayat sub-castes — priests, traders, weavers, etc. — own little or no land. But one of them, the Sadar Lingayats, has huge numerical strength and traditionally cultivated land and dominated village life in the manner of the Vokkaligas (Manor 1977a).

We need to provide a little more detail on these matters in order to explain regional variations within Karnataka. In what before independence was the princely state of Mysore (roughly the southern-half of contemporary Karnataka), Brahmins stood at the apex of the caste hierarchy by virtue of the traditional priestly roles which they continued to perform unchallenged in areas dominated by the Vokkaligas. Because they were traditionally literate and often learned, they made great progress in Western education and eventually migrated in significant numbers to urban centres like Bangalore and Mysore, giving up, in the process, whatever little land they had. They had always constituted a tiny portion (3.5 per cent) of the total population, and this migration reduced their numbers in rural areas still further. Those who remained in villages had to defer in temporal matters to the Vokkaligas, whose landed wealth and numerical strength ensured their dominance of village life. Despite this, the Brahmins' position atop the ritual hierarchy was seldom challenged in southern Karnataka as it was in neighbouring Tamil Nadu, where the caste system was ridiculed by elements of the Dravidian movement. Here, a reasonably congenial relationship existed in which the Vokkaligas accepted the superior ritual status of the Brahmins, and the Brahmins accepted the economically and politically dominant position of the Vokkaligas within villages.

Things were different in the northern half of the state. Nearly all of it was divided before independence between areas directly ruled by the British as part of the Bombay Presidency (called, to this day, Bombay

Karnataka) and areas that formed part of the largest princely state, Hyderabad (called Hyderabad Karnataka), the government of which was (in sharp contrast to that of the princely state of Mysore) harshly autocratic and unconcerned about development.[2] Village life in both these northern regions was dominated by the Lingayats, since there were very few Vokkaligas here.

In contrast to old Mysore,[3] northern Karnataka witnessed considerable conflict between the Brahmins and the Lingayats. This occurred because the Lingayat caste-cluster, which was also a Hindu sect (McCormack 1963), sprang from a religious reform movement that challenged the ritual authority of the Brahmins, and because they had their own priestly sub-caste which performed religious ceremonies reserved for Brahmins in old Mysore.

Since the maharajas' small caste had no links to the Vokkaligas or the Lingayats, princely governments in old Mysore took care to avoid interference in village life, lest they inspire resistance.[4] They left power relations at the village level largely untouched. So, for the most part, did the British authorities in Bombay Karnataka. The government in princely Hyderabad intruded unhelpfully at times, but in the main, it was oblivious to the rural social order.

---

[2] Present-day Karnataka also includes a few smaller areas. The most important of these are two coastal districts, which before independence were governed directly by the British as part of the Madras and Bombay Presidencies. The composition of society in these districts varies markedly from the rest of Karnataka. There are, for example, very few Lingayats or Vokkaligas in these districts. Another area, but one which was not socially untypical, was the tiny princely state of Sandur. The British also directly administered the eastern half of the city of Bangalore, as a 'civil and military station'.

[3] 'Old Mysore' refers to, roughly, the southern half of contemporary Karnataka, which was a princely state until 1947 and a state within the Indian federation between 1947 and 1956, when it was merged with other Kannada-speaking areas to form a new, enlarged state. The use of the term 'old' is intended to distinguish the area called Mysore (until 1956) from the enlarged state also called Mysore until 1972, when the name was changed to Karnataka.

[4] Unwise interference and maladroit governance had once triggered a rebellion in 1830 which, in the following year, persuaded the British to oust the princely house of Mysore from power for half a century. The painful memory of this lived on after it resumed control in 1881, and inspired its policy of non-interference.

In old Mysore, the creation of a Representative Assembly in 1882 enabled the Vokkaligas (and to a lesser extent the Lingayats, who were fewer in number in the princely state) to translate their rural dominance into significant influence in this elected body (which had quite limited powers), even as they remained loyal to the princely rulers. The Brahmins, on the other hand, had used their unrivalled advances in education to occupy a premier position — indeed, one of dominance — within the princely administration. An increasing awareness of the nationalist movement led some Brahmins, particularly those who had taken to the legal profession, to join it and to press for a less autocratic government in princely Mysore.

At the same time, the Vokkaligas and Lingayats who had captured seats in the Representative Assembly, and then in the (again, only modestly powerful) District Councils which the princely government had created in the 1930s, banded together to form a non-Brahmin alternative to the emergence of a Brahmin-dominated party called the 'Mysore Congress' that had tentative links to the national organisation of the same name. They were sympathetic to the nationalist move-ment, but hesitated to join the Congress where they feared they might have to share a considerable part of the power with the Brahmins. However, in 1937, the princely authorities unwisely arrested a Congress leader on the eve of a Representative Assembly meeting, and in reaction, the non-Brahmin party and the Mysore Congress merged to form a much more formidable Congress organisation. After independence, it came to dominate the state's politics. This organisation was soon taken over by the Vokkaligas because of their numerical strength and their dominance of village life in old Mysore, and to a lesser degree, by the Lingayats.

To the north, in Bombay Karnataka, despite tensions between Lingayats and Brahmins, nationalists from these two groups made common cause before independence in a regional branch of the Indian National Congress. Lingayats eventually came to predominate within this organisation. The repressive princely regime of Hyderabad Karnataka, on the other hand, prevented nationalist activity from developing much strength. But soon after independence, the Lingayats (who dominated village life here) swiftly built and came to dominate a Congress organisation in this region. In 1956, state boundaries inherited from the British were redrawn to conform roughly to the lines separating linguistic regions, and the present-day state of Karnataka (called Mysore until 1972) came into being.

Since in the newly enlarged state Lingayats outnumbered Vokkaligas, the former assumed a pre-eminent role in Lingayat/Vokkaliga-dominated governments. After 1956, Vokkaligas occupied many powerful posts in state cabinets, but all chief ministers, until 1972 (when Urs assumed this role), were Lingayats.

How was the Lingayat–Vokkaliga dominance sustained at the state level, and how did it influence the character of successive governments before 1972? Lingayats (mainly from land-owning sub-castes and the numerically and economically powerful Banajiga (trading) sub-caste) and Vokkaligas were elected to the state assembly in numbers far greater than their shares of the state's population, thanks mainly to the influence which their caste fellows exercised at the village level. They then banded together at the state level to ensure that the lion's share of the political spoils flowed down to the Lingayats and Vokkaligas at the grassroots. This system of patronage distribution enabled them to translate their dominance in terms of ownership of land into dominance over successive state governments. It also ensured their dominance over the Congress Party, which in turn occupied a dominant position among political parties from independence until 1972, when Urs became Chief Minister, as leader of Indira Gandhi's version of the Congress which had split in 1970.

Despite the potency of the Lingayats and Vokkaligas in state politics before 1972 — which led members of both castes to see their dominance of the state government as their right — three features of state politics in that era are worth noting, since they provided Urs with favourable political opportunities once he assumed power.

First, here as in most other Congress-ruled states, the party's political 'machine' distributed modest amounts of patronage to disadvantaged groups and gave leaders from these groups symbolic posts in the party and the state government. These were mainly token exercises which were aimed at keeping such groups content, while most resources served the interests of the dominant landed castes. Even the elected representatives from the disadvantaged groups had to protect the interests of the dominant castes at the constituency level as well as within the party system in order to get a share, however little, in the power structure. But by 1972, the political awakening among lower-status groups had inspired growing impatience with the prevailing arrangements. The inspiration for this largely came from Mrs Gandhi who had identified herself with the 'have-nots' in her battle with the old guard in her party. Urs sought to intensify this impatience in order to maintain himself in power in the face of a Lingayat–Vokkaliga backlash against his government.

Second, the flow of political patronage to the Lingayats and the Vokkaligas at the local level had mainly benefited the prosperous members of these caste-clusters. Poorer people within both castes, and especially among the Vokkaligas, had been somewhat left out. This created the possibility that redistributive, anti-poverty policies, which Urs pursued after 1972, might attract votes from those who felt excluded. This was not a major opportunity for Urs, but he set out to make the most of it, especially among poorer Vokkaligas.

Finally, during the era of Lingayat–Vokkaliga dominance at the state level before 1972, several politicians from these castes had failed to rise as high in the state-level pecking order as they had hoped. A handful of such people joined Urs and Mrs Gandhi's version of the Congress when it split in 1970, in the hope that they might achieve senior posts which had so far eluded them. Many calculated that Mrs Gandhi's anti-poverty slogans might enable her version of the party to garner election victories, as indeed it did at the national election of 1971 and the state election of 1972. They also reckoned (mistakenly, as it turned out) that despite these slogans, Lingayats and Vokkaligas would continue to loom large in the leadership of the party and the government. Urs found it advantageous to play upon the ambitions of these disgruntled Vokkaligas and Lingayats since they had networks of clients in different sub-regions of the state. But while he gave some of them important posts in his government, he ensured that substantial numbers of leaders from disadvantaged groups also held key posts. As a result, the Lingayat–Vokkaliga dominance at the state level gave way to rainbow coalitions at the cabinet level in which he and politicians from other social groups predominated.

Urs's Early Career

Devaraj Urs grew up in a middle-class family in the city of Mysore, which until 1947 was the capital of the princely state (India's second largest) of the same name. After school he attended Maharaja's College (an institution of high quality) in the University of Mysore where he studied for a Bachelor of Arts degree. He was also an accomplished member of the college wrestling team, a pursuit which others (and, in his lighter moments, Urs himself) believed inculcated in him the pugilistic instincts that shaped his later approach to politics.

As a member of the maharajas' small Arasu sub-caste, he was an unlikely recruit for the Mysore State Congress, an affiliate of Mahatma Gandhi's national organisation. It supported the struggle for Indian independence and coupled this with a campaign for the democratisation of politics within Mysore state. In most princely states, oppressive governments prevented such bodies from developing much — and often any — substance. But Mysore was the most liberal of these states, which was in keeping with its advances in the sciences, industrialisation and economic development. So, Congressmen here were permitted to operate relatively freely. The young Urs developed pro-Congress sympathies in his student days and enlisted in the organisation. He was a prize catch since he was a rebel from within the maharajas' community, campaigning against what was, despite its enlightened ways, a substantially autocratic regime. Urs later said that as a result of his association with the Mysore State Congress, he was persona non grata in the palace for a number of years.

He still holds the record in post-independence Karnataka for representing the same constituency, Hunsur, from 1952 to 1982.[5] But his record is still more impressive than that, since he was actually first elected in 1942 to the (pre-independence) Mysore Representative Assembly, which the state's princely rulers had established in 1882 to establish their progressive credentials.[6] He won his seat on a Congress ticket at a time when the Congress was demanding that the then Maharaja permit the people to elect their own government.[7]

But despite this remarkably long innings in public office, he was a relatively inconsequential politician until 1971. He was treated somewhat dismissively by S. Nijalingappa, the first Chief Minister after the state was enlarged in 1956 to embrace all Kannada-speaking areas, because he was neither a Lingayat nor a Vokkaliga. His stint in Nijalingappa's governments at various points during the 1960s, during which he held the portfolios of housing, labour, transport, information, sericulture

---

[5] N. Hutchamasti Gowda, a Vokkaliga leader and former minister, served in the legislature for a longer period, but not in an unbroken spell. He was defeated in 1978, and again in 1985.

[6] Representative Assembly members were elected on a restricted franchise of which tax-paying land-owners constituted a majority of voters.

[7] For a detailed account, see Manor (1977c).

and animal husbandry, was uneventful except for a minor controversy over the misuse of office while he was Transport Minister. This was a respectable set of assignments, but Urs still felt rather marginalised, and clearly disgruntled. His disenchantment deepened in 1967, when Nijalingappa sought to deny him the party nomination in the state election. Only the intervention of one of Urs's formidable friends prevented this from actually happening.

Nijalingappa had led the campaign to unify Karnataka (then called Mysore), and had been the main beneficiary of this change, becoming Chief Minister and the pre-eminent figure in the state's politics for many years thereafter. His doubts about Urs were partly based on the latter's reservations about unification. Urs identified with the old, smaller state where he had grown up and entered politics. He was a typical Mysorean who believed that the residents of that region had a certain cultural sophistication and that people from the integrated, northern areas were somewhat rustic by comparison. And, even though he had joined the Congress opposition to princely rule, as a member of the princely caste, he was sentimental about the old principality. He had little in common with those from the newly integrated areas.

Strictly speaking, Nijalingappa was also from old Mysore — a respected Lingayat lawyer from Chitradurga district, which bordered the integrated areas.[8] But in reality, he derived most of his political strength from the Lingayat-dominated areas of Bombay Karnataka and Hyderabad Karnataka that were newly included in 1956. He had also developed enough contacts in the Congress at the national level to be recognised as an important south Indian leader. When the state was enlarged, it was obvious that the chief ministership should go to him since he was the only leader who could knit together the different parts of the new state. Moreover, as the man who had led the drive for unification, his claim could not be ignored.

When Nijalingappa became Chief Minister, Vokkaligas and especially fellow Lingayats (who outnumbered Vokkaligas in the enlarged state) dominated the ruling Congress, and the party, in turn, thoroughly dominated politics in the state. In those days, the Congress occupied not only the centre ground of politics, but most of the left and right as well, although it was essentially a party of the centre–right, since the lion's share of the spoils (passing through its efficient political machine) went to

---

[8] For an account of his early years, see Manor (1977b).

the two landed caste-clusters. The main conflicts in Karnataka took place not between the Congress and other parties but 'within' the Congress. Similarly, in an era in which the Lingayats were pre-eminent over the Vokkaligas in state politics (1956–72), many key conflicts occurred not between the Lingayats and the others, but 'within' the Lingayat caste-cluster. When the Lingayat influence was challenged by other groups, as it was throughout the period after 1972, they would swiftly unite to meet the threat. But in the years between 1956 and 1972, it was hardly ever challenged, so sometimes a serious conflict developed between the two most influential Lingayat sub-groups.

Nijalingappa had mainly to deal with a dispute between two sizeable factions. Both were dominated by Lingayats, but to maximise their leverage, both drew upon legislators from other castes and all regions of the state. Nijalingappa, who belonged to the Banajiga sub-group among Lingayats, himself headed one of these factions, and the other was led by B. D. Jatti, who was a Panchamsali, another Lingayat sub-group.

One of Jatti's many camp followers was Urs. He was disgruntled over Nijalingappa's refusal to entrust him with the ministerial responsibilities that he thought he deserved. To manage the factional struggle, Nijalingappa offered key dissidents important roles in his government, and Urs was one of the beneficiaries. But his portfolios did not enable him to distribute much patronage to legislators and other clients, or to build up his public image by initiating popular programmes.

As a result, Urs remained on the periphery of the state-level elite until the split in the Congress in 1970. By then, crucial changes had occurred. Nijalingappa had moved to the national level where he was a key figure in the 'Syndicate', the group of regional Congress barons who first selected Indira Gandhi as Prime Minister and then clashed with her in a conflict that culminated in the party schism. Indeed, at the time of the split, Nijalingappa was the national president of the Congress. Despite his absence, he exercised potent influence over practically everything that happened within the ruling party in Karnataka. He had seen to it that his loyal lieutenant, Veerendra Patil (also, of course, a Lingayat) was made Chief Minister, although Jatti had offered him stiff resistance.[9] To get Jatti out of Patil's way, Congress bosses at the national level

---

[9] On one earlier occasion, when Nijalingappa had been forced out of office for a short spell, Jatti had headed the government. But he eventually had to make way for Nijalingappa again.

made him Lieutenant-Governor of Pondicherry. At a reception in Bangalore to celebrate his new appointment, Jatti openly said that the dissident leadership would now pass on to Urs. This led Patil to exclude Urs from his state cabinet. Ramakrishna Hegde, his Finance Minister, who was often described as Patil's political twin, later told Raghavan in Bangalore that the Chief Minister had acted against his advice.

> I had suggested that he should retain all those who were in Nijalingappa's cabinet. He chose to ignore my advice. Had Urs been retained, probably it would have been difficult for Mrs Gandhi to set up her party here in 1970.

The Congress Split and the Parliamentary Election of 1971

The seeds for the split in the Congress had been sown soon after Indira Gandhi became Prime Minister in 1966. The regional barons in the Syndicate had preferred her to the rigid, truculent Morarji Desai, because they thought that she would be meek and pliable. They were mistaken. In time, she aggressively challenged them as 'reactionaries', and increasingly turned to Young Turks in the Congress, and to the Left, for support. When the All India Congress Committee met in Bangalore in 1969, Mrs Gandhi put forward a rival to the Syndicate's choice for the party's candidate for India's presidency. After her candidate won, the barons expelled her from the Congress. By then she had virtually established a parallel party organisation, and when the formal split occurred soon afterwards, she merely had to formalise these arrangements.

However, Karnataka was one state which posed problems in this regard. Since its former Chief Minister, Nijalingappa, was president of the Syndicate's version of the party, now called the Congress (O) ('O' for 'opposition', since it sat in opposition to Mrs Gandhi's Congress (R) or 'ruling' Congress[10] in Parliament in New Delhi), most Congressmen in the state remained loyal to the Congress (O). They did so also because Mrs Gandhi's abilities as a vote-getter were unknown, and because by remaining with the party in power in the state, they retained access to the system of spoils. Those who stayed with the Congress (O) included practically all the prominent Lingayat and Vokkaliga politicians.

---

[10] The 'R' initially stood for 'requisitioned', which referred to a requisitioned meeting of the party called by Mrs Gandhi at the time of the party schism, but it soon became based on the word 'ruling' (Brass 1990: 68).

A tiny number of second-line leaders from these castes joined Mrs Gandhi's Congress (R). They included, apart from Urs, H. Siddaveerappa, H. M. Chennabasappa (both Lingayats) and N. Hutchamasti Gowda (a Vokkaliga),[11] none of whom had ideological reasons for doing so. They made this choice because they had virtually no role to play in the politics of Patil's ruling clique. The leadership of the Congress (R) in the state legislature went not to Urs (who was made ad hoc president of the state-level unit of the party) but to Siddaveerappa, who belonged to the land-owning Sadar Lingayat caste and exercised considerable influence over the politically important Sirigere *math* (monastery).[12]

Both Patil and his sophisticated alter-ego, Finance Minister Hegde, who was considered to be quite close to Mrs Gandhi, had tried to avert the split in the Congress. But when it occurred, Patil's loyalty to Nijalingappa weighed heavily on him and he remained with the Congress (O). His party, which enjoyed numerical superiority in the state assembly, held on to power until the 1971 parliamentary election. But he had been pitched into a new, unnerving situation. For the first time since independence, the ruling party in the state was different from that at the national level. Consequently, he had to deal with decidedly hostile interventions from New Delhi. Mrs Gandhi, in her desperate and ultimately successful attempt to secure her hold on power, operated with such ruthlessness that many political norms were completely ignored. Patil and his colleagues, who were used to the old, gentler politics, found it very difficult to adjust to this, as also to Mrs Gandhi's charges that the Congress (O) was a reactionary impediment to her progressive plans to 'abolish poverty' — the key slogan of her election campaign in 1971.

---

[11] Mrs Gandhi also retained the loyalty of a formidable Vokkaliga leader and former Chief Minister of the state, K. Hanumanthaiah. But he was a minister in her cabinet in New Delhi and preferred to remain at the national level. So he did not become a key player in state-level politics.

[12] The Sadar Lingayats were one of the two most politically powerful subsections of the Lingayat caste-cluster or sect. Most Sadars were prosperous cultivators in northern Karnataka. The *swamiji* (religious head) of the Sirigere *math* was arguably the most powerful religious leader in the state, since his followers were spread across 40 to 50 assembly constituencies. It had long been believed that he had the ability to ensure the victory or defeat of candidates in these constituencies merely by sending a directive to his followers who, in turn, were mostly Sadar Lingayats. Such influence, however, stopped working in the mid-1970s (of which more later).

Long before the national election, she toured the country extensively, and found that people responded with spontaneity and warmth on a scale that even she could not comprehend. When she made a whirlwind tour of Karnataka, she found that enthusiastic mass gatherings would wait several hours to catch a mere glimpse of her. Once, when she arrived in Bangalore well past midnight (after touring the northern districts), enormous crowds waited for her on the streets.

This kind of popular response surprised Patil and his colleagues, but they did not take it too seriously. When a parliamentary election was called for in early 1971, the Congress (O), with its well-knit organisation, expected to win a clear majority of seats from the state. By contrast, the Congress (R) had to field numerous new faces, and it lacked a strong organisation in the districts.

Urs played a role in the Congress (R)'s campaign, although other leaders loomed larger. He had difficulties with national-level Congress (R) leaders like Umashankar Dixit. As he later explained to Raghavan:

> When I wanted money to run the organisation or manage the elections, Mrs Gandhi used to direct me to Dixit or some other senior leader. I had to beg for more money as they were generally stingy. I had to meekly accept whatever they gave and manage with it.

The Congress (R) was opposed not just by the Congress (O), but by a 'grand alliance' that included the Jan Sangh, the Swatantra Party and the Socialist Party. But Mrs Gandhi's campaign promises of radical pro-poor policies carried her to a sweeping victory across the country. The Congress (R)'s triumph in Karnataka was astounding. It won every parliamentary seat and secured a massive and unprecedented 70.87 per cent of the votes.[13] Urs had little to do with this. His efforts at organising the party had helped, but the key was Mrs Gandhi's image and her ability to portray her opponents as tired traditionalists.

Only hours after the announcement of the result, two ministers in Patil's government defected to the Congress (R). This opened the floodgates. Within a few days, Patil had lost his majority in the state assembly and was forced to resign. The Congress (R) was plainly in a position to form a new government with the support of the defectors

---

[13] By contrast, the Congress (O) gained 43.68 per cent of the popular vote across all of India.

and some favoured the idea, not least Siddaveerappa who, as a Lingayat and the party's leader in the legislature, was the logical choice for the post of Chief Minister. He set out for Delhi where Mrs Gandhi would make the decision. But since what was then India's only airline was on strike, he went by train, which took almost two days. Urs knew that if a government was formed immediately, he had no chance of becoming Chief Minister. He needed to persuade Mrs Gandhi to call for a fresh state election and to clear out the old guard represented by the defectors. He remained in Bangalore, gambling that the airline strike would end. It paid off. The strike was called off and he reached Delhi well before Siddaveerappa. He convinced Mrs Gandhi to impose President's Rule[14] until a state election could be held, which eventually was, a year later in March 1972.

The Rise of Urs and the State Election of 1972

The resulting dissolution of the assembly deprived Siddaveerappa of his key post as leader of the Congress (R) in the legislature. It left Urs, the ad hoc president of the state unit of the party, as the only senior leader with an official post. Twelve months of President's Rule gave him the time he needed to construct a solid organisation for the party at the district and *taluk* (sub-district) level. Before Mrs Gandhi's sweeping victory in the 1971 national election, Urs had had great difficulty finding recruits for the new Congress (R). As he later put it, 'In those early days, my unit of the party was only the sign board outside the office.'[15] But once the 1971 election result had shown second- and third-tier politicians the writing on the wall, he had far less trouble, and his supreme management skills soon ensured that the party developed a solid organisation across the state.

Despite the stunning outcome for the Congress (R) in the national election, many key Lingayat and Vokkaliga politicians remained with the Congress (O). Urs found that as a result, many district- and sub-district-level leaders from these castes, who were clients of important state-level leaders, also refused to join him. But he was now confident enough of two crucial changes to look beyond the two dominant landed castes. The first was Mrs Gandhi's ability to win votes by making direct, personal

---

[14] Direct rule from New Delhi, under the leadership of the state's Governor.
[15] Devaraj Urs, interview by James Manor, Bangalore, 12 August 1978.

appeals to ordinary people. Lingayat and Vokkaliga leaders of the Congress (O) could not compete with this, and were thus effectively bypassed. The second was a political awakening that had clearly occurred among the less prosperous social groups, which made them less deferential to the dominant castes and more willing to defy their wishes by responding to Mrs Gandhi's appeals.

Urs systematically recruited bright political activists from among the Backward Classes[16] and the Scheduled Castes, both of which stand below the Lingayats and Vokkaligas in the traditional social hierarchy.[17] These groups outnumbered the dominant castes, and had long suffered at their hands, in part because the political spoils had mainly gone to the dominant landed castes.

Urs had one other compelling reason to draw these disadvantaged groups into his organisation. His own caste status ensured that the Lingayats and the Vokkaligas would be hostile to him. The chances that he, rather than a Lingayat leader like Siddaveerappa, might become and remain Chief Minister would be greatly enhanced if the non-dominant groups loomed large in the Congress (R) organisation. Siddaveerappa would still be an important player, and so would his fellow Lingayat, Chennabasappa. But since most dominant-caste leaders stuck with the Congress (O), these two would be unable to emerge as convincing leaders with state-wide networks of caste fellows. Urs had conjectured well, for their influence in fact remained limited to their respective districts and even there, other powerful Lingayat politicians countered them.

When the state election campaign finally kicked off in early 1972, Mrs Gandhi toured the state extensively, since she was eager to trounce the Congress (O) in one of its last bastions. (Karnataka and Gujarat were the only two states that remained under its control.) She continued to promise change: greater justice for the poor and the excluded. However, being Jawaharlal Nehru's daughter, she also represented continuity, and she appealed to the electorate to vote for a party that could ensure

---

[16] Backward Classes refers to castes which occupied the middle and lower-middle levels of the traditional caste hierarchy, with the Lingayats and Vokkaligas above and the Scheduled Castes or Dalits below them. As we will explain later, Urs eventually expanded the official definition of Backward Classes — for political reasons — to include the Vokkaligas as well.

[17] Karnataka has only a small number of residents (6.7 per cent of the population) from the Scheduled Tribes.

stability at the state level, as it had done at the national level. This combination of offering both change and continuity has always been unbeatable in Indian elections. Nehru, a sitting Prime Minister proposing socialist reform, had won repeated majorities in this way. Mrs Gandhi and later her son Rajiv would do so again in the national elections of 1980 and 1984, respectively.[18]

This combination served the Congress (R) well in the 1972 state election in Karnataka as well. The party won 162 of the 224 seats in the assembly — a crushing humiliation for the Congress (O). The latter had, as always, activated its networks of district- and sub-district-level leaders, and its links, mainly, to the Lingayat and Vokkaliga heads of village leaders who had influenced significant numbers of voters from lower-status groups in previous elections. But this kind of politics no longer worked. The political awakening among ordinary people from every section of society, which made them more aware of political issues, of their rights and interests, and of the power and secrecy of their votes, had proceeded far enough to erode the persuasive power of Congress (O) activists. This awakening made it possible for Indira Gandhi's direct appeal to evoke a mass response, and for Urs's new recruits from the non-dominant groups to win seats in the legislature.

Another key reason for this dramatic result was that, for the first time, a realistic alternative existed to the old Congress Party machine; voters now had a genuine choice. Until 1972, the state's politics had centred around a single, dominant party: the Congress. Opposition parties had always existed, but they had offered meek challenges with no hope of success. In 1972, an alternative, even if it was a splinter of the Congress, not only emerged but prevailed resoundingly by projecting new, progressive policies which suggested that the end of the Lingayat–Vokkaliga dominance was at hand.

The 1972 election did not, however, usher in an era of multiparty competition. The victorious Congress (R) had won a majority large enough to restore one-party dominance. In fact, it sustained this victory in the next state election in 1978. So while Urs broadened and deepened democracy in ways that seemed unimaginable before 1972, the end of dominant-party politics which would complete this process had to wait yet awhile.

---

[18] See a discussion of this in Manor (1982).

As the state election of 1972 had approached, Urs was told by the party high command in New Delhi that he had to choose between continuing as president of the state unit of the party and contesting for a seat in the legislature. This posed a painful dilemma. He thought he could win easily from Hunsur. He had done so at every election since independence, sometimes without a contest, because other parties regarded him as unassailable. So, he did not expect to be tied down to his constituency. But it was crucial that he remain state party president, since that would ensure huge influence over the selection of candidates. Unable to make up his mind or to consult his followers on such a sensitive issue, Urs consulted, of all people, Hegde, a prominent figure in the rival camp. Hegde explained this to Raghavan a decade later:

> Before the election, Urs shared his dilemma with me and sought my advice . . . I told him he should keep the party position and not contest. In the event of his party coming to power, the credit would go to him and he would be in a position to have full sway over elected legislators if he wanted to become Chief Minister. He could always get an elected member to vacate a seat for him later. He took my advice.

Hegde was right. As party president, Urs had enormous clout, and used it to ensure that men of his choice were given party tickets. He saw to it that candidates from the Backward Classes, who had long received only tokenism from the Congress when it was controlled by the dominant castes, got a sizeable share. Other important leaders like Siddaveerappa had their say, but in the final analysis Urs prevailed, and the party's central election committee in New Delhi endorsed his choices.

After the election, Urs had little difficulty getting elected as leader of the legislature party. There was a meek attempt by Siddaveerappa to oppose him, but Urs overcame it effortlessly since he had the personal loyalty of many newly elected members and, more crucially, the backing of Mrs Gandhi. By this time, she had so centralised power within the party that it had adopted the practice of authorising her to select state-level leaders. She, on the advice of a central observer who had assessed the strength of each contender, chose Urs. He was duly sworn in as Chief Minister.

He was the first Chief Minister in the quarter-century since independence who was neither a Lingayat nor a Vokkaliga. He believed that less privileged groups, who had suffered at the hands of the two landed castes, saw in his election some hope of their own liberation. But to capitalise on this, he had to deliver tangible changes. Mrs Gandhi had changed the rules of politics at the national level, and Urs now had to ensure a similar change in Karnataka. Imaginative new policies would soon emerge, but he first had to select a ministerial team.

He acted assertively, choosing not to strike compromises with factions or other leaders in the party. The two ministers initially inducted into office with him were Chennabasappa (a Lingayat) and K. H. Patil (a Reddy, considered a Vokkaliga), but not Siddaveerappa (also a Lingayat) who had been his rival for the party leadership. Siddaveerappa had to wait until the first expansion to get into the ministry. By including the Lingayat Chennabasappa, Urs saw to it that Siddaveerappa could not drum up a campaign by claiming that Lingayats had been left out in the first phase of cabinet formation. He could only complain over his exclusion on personal grounds, which would have placed him in a poor light.

By constituting the initial three-member ministry in this way, Urs indicated first, that he would not shut Lingayats and Vokkaligas out of his government, and second, that he was in command and their inclusion was not something that occurred automatically. He also shrewdly selected a Lingayat from old Mysore (where Vokkaligas predominated) and a Vokkaliga from northern Karnataka (where Lingayats predominated). This was a striking reversal of traditional practice in cabinet-formation. This, again, was a clear signal that Urs would do things his way. And as we shall see in Chapter 2, it soon became unmistakably clear that ministers from the once-dominant castes would be treated on an equal footing with colleagues from lower-status groups, and that the new government's policies would mainly serve the interests of these latter groups.

Before 1972, every state cabinet had primarily been dominated by Lingayats and Vokkaligas. In 1967, for example, 10 out of 14 ministers came from these castes. Urs changed this by giving strong representation to the Backward Classes, the Scheduled Castes and the other minorities. When the cabinet was expanded soon after the original three were inducted, seven of his ministers were drawn from these groups, compared to six who were Lingayats or Vokkaligas. For over two decades after independence, not more than one Scheduled Caste leader and one Muslim had held ministerial rank. During Veerendra Patil's tenure, Scheduled Caste representation had been increased to two. Urs increased it to four, and included two Muslims.

In another departure, he promptly issued informal 'instructions' to the bureaucracy that they should treat these less privileged groups with respect. This was an indication that in his actions and policies, as well as in his recruitment of legislators and ministers, he would bring an end to the landed castes' dominance of state-level politics. He was sinking his party's roots deeper into society and deepening democratic processes.

Changing the Power Structure at Lower Levels

Urs knew that cabinet-formation and executive instructions from on high were only the beginning. Over time, he would need to induce deeper changes at lower levels in the system, and in his eight years at the helm, he would gradually achieve this. But it is worth pausing here briefly to explain how the old system worked at the taluk (sub-district) level and below, since it will show how difficult his task was.

Although numerous officials from various government departments are involved in the administration at the sub-district level, state legislators (whose constituencies usually conform roughly or precisely to sub-districts) must develop particularly close, congenial ties with three officials. The three who exercise the greatest influence over rural life are the sub-inspector of police, the engineer from the Public Works Department and the block (sub-district) development officer or BDO. They are important because it is mainly through them that a legislator can distribute patronage and cultivate popular support.

Villagers commonly get embroiled in personal feuds on all kinds of issues. Often, matters which should not concern the police are taken to them for intervention. These might include a domestic quarrel within a family, or a dispute over land or livestock. A sub-inspector of police is considered to be powerful enough to resolve such issues. The police must also deal with the law and order problems and criminal complaints that loom large in village affairs. The villagers who lodge such complaints as well as the accused rely upon politically active leaders to assist them with the police. A legislator who has a good working relationship with the senior sub-district police officer (that is, the sub-inspector) can acquire potent influence among the villagers because of his ability to intercede on behalf of those who seek his assistance. A legislator who is on good terms with the sub-district engineer gains influence because the engineer can influence decisions on what public works will be taken up. Equally importantly, he also has the ability to allocate resources selectively to such works. A legislator who can affect decisions about the creation of visible assets through public works will win the respect of his constituents. The third official, the BDO, is equally useful because he is responsible for development projects within the sub-district. He, like the engineer, has immense influence over investments of public resources in various villages.

Each year there is a 'transfer season' (usually in March and April) when a large-scale reshuffle of officials across the state is ordered from Bangalore — a process dominated by senior politicians, not least the Chief Minister. Legislators spend a lot of time here trying to get senior administrators to post people of their choice, especially, but not only, to these three key posts in their constituencies. If they succeed, they can dominate government actions within their bailiwicks and make illicit profits by extracting payments from low-level bureaucrats who seek postings from them.

But in order to succeed, they often need support from senior politicians who exercise leverage over senior administrators in the state capital. Urs was intimately familiar with this process, and he and his senior colleagues devoted much time and energy to ensure that their party's legislators got what they wanted. They also used this opportunity to erode the old Lingayat–Vokkaliga dominance of key posts at the sub-district level, since such a measure enhanced the chances of Urs's policies (to address the needs of non-dominant groups) penetrating the grassroots. It took time to change the vast, sprawling administration, but persistence ultimately produced substantial results. Legislators from disadvantaged groups now used the methods that their dominant-caste predecessors had employed to enable their caste fellows at the local level to assert themselves more forcefully. In the process, some of them meted out the kind of harassment that the Lingayats and Vokkaligas had once indulged in. This was regrettable, but it became apparent in time that the overweening power of the dominant castes at all levels of the system had ended.

Urs and the Dominant, Landed Castes

These changes at the sub-district, and indeed the village level, were only possible because of Urs's determination and ferocious attention to detail from the top. In handling many other issues, he operated with subtlety and guile. But in this matter, and in his other dealings with the dominant, landed caste-clusters, he had to act blatantly, to drive home a message about the very fundamentals of his new politics. He made it vividly apparent that he regarded the Lingayats and the Vokkaligas as the 'haves' and the rest (excluding the Brahmins) as the 'have-nots', and that he was on the side of the latter.

This may sound like a class-based argument, but in his early years as Chief Minister, he analysed everything in terms of caste and fashioned his policy innovations on this basis. His views on this key issue evolved over time, however. Towards the end of his tenure, he began to equate caste with class, to speak more often of class, and to give a class complexion to his brand of caste politics. In particular, he began to stress that even the Lingayat and Vokkaliga caste-clusters (especially the latter) contained many poor people. They had gained little in the era when leaders of their respective castes had dominated state politics, but they now benefited more from his redistributive policies.[19] There was considerable evidence to support this claim. But despite this new emphasis, caste remained uppermost in his calculations.[20]

Urs was less sympathetic towards the Lingayats than the Vokkaligas. He often managed to forge political accommodations with the latter without departing from his commitment to give preferential treatment to the Backward Classes and other groups of still lower status. And, he eventually sought to divide the two land-owning caste-clusters, somewhat disingenuously, by including the Vokkaligas within the official Backward Classes category that would benefit from reservations in government employment and educational institutions.

The explanation for Urs's hostility towards the Lingayats remains unclear. When asked about it, he offered deliberately inadequate answers. For instance, he once told Raghavan that he had developed deep suspicions of Lingayat politicians simply because they had no respect for leaders from other communities. He gave an example of how cabinet meetings were conducted during Nijalingappa's time:

> Even before the meetings, the Lingayat lobby in the ministry . . . decided which subject should be approved and which should not. I can understand lobbying before the meeting among ministers interested in having some

---

[19] Devaraj Urs, in interviews with James Manor between 1979 and 1981.

[20] The inter-relationship between caste and class is extremely complex, and we lack the space to examine it fully here. It is discussed in detail, in Frankel and Rao (1989–1990), a set of books that considers this issue for many different Indian states.

project or proposal approved by the cabinet. But the way they did it was so patently casteist that I began to dislike them. Even if no major issue was to be discussed, Lingayat ministers would exchange views just before the meeting and decide what they should accept and what they should disapprove. In that system, some of us had a hard time pushing through subjects we were interested in. I told myself then that if I ever got a chance, I would break the monopoly of the Lingayats.

Raghavan then asked him what he thought about Vokkaliga politicians, to which Urs had the following to say:

They were slightly better in that they would always try to protect their own caste group's interest, but when it was not in jeopardy, they were willing to accommodate others. Not so the Lingayat ministers. Their constant attempt was to first protect their interests and, equally importantly, try to stop others from deriving any benefit.

Urs could go on endlessly about how the Lingayats had tried to dominate politics to the exclusion of others who deserved a voice. But this could not have been the sole reason for his intense distaste for them. It is also likely that he thought that Lingayat leaders were responsible for frustrating him until he broke loose from them. Moreover, he was painfully aware that in the elections to the Lok Sabha in 1971 and to the state assembly in 1972, both the Lingayat leadership and Lingayat voters had, by and large, opposed his party.

From the Lingayats' point of view, this was perfectly logical. After all, they had seen their leaders dominate state politics since 1956, and could not be expected to back a party that appeared likely to end their control. They created huge problems for Urs, who found it impossible to draw into his party second- or even third-tier Lingayat leaders in substantial numbers. In the state election of 1972, few Lingayats were willing to contest on his party's ticket, so that he was forced to fall back on candidates from other castes, particularly in northern Karnataka (the Lingayat heartland).

This deepened his estrangement from the Lingayats and reinforced his inclination to make a virtue of his (partly enforced) reliance on lower-status groups. He initially adopted this progressive approach not out of any ideological commitment, but for pragmatic reasons; such a measure was essential to his political survival. He was thus labelled a 'pragmatic progressive' (Manor 1980). But soon, his inclination to champion the interests of the less privileged hardened into a firm conviction. His land reforms and his policies to support the Backward Classes also stemmed, in part, from his desire to settle scores with the Lingayats. We shall discuss this in greater detail in Chapter 2.

Urs in a Broader Context

Until 1972, when Devaraj Urs took office as Chief Minister, the credit for the Congress (R)'s success in Karnataka had overwhelmingly gone to Indira Gandhi. Her promise to 'abolish poverty' had won her a sweeping victory across India and in Karnataka in the national election of 1971. The momentum that this provided, besides a boost from the defeat of Pakistan and the creation of Bangladesh in the war later that year, carried the party and Urs to victory in the state election of 1972. But it soon became apparent that Urs was no ordinary leader. His adroit machinations, his capacity to operate both subtly and forcefully as changing circumstances demanded, and his shrewd sense of what the times required and would permit, enabled him to achieve more progressive change than any other Congress Chief Minister, and than Indira Gandhi herself.

He soon became an immensely formidable leader in his own right, and the pre-eminent force in the politics of Karnataka. But he chose not to over-reach himself by seeking to establish the kind of personal rule which Mrs Gandhi had then sought and achieved — a process that did severe damage to the institutions of government and, ultimately, to her own party. Urs made himself indispensable in state politics, but his indispensability, and the key to his political survival in the exceedingly difficult times to come, lay in his determination to sustain and indeed to strengthen the institutions which were essential to his drive for progressive, redistributive change. Indira Gandhi weakened the Congress (R) by undermining its internal institutions and by turning increasingly to second- and third-rate lieutenants who qualified for important posts through abject pledges of personal loyalty to her. By contrast, Urs bolstered the strength of the party in his state by raising up promising new leaders from disadvantaged groups, and by promoting those who proved most effective. The result, as we shall see, was a Karnataka Congress that continued to win elections even after Mrs Gandhi's excesses had consigned her party to a humiliating defeat at the national level.

The emphasis in this chapter and in the two which follow is, rightly, on Urs as an agent of change. That is mainly what he was, but it is important to stress that in two crucial respects, he was seeking, in the preservation of certain important features of Karnataka's politics, not change but continuity.

First, by pursuing change, he was reviving a tradition which the enlightened princely governments in old Mysore had established. This tradition was the policy of introducing reforms in order to anticipate and, thus, defuse future conflicts. The political awakening among the Backward Classes, the Scheduled Castes and the minorities, all of whom had long faced Lingayat and Vokkaliga dominance, was bound, eventually, to become a potent element of the state's politics. By anticipating and incorporating it into the mainstream, Urs prevented it from wreaking the havoc that it produced across north India after 1990.

Just as old Mysore's princes had opened the system up to non-Brahmins, which in that early phase mainly meant Lingayats and Vokkaligas, Urs opened up the system, and his ruling party, to other less privileged groups. He did so for the same reason that had earlier animated the maharajas. They had had no connection to the landowning castes that dominated village life, so unlike the princes in many other parts of India, they could not derive their legitimacy from ties of caste and kinship to the most formidable landed castes. They therefore attended to the needs of these castes and created space for them within the state's political elite. Urs also lacked such ties, so he sought to anchor his authority in new links to less-prosperous groups who outnumbered the landed castes. This was a startling change, but it was also a return to a time-honoured tradition of accommodation and inclusion, to which Vokkaliga and especially Lingayat politicians had, in their heyday atop the state government, become largely oblivious.

Second, he sought to preserve one-party dominance within Karnataka's politics. The social composition and the electoral base of the Congress (R) he headed at the state level differed markedly from that of the Congress before his time. During his eight years as Chief Minister, other parties remained relegated to the margins of state politics. So here again, the dramatic changes that he introduced also served to maintain a certain continuity. The party had to be transformed in order to remain dominant. It was not until 1983, after his Congress successor had indulged in a prolonged spell of extravagant misgovernment, that the party's dominance ended and the people of Karnataka were given a realistic choice at election time. We will discuss this again in some detail in Part II of this book.

2

Consolidating a Broad Social Base:
Land Reform, Caste Reservations and the Emergency

Developing a Progressive Strategy

It would have been possible, indeed easy, for Urs to continue in office for a considerable time without introducing major policy innovations. Even if he had merely implemented the (mostly modest) new programmes that Mrs Gandhi was formulating, which very few of her Chief Ministers were actually doing, he would have been considered a success.

But he recognised that the immense popularity of the Congress (R), and his solid majority in the legislature, together with the demoralisation that had overtaken the Congress (O), gave him an opportunity to initiate a change of historic proportions. It would entrench power-sharing at the state-level among all important social groups as an accepted practice, which politicians would then disregard at their peril. It would broaden the social base both of his party and of state politics. In addition, not incidentally, it would thwart efforts (which he rightly anticipated) by the Lingayats and the Vokkaligas to oust him, by making a restoration of their dominance over state politics impossible.

Quite soon after he assumed office, Urs began speaking of the need for constructive change on two fronts which, over time, became the main reforms that he undertook. They were intended to erode the power of the two dominant landed castes, especially the Lingayats, and to attract support from the disadvantaged. The first was a policy of 'land to the tiller'. This kind of land reform would give tenants who worked the lands of others (mainly Lingayats and Vokkaligas) ownership of them. The second would provide more meaningful and substantial reservations in government employment and educational institutions for the Backward Classes. They, unlike the Scheduled Castes (ex-untouchables, who in more recent years have come to be called Dalits), had never fully enjoyed such advantages. In Karnataka, a reservation policy of sorts for the Backward Classes was in place long before independence, but in practice it had been diluted to such an extent that it had had only a marginal impact.

It is important to add that Urs was perceptive enough to see that if his policies were to succeed, they required support from two structures linking the apex of the state government to the local level. These were the bureaucracy and his party's organisation. The mere passage of laws in the state assembly and the design of new policies atop the administration could achieve little without such backing. As he well knew, India's post-independence history was littered with examples of laws and policies that went unimplemented because these intermediate structures remained inert or obstructive.

He therefore put heavy, unrelenting pressure on senior civil servants to push ahead with his new policies, and asked his party colleagues at lower levels to keep the heat on bureaucrats. But this latter effort would bear fruit only if he could forge his party into a force that was inclined and empowered to perform this task.

Urs had already done much to remake the party, or rather to build it from scratch, since at the outset he had found relatively few takers for Mrs Gandhi's version of the Congress. This was initially a disadvantage, but now that he needed an organisation that would respond to him, he was glad that he had had the opportunity to construct it anew. He had recruited many new faces, most of them people from lower-status groups who tended to sympathise with his new policies which benefited their respective groups. When defectors poured in after the party's victory in the 1971 national election, Urs acquired numerous politicians who were not very sympathetic to his progressive programmes. A few of them were Lingayats, and those who came from the dominant, landed castes were susceptible to pressure from the Chief Minister. He held the key to their promotion to ministerial jobs and other cherished postings on state boards and corporations, and they mainly depended on him to approve the transfer of key officials within their constituencies which, as we saw in Chapter 1, was vital to their interests.

Urs applied such pressure systematically, but he also deployed another resource which had been relatively little used by previous Chief Ministers — money. Urs quickly developed a centralised system of illicit fund-raising, which sent corruption soaring well beyond its previous levels. He spent some of this money on himself, but most of it was used for progressive political purposes.[1]

---

[1] The comments that follow are mainly based on remarkably candid comments made by Urs himself in interviews by James Manor in London (1979) and Bangalore (1981).

Three of these were especially important. First, he made regular, very generous tributary payments to the national leadership of the Congress (R). His aim was to prevent Mrs Gandhi and her inner circle from intruding unhelpfully in Karnataka. After abandoning intra-party democracy, which had prevailed in the Congress since Mahatma Gandhi had introduced it in 1919, she had made a habit of interfering in party affairs in nearly all the other states. She harboured extravagant fears of challenges from potent regional Congress (R) leaders, so she frequently encouraged dissident factions in most states to keep her Chief Ministers from becoming too formidable. This undermined their ability to implement her earlier promises of poverty reduction and other national programmes, but she persisted nonetheless. Urs, by maintaining a substantial flow of funds to the high command, and by applying his considerable personal charm to persuade Mrs Gandhi of his unflinching loyalty, achieved much more autonomy than most of his counterparts in other states. He used it to pursue progressive programmes, mainly of his own making.

Second, he distributed funds to legislators, with three aims in mind. The money was partly intended to persuade them to spend less time manipulating their networks of clients to raise illicit profits from small-scale bribes, so that they would concentrate on their role as his agents in pressing low-level bureaucrats to implement his programmes. He also asked them to spend some of these funds in ways that benefited disadvantaged groups in their constituencies. And in cases where legislators came from such groups and therefore tended to have little private wealth of the kind that was often available to Lingayat and Vokkaliga legislators, the money was intended to bankroll their election campaigns and their political activities between elections.

Finally, Urs spent some of his illicit funds on low-status groups themselves, especially on their caste associations. Some of these associations had existed before he assumed power, but had weak structures, few members and little money. Others had to be formed anew by Urs himself and his lieutenants who, in turn, badly needed funds. By pumping cash into these bodies, Urs sought to strengthen the capacity of disadvantaged groups to acquire influence at lower levels, to cement their loyalty to him, and to enable them to apply pressure from below on legislators and low-level bureaucrats to implement his progressive policies.

The steep increase in corruption during his time in power was understandably distasteful to many observers. But in assessing it, we must also pay attention to the enlightened purposes to which much of the money was put. Very few other Indian politicians who have engaged in large-scale profiteering since the early 1970s have committed funds to such purposes on a scale like Urs's.

Let us now consider his two main progressive initiatives: land reform and reservations for the Backward Classes in educational institutions and government employment.

Land Reform

Urs was not the first to attempt land reform in the state. In 1961, Revenue Minister Kadidal Manjappa, a Vokkaliga who had developed Left-of-Centre views while growing up in the only district of old Mysore with marked inequalities in landholdings,[2] had authored a bill to standardise land law across the various parts of the newly united state. However, it went beyond homogenisation and introduced reforms by way of banning the lease of agricultural land, giving tenants considerable security from eviction, and fixing a ceiling on the amount of land that any person could own. But the legislation had little impact, partly because it contained loopholes that enabled people to elude the provisions on land ceilings, and mainly because subsequent governments lacked the will to implement it, given their bias towards the land-owning groups. Even absentee landlords remained unmolested.

Urs was determined to strengthen this law and, more crucially, to implement it aggressively. He introduced substantial amendments to it which came into force in March 1974. All tenanted land was to pass to the government which, in turn, was to transfer it to the tenants after an examination of claims by specially constituted, powerful tribunals. The amended act also barred the leasing of land, abolished sharecropping, prescribed ceilings for various categories of land and, not incidentally, closed the earlier loopholes.

---

[2] He felt strongly about the issue and wrote a novel to dramatise it, which in English was entitled *The Flame of Panjaravalli*. James Manor interviewed Manjappa, who had briefly served as caretaker Chief Minister, on his youth in Shimoga district and his later career on numerous occasions in Bangalore in 1972 and 1973.

To provide tenants with swift resolutions of their claims, 193 land tribunals were created, at least one per taluk (sub-district). Each consisted of a civil servant as chairman besides four other non-official members, including representatives of subaltern groups, at least one of whom came from the Scheduled Castes. This last provision was not merely symbolic. Even though Urs packed the tribunals with people who were committed to land reform, he feared that the Scheduled Castes might not receive full justice if members sided with the dominant landed castes, who were the main losers in this exercise. The Scheduled Caste member and those from other low-status groups were supposed to protect the interests of tenants from their respective communities. To prevent the tribunals' decisions from being mired in lower courts where corruption was a serious problem, the law prohibited both the participation of lawyers in these tribunals and appeals against decisions arrived at in the tribunals to any court.[3]

The newly amended act was a great success in creating new political space and leverage for disadvantaged groups, in abolishing tenancy and in providing 'land to the tiller'. By 1979, roughly 800,000 tenants' applications had reached the tribunals and, of these, over 500,000 had been dealt with. Approximately 60 per cent of these cases were resolved in favour of tenants, who received ownership of over 1.25 million acres. These are impressive figures. Tenancy and sharecropping had effectively been abolished and a massive transfer of land had occurred.

This change in one of the fundamentals of agrarian life, and in thousands of villages scattered across the state, could not have been achieved without fierce, relentless pressure from the Chief Minister. Urs made land reform the focal point of his anti-poverty programmes, and in this way gave the most vivid, tangible demonstration to the rural electorate of his seriousness about assisting the 'have-nots'. He spoke of the issue day in and day out and frayed the nerves of bureaucrats with demands for forceful administrative action.

If we compare this reform to the most radical options available, it falls short, as Left-wing critics have often stressed. The act did not

---

[3] Some who lost land sought to get round the prohibition on appeals by approaching the Karnataka High Court in its writ jurisdiction, which is different from an appeals provision. But they made little headway. We are grateful to V. K. Natraj for insights into these issues.

lower land ceilings as markedly as it might have done, and this placed limitations on the government's capacity to redistribute surplus land to landless people. As a result, the reform benefited tenants far more than the landless. While most of the former were distinctly 'poor', they were better off than those who lacked land. (However, it must be stressed that a large number of Karnataka districts have an exceedingly low incidence of landlessness, so that tenancy was indeed the main problem in these areas.) But if we compare this reform not to an ideal, radical blueprint but to the pre-existing realities of daily life at the grassroots, then it can be said to have produced startling change, the like of which had never been witnessed in rural Karnataka.

Critics have also pointed out, accurately, that some tenant-beneficiaries of this reform were Vokkaligas. But Urs welcomed this for two reasons. First, he argued that any tenant-farmer is in a condition of dependency and disadvantage, in that he cannot obtain the full reward for his labour. If some Vokkaligas suffered from these injustices, it was only right that they too be liberated along with tenants from other groups. Second, the benefits which went to Vokkaliga tenants helped Urs make headway towards one of his other important political goals — attracting electoral support from poorer Lingayats and especially Vokkaligas, of whom there were many.[4]

Reservations for the Backward Classes

Along with land reforms, Urs zealously forced through a policy of positive discrimination in educational institutions and government employment for the Backward Classes (the social groups found in the middle-to-lower reaches of the traditional caste hierarchy, but above the Scheduled Castes for whom reservations had long existed). The term Backward Classes covered a large number of castes, many of which were quite small, but which, taken overall, constituted nearly a third of the population. On their own — without counting the Scheduled Castes (16.7 per cent) and Muslims (11.6 per cent), whose support Urs also sought — the Backward Classes outnumbered the Lingayats and Vokkaligas combined. They were a huge potential source of votes which he could not afford to ignore.

---

[4] Devaraj Urs, in interviews with James Manor in Bangalore, 1980 and 1981.

This was not the first time that the issue of reservation for the Backward Classes had arisen in the state, although an earlier episode had come to nothing. An official commission to consider reservations for the Backward Classes had been set up during the early 1960s, in the days of the Lingayat–Vokkaliga dominance, by the Nijalingappa government. It had recommended that the Lingayats be excluded from this category. The government rejected this and included them in a scheme which earmarked a certain percentage of jobs for each caste group, so that only the Brahmins were excluded. When this was repealed by the Supreme Court, the government adopted a reservation policy based solely on economic criteria and promised to set up another commission to study the issue. This never happened.

Urs was determined to make reservations for the Backward Classes the second of his flagship policies. Soon after he came to power, he appointed a commission headed by L. G. Havanur, a lawyer and an important activist belonging to the Backward Classes. After an elaborate survey, the initial inclination of the commission members was to exclude both Lingayats and Vokkaligas from reservations for the Backward Classes, but Urs privately told Havanur that it was politically impossible to do so. In late 1975, the commission recommended the inclusion of the Vokkaligas. In 1977, Urs implemented this recommendation. The report also called for the exclusion of Muslims (a patently disadvantaged group) because they were not part of the Hindu caste hierarchy. Rejecting this recommendation, Urs included Muslims, a key element of his electoral base. The inclusion of Vokkaligas ensured that the two dominant caste-clusters did not combine against him. He also established an agency to assist disadvantaged people from all groups, regardless of caste, to allay fears that his policies were too caste-centric.[5] And, since he had waited to give effect to the policy until the Emergency was in force, he was able to proceed at a time when opponents were extremely reluctant to mount popular protests.

To reinforce the psychological and material impact of his two main initiatives, Urs pursued a range of other policies to benefit disadvantaged groups. One largely symbolic act is worth noting. It sent a powerful signal to everyone about his commitment to low-status groups, and

---

[5] We are grateful to V. K. Natraj for advice on this set of issues.

specifically to the one key element of his social base that had not benefited from his policy of reservations (since reservations for them had long
existed): the Scheduled Castes. All across Karnataka, members of the
Scheduled Castes were employed by local authorities in the degrading
occupation of having to remove night soil from dry latrines in areas
where modern sewage systems had not been constructed. With considerable fanfare, Urs issued an executive order banning this practice.

In fact, he went further and lent real substance to his claim of being
a champion of Scheduled Caste interests by giving leaders from these
groups important cabinet posts. One of these, B. Basavalingappa, a
distinctly aggressive and thus controversial figure, had suggested the
night-soil ban to the Chief Minister. Urs's willingness to place such a
forceful Scheduled Caste leader in a position of real influence was highly
unusual within the Congress (R), which in most other states appointed
moderate, easily manageable Scheduled Caste politicians to ministerial
posts of limited power.

The Chief Minister followed this with a programme to provide free
houses to the Scheduled Castes and then, to reach out to poor people of
all castes, distributed free sites for houses to all landless labourers, many
of whom came from the Scheduled Castes. These initiatives were pursued
quite vigorously. Their impact was, however, undermined somewhat
by leakages in resources, which indicates that Urs's efforts to motivate
legislators and low-level bureaucrats to support these policies sometimes
yielded disappointing results.

We now consider some of Urs's actions which were intended to
cultivate popularity among both the 'haves' and the 'have-nots'.

Renaming the State

One of the first things that Urs did after assuming office was to change
the name of the state from 'Mysore' to 'Karnataka'. This might have
occurred in 1956 when all the Kannada-speaking areas were united in a
single state. These included the former princely state of Mysore, besides
northern and coastal areas which before independence had been directly ruled by the British or by another prince, the Nizam of Hyderabad.
The change to 'Karnataka' in 1956 would have made sense for two
reasons. The majority of the population of the enlarged state lived
outside former princely Mysore and favoured such a change. And in the
pre-independence period, the Indian National Congress had called its

regional committee for *all* these disparate areas the 'Karnataka Pradesh Congress Committee'. But the first Chief Minister of the enlarged state, Nijalingappa, decided to retain the name 'Mysore' in order to reassure the large minority who lived in the former princely state of the same name (that is, the southern part of the newly unified state), many of whom were reluctant about the enlargement.

Urs decided to adopt the name 'Karnataka' in order to do the opposite, that is, to reassure those in the north that their interests would not be ignored. Urs came from former princely Mysore, his caste links to the former maharajas were well known and the capital of the state was in Bangalore, which was located in the south. He was therefore concerned that the majority outside former princely Mysore might feel that their regions would be neglected. So his decision (which surprised most observers) was, despite its cosmetic nature, a shrewd gesture to ease their anxieties.

Pursuing Reform from atop a Fractious Party

Urs was able to pursue his various initiatives, partly because he presided over reasonably strong administrative structures which functioned quite smoothly. Managing his party and a political scene that was rendered turbulent by his policy innovations was a more daunting prospect. He had assumed office with immense leverage over his ministers, legislators and party. His cabinet consisted of a few heavyweights like Siddaveerappa and Chennabasappa and a couple of zealous ministers like K. H. Patil, but the others lacked experience. And Urs himself was largely untested in the art of statecraft since he had held relatively insignificant posts before 1970.

He was repeatedly troubled by conflicts and crises within his party. But he soon demonstrated a capacity to cope. He turned out to be an adroit machinator, and was also lucky in some ways. When crises loomed in Karnataka, Mrs Gandhi usually faced even more severe tests at the national level, so that she held back from undermining Urs as she did with many of her other state-level lieutenants.

Within months of taking power, Urs faced his first serious skirmish. He was instructed by Delhi not to cling to both his offices: the chief ministership and the presidency of the state unit of the Congress (R). The choice of a successor to head the party organisation was not easy. Like any Chief Minister, Urs preferred either a yes-man or a moderate in this key post so that he could maintain effective control over the party while running the government. A potent group of Congress (R) leaders, however, preferred a formidable candidate of their choice. They chose K. H. Ranganath, a man with excellent credentials and a highly respected Scheduled Caste leader known for his sincerity and integrity. Those who backed him came from the erstwhile Praja Socialist Party to which Ranganath himself had also belonged. Urs had nothing against him, either personally or in caste terms. But to buckle under the pressure of one faction would have been seen as a sign of weakness. So, to retain control over the organisation, he drew up his own plans.

He pressurised Ranganath to withdraw. Until the last moment, the latter stood firm, but then he lost heart and stood down. The Chief Minister's choice, K. H. Patil, who left the cabinet to take up the presidency of the Congress (R)'s state unit, was thus installed. It was a tainted victory, since money and muscle had allegedly been employed by Urs's supporters. Indeed, one of his close confidants had actually carried a briefcase stuffed with rupees to what turned out to be a very turbulent meeting to elect the new president. This was discovered when a melee broke out and someone snatched it from him. But Urs prevailed and, for a time, the party's affairs appeared quite settled.

He believed, however, that if he was to dominate (as he needed to do to force through his ambitious policies to broaden the social base of his party), he had to resort to manipulations on a scale never seen before in Karnataka. He continuously set one minister against another, set groups of legislators against particular ministers and favoured carefully selected legislators.

It took some time, but he effectively neutralised Siddaveerappa and his supporters, so that by their third year in power, Urs had moved him from a key portfolio to a relatively minor charge. To accomplish this, he used the Youth Congress to mount attacks on conservative leaders, including Siddaveerappa and Chennabasappa (both Lingayats). He even used members of opposition parties to embarrass Chennabasappa by feeding them vital information about his misuse of office.

Another problem proved more intractable, however. K. H. Patil, his hand-picked president of the state Congress (R) unit, did not turn out to be a yes-man as expected. He took his job very seriously and saw the party's task as one of monitoring the state government to ensure that it delivered on its election promises. He often wrote to ministers, pulling them up for what he saw as lapses. Not surprisingly, this was resented by Urs. Patil's interventions made it seem as if the party was eternally in conflict with the government, often behaving like an opposition party. Urs and Patil began a game of one-upmanship, supplying the media with stories of factional squabbles. Even though the two men publicly differed little on policy (we say this since both of them were articulating the party's programmes and policies), Patil came to be identified with the formerly dominant castes and Urs with the Backward Classes. As a result, the Congress (R) became, and was seen to be, faction-ridden.

The conflict between Urs and Patil often assumed comical proportions. For instance, when the Backward Classes Commission, headed by Havanur, circulated a draft of its final report among its members, one of them slipped Patil a copy. He hurriedly set up a small committee to propose its own recommendations, or — should we say — to pretend to do so. What it really did was to reproduce Havanur's draft recommendations. Patil believed that Urs would accept Havanur's findings, so he sought to give the impression that the government (led by Urs) was acting on the party's (led by him) advice, and in this way take the credit. His game, however, was so transparent that it was seen by the public as a crude attempt to steal Urs's thunder.

None of this posed any real challenge to Urs's leadership. He maintained his pre-eminence through a shrewd distribution of patronage. To keep his followers happy, he created a number of statutory boards and corporations (almost 80) and appointed partymen loyal to him to these bodies. Urs ensured the smooth running of these institutions by seeing to it that their actual control remained with bureaucrats. A person given a post on one of these bodies enjoyed perks such as a salary, a car, a rented house, and travel expenses. They were also able, on a small scale, to provide clients with the favours that these bodies had to offer. As a result, the partymen who benefited (some of whom held no elective office) backed Urs in his encounters with rivals.

Urs carefully saw to the other interests of his legislators as well. In selected cases, regular monthly payments were made to them. He ensured that the funds did not flow from the party, where his control was less than complete. Instead, favourably inclined senior bureaucrats in the legislators' districts, belonging to the departments of Excise or Public Works (both of which yielded substantial illicit funds) supplied the payments. These bureaucrats received protection as long as they kept both the misuse of office and corruption within limits. To secure tight control over such 'wet' departments (that is, those which brought in large contributions for political activities), Urs kept them in his own hands. These included Major Irrigation and Excise (the department dealing with alcoholic drink, from which the state government derived roughly half of its revenues[6]). At times, these departments were nominally in the charge of another minister, but no proposal could be cleared by the minister himself. It had to be referred informally to the Chief Minister. Urs once admitted this practice, in private, to Raghavan:

> I am accused of institutionalising corruption. That is not true. It was institutionalised long before I assumed power. I have to admit that I asked some officials to make regular payments to legislators. Even if I had not asked these officials to finance my partymen, they would have remained corrupt. The bribes they would receive would have gone to their personal coffers. I diverted part of it to the legislators and, in some cases, to other partymen. You may find this explanation illogical. I could not eradicate corruption. Instead of letting the officers make money for themselves which, in any case, they would have done, I allowed some of my men to have a share. I know it was wrong, but I had no choice because in my fight against politicians with vested interests, I needed to cultivate a large number of legislators and not all of them were motivated by altruistic sentiments or ideological reasons to be with me.

Urs's troubles with the party during his first three years in office were compounded by Basavalingappa. Despite having served only a brief stint as a junior minister during Nijalingappa's tenure, he was aggressive enough under Urs to transform himself into the government's leading spokesman for the Scheduled Castes. He confined himself to Scheduled Caste issues, but also launched very public verbal attacks on the dominant landed castes. For quite some time, this suited Urs since Basavalingappa reflected the line Urs was pursuing, and in doing so he was making controversial statements that Urs himself could not make.

Eventually, however, Basavalingappa went much further. For instance, he once suggested that the Scheduled Castes throw all the pictures of gods and goddesses into dustbins. This was clearly derived from the radically rationalist, anti-religious repertoire of E. V. Ramaswamy Naicker,

---

[6] See Manor (1993b: Chapter 2).

a leader of the anti-Brahmin Dravidian movement in neighbouring Tamil Nadu. Such sentiments had never had much support in Karnataka. For a majority of Hindus, who resent any attack on gods, his statement was shocking. Moreover, he reinforced the sense of popular outrage against him by criticising Mahatma Gandhi.

Later at a students' meeting in Mysore, when a participant began speaking in English, a section of the audience heckled him, demanding that he speak in Kannada. (This had become a common practice at meetings which pro-Kannada activists attended.) This provoked Basavalingappa into some plain speaking. He suggested that the hecklers not be so narrow-minded. Kannada, he said, would only be richer if it borrowed ideas from other languages and literatures. His comments were uncontroversial until he added, 'If we do not borrow rich ideas from other languages, what would remain in Kannada is cattle-feed.' This sentence caused him enormous problems. The next day, a Kannada daily highlighted his statement and quoted his expression — '*boosa*', meaning cattle-feed — in its headline. This triggered an agitation in Mysore and Bangalore. Many writers and pro-Kannada activists joined in. Despite support from Scheduled Caste associations, the incident was so embarrassing that Urs asked Basavalingappa to resign.

Other party colleagues also caused Urs problems. A junior minister had to resign when an unknown woman who was staying in his house disappeared for a brief period of time. This became a scandal. Another junior minister also had to go because he got into trouble with a streetwalker.

As factionalism grew and certain other important leaders began forging close contacts with Congress (R) leaders at the national level, politics within the party became quite lively. In his own home district, Mysore, the pro-Urs faction faced a formidable challenge from dissidents which lasted several years. Some of the rebels privately admired Urs, and he reciprocated the sentiment. But when it came to district politics, the rival factions did not mince words. Similar trends emerged in several other districts. The occasional meetings of the state unit of the Congress (R) provided opportunities for various factions to lash out at one another.

Despite all this, and opposition from the state Congress (R) president, Urs never lost control over his government. He staved off challenges by shrewdly cultivating Mrs Gandhi and relying on her in times of crises. In achieving this, his efforts to deliver on her promises of progressive change counted for surprisingly little. What mainly won her backing were his consistently hearty pledges of loyalty and the massive tributary payments which he gave her on a regular basis.[7]

One serious challenge came in the form of a memorandum that some of Urs's party colleagues drew up for submission to Mrs Gandhi in late 1974. It contained as many as 99 accusations of corruption and nepotism against him. Urs ignored it altogether in public, but privately he was worried. It was becoming clear that the articulate and powerful among the disgruntled leaders were being drawn towards K. H. Patil. These included H. N. Nanje Gowda, Siddaveerappa and S. M. Krishna, a sophisticated Vokkaliga leader from Mandya, the Vokkaliga heartland. By early 1975, their efforts appeared to pose a grave threat. Urs privately told some of his associates that it looked like his days as Chief Minister were numbered. He was saved soon thereafter by virtue of the fact that Mrs Gandhi, who had by then become the sole arbiter of the destinies of her partymen, found herself in even bigger trouble. The Allahabad High Court had found her guilty of corrupt electoral practices. In order to save herself, on 25 June 1975 she imposed a state of Emergency. By backing her to the hilt, Urs retained her confidence and saved himself.

The Emergency in Karnataka: A Study in Ambiguity

The Emergency was the most thoroughly vile episode in India's recent past, although it established that autocracy could achieve little and was unacceptable to the masses. Like in the other states, outrages occurred in Karnataka, but as we shall see, they were substantially (though not entirely) checked, mainly by Urs himself. And yet in political terms, he found it a godsend in two important ways.

First, it completely stifled dissidence within the party. He virtually had a free hand in the state until the Emergency was lifted in February 1977. He used his extraordinary powers to neutralise his rivals: reshuffling the cabinet to leave leaders like Siddaveerappa holding relatively inconsequential portfolios, and giving his own supporters crucial posts. He also managed to have K. H. Patil (the state party president) replaced by a political lightweight. He did all this in a manner that maintained the balance between different regions and castes. He thus further entrenched rainbow coalitions as standard practice at the state level. They

[7] Devaraj Urs, interview by James Manor, 24 January 1980.

have, with some variations, remained so ever since. In other words, Urs's great achievement, that of bringing the Lingayat–Vokkaliga dominance over state politics to an end, has endured.

Second, the Emergency greatly assisted Urs in implementing two of his major policy innovations which were designed to consolidate support among lower-status groups: land reforms and caste reservations. Civil liberties were sufficiently curtailed to make popular protest on any issue unthinkable. Stifling Emergency laws also censored the press, preventing the dissemination of any news of dissent.

A year after he left office, Urs told Raghavan that without the Emergency he would have found it difficult to implement land reforms, and impossible to deliver reservations for the Backward Classes. 'I know the Emergency was bad for the country in many ways. But you must credit me for using it for good purposes and not misusing it.' He could have committed severe abuses like the central government and Chief Ministers of most (though not all[8]) other states did. But he restrained himself because in his heart of hearts he was opposed to draconian measures, which he rightly believed would prove to be bad politics over the long term. When we compare Karnataka with other states, it becomes apparent that excesses were far rarer here than elsewhere (Manor 1978). Much of the credit for this moderation goes to Urs. During the Emergency, an over-enthusiastic colleague suggested that he should put all opposition leaders, including those at the district and sub-district levels, behind bars. Urs bluntly and firmly refused this because he knew the Emergency would not last forever, and someday everyone responsible for the abuses would be held accountable.[9]

Urs seized this opportunity to ram through caste reservations and land reforms, for example, by removing the right to appeal against decisions of the land tribunals, something that would not have been permitted in normal times. He also used his coercive authority to liberate many of the 26,000 bonded labourers who were serving as serfs of land-owners or merchants, a task which had long proved impossible because governments lacked the draconian powers which the Emergency provided.

---

[8] There were exceptions in a few other states, notably Andhra Pradesh. This is discussed in detail in Manor (1978).

[9] This incident was narrated to Raghavan at the height of the Emergency by a cabinet minister who wished to remain anonymous.

He made headway against rural indebtedness, another intractable problem. Unlike nearly all other Congress Chief Ministers who settled for cosmetic measures, Urs actually worked hard to implement Mrs Gandhi's 20-point programme, a package of measures mainly aimed at the poor. Indeed, he appears to have been more committed to it than the lady herself, since she tolerated inaction from many of his peers.[10] Urs also used his immense leverage to push for a housing programme for the Scheduled Castes and the distribution of free sites for the rural poor with renewed vigour.

He energetically juggled the bureaucracy to position officers who were firmly committed to his pro-poor policies in key administrative posts at all levels. Those who were unreliable or inefficient were posted to departments unconnected with programmes to promote social justice and support disadvantaged groups. To consolidate his broad social base, he channelled patronage to the Backward Classes more aggressively than in normal times. He increased the provision of illicitly raised funds to groups which came under the category of Backward Classes, added government funds to the flow, organised conferences for them, and provided their caste associations with sites and funds from the state government to construct buildings.[11]

It is also worth stressing what Urs did *not* do during the Emergency. He did not undertake a campaign of forced sterilisations — the most politically insane scheme concocted by Mrs Gandhi's destructive son, Sanjay. Every month, Urs would send reports to the Congress (R) high command of large numbers of sterilisations, and saw to it that the numbers reported rose each month. But these reports were works of fiction. They were submitted in order to minimise hare-brained intrusions in Karnataka's politics from his party's national leaders. Together with the vast payments which Urs regularly provided to Mrs Gandhi, these reports earned him substantial autonomy. He was also helped in this by

---

[10] For evidence of Mrs Gandhi's indifference in 1975 to land reforms and policies to help disadvantaged groups, see Tandon (2006: 172). This is further reinforced by James Manor's interview with an aide to the then Chief Minister of West Bengal, in Cambridge, Massachusetts,12 November 1985.

[11] These comments are based on numerous discussions which E. Raghavan had with Urs over the years, and on an interview with Urs by James Manor, 8 August 1979, Bangalore.

the huge distance between Karnataka and New Delhi. He recognised that Congress Chief Ministers in states close to the capital suffered more intense surveillance and greater interference than he did.[12] He used this autonomy to protect the people of Karnataka from most of the brutish excesses which Sanjay and Indira Gandhi wished to see implemented, and got away with it.

So apart from some glaring aberrations, the Emergency in Karnataka entailed few gross abuses and was, in part, turned to positive effect by Urs. This largely explains how his party could garner sweeping election victories to the Parliament in 1977 and to the state assembly in 1978, while it suffered crushing defeats in most other states (Manor 1978). There is a parallel here with his use of illicit funds. Both the Emergency and the soaring corruption under Urs were outrageous, but both were partly used for constructive purposes.

To understand this ambiguity fully, it is important that we consider the darker side of the Emergency in Karnataka. When it suited him, Urs acted in an authoritarian manner. In his dealings with party colleagues, he often behaved imperiously. With others, he was often arrogant. When journalists and newspapers protested against constraints, they were denied customary facilities. The official in charge of press relations in the Chief Minister's secretariat barred a political correspondent from the *Deccan Herald* from press conferences. Newspapers which were not pro-Congress (R) or pro-Urs, for instance the *Indian Express*, also suffered in many ways. Censors applied their scissors indiscriminately, and deliberately cleared news stories so late that many newspapers could not bring out their editions on time.

Powers to curtail civil liberties were also used arbitrarily, and there were several instances of detention and physical harassment by the police in different parts of the state. By far the most notable cases of detention under the Maintenance of Internal Security Act were those of Lawrence Fernandes and Snehalata Reddy. But it must be stressed that the gross mistreatment of both occurred under heavy pressure from Congress (R) leaders at the national level who were eager to track down

---

[12] These comments are based on James Manor's interviews with Urs, in Bangalore, from 1978 to 1981. Manor also interviewed Vengal Rao of Andhra Pradesh, another Congress Chief Minister who submitted false reports of sterilisations. When asked why he did it, Rao replied, 'I didn't want a war.'

the opposition leader George Fernandes (brother of Lawrence and friend of Snehalata Reddy), who had gone underground to organise resistance to the Emergency. Lawrence Fernandes was physically maimed by the Bangalore police in a bid to extract information about his brother's whereabouts. Snehalata Reddy, a highly talented stage and screen personality, was picked up for the same reason and detained in appalling conditions. The physical and psychological hardship made her so ill that she finally died a few days after she was hurriedly released from prison. She was set free only when Urs heeded appeals by her friends. Apart from these two extremely obnoxious cases, it was mostly RSS[13] activists who received rough treatment from the police.

Urs also set out to undermine rival political parties, by quietly negotiating the entry of ten middle-level opposition leaders into the Congress (R). Among them was S. Bangarappa, a one-time socialist with a base among the Idigas (a prosperous 'Backward Class') in Shimoga and North Kanara districts. The prize catch, however, was H. T. Krishnappa, acting leader of the Congress (O) legislature party.

Krishnappa had been given this post because H. D. Deve Gowda, the official leader, was jailed during the Emergency. When Krishnappa joined Urs's Congress, it was rumoured that he was only the first Congress (O) leader to switch sides and that others, including some in jail, would soon follow. The names mentioned included former Chief Minister Veerendra Patil, and Deve Gowda himself. Patil had not been jailed, and it was believed that this was done deliberately at the instance of Mrs Gandhi, who wanted to use him to bring other Congress (O) leaders into her party.

Soon after the Emergency was lifted, Urs claimed at a public meeting that Patil had negotiated with him about defecting. Years later, Krishnappa also stated that he had been asked to join Urs's Congress by Deve Gowda, who had expressed an intention to follow suit. This had not happened because the Emergency was lifted before negotiations could be completed, but when this disclosure was made in 1989, Deve Gowda did not deny it.

The man responsible for preventing a mass defection from the Congress (O) was Hegde. He was in jail throughout the Emergency and

---

[13] The RSS is the Rashtriya Swayamsevak Sangh, a highly disciplined, hardline Hindu nationalist organisation.

when Veerendra Patil sent word to him suggesting a merger with Urs's Congress, he bluntly rejected the proposal. Even though no formal merger took place, Urs wrought immense damage within what little was left of the opposition. Indeed, he was reportedly happy that leaders like Veerendra Patil had not defected (something that had almost certainly been Mrs Gandhi's idea[14]), because had they done so, they would have formed a separate faction within the Congress (R), with the potential to threaten his hold.

The Lifting of the Emergency and the Parliamentary Election of 1977

When the Emergency ended in February 1977 and a parliamentary election was ordered, Urs had to run his campaign in Karnataka in the teeth of intense hostility from the media. In the free atmosphere that gradually replaced the suffocating Emergency rule, newspapers began hounding Mrs Gandhi at the national level and Urs at the state level by highlighting recent excesses.

Although Mrs Gandhi campaigned in the state as always, covering several key constituencies, Urs had more or less to fend for himself since she had her hands full dealing with a deeply embittered electorate in north India. In Karnataka, the choice of Congress (R) candidates was quite a simple affair. Almost all the sitting members (Congress (R) held every seat) were renominated without much fuss.

Despite massive negative publicity in the run-up to the election, Urs ran a smooth campaign. Yet, he was unsure of his party's fate because he, like everyone else, sensed a wave of sympathy for opposition parties. Their leaders who toured the state drew massive crowds while the turnout at Congress (R) rallies was disappointing. And often, the latter gatherings became embarrassing due to dramatic displays of anger by members of the public.

The general election in March 1977 was the most bitter since independence. A fragmented opposition swiftly came together at the national level in the newly created Janata Party, and offered Mrs Gandhi a challenge the like of which she had neither seen earlier nor expected. She had centralised power in her party and government to such a degree,

---

[14] For compelling evidence of this, see Tandon (2006: 114 and 281–82).

and reacted so heatedly to disappointing news, that people tended to tell her what they thought she wanted to hear, even if it was inaccurate. Thus, by pursuing unprecedented power, she had unwittingly weakened herself by cutting herself off from reliable intelligence.

Karnataka was not insulated from the national resentment against those who had curbed civil liberties during the Emergency. The election here was so keen that on polling day there was great tension, and a few incidents of violence also took place.

When the counting of votes for half of Karnataka's seats began and initial trends emerged, Urs, who had been worried, was stunned. His party was leading in almost every constituency. He also got word from neighbouring southern states that the Congress (R) and its allies were doing well there too. But at that point, he still had no inkling of what was happening in the north. He was, rather surprisingly, in two minds about what initially looked like a Congress (R) sweep. Years later, he told Raghavan about what he felt that afternoon:

> I was immensely pleased that my party was doing much better than I expected in Karnataka. But I was equally unhappy. After all, I thought if we are doing well in Karnataka, we must do well elsewhere too. In that case, the lady would not only continue in power, she would be ruthless. I could not share this anguish with anyone because I was supposed to be — I was — a true Congressman. However, I could not be a true Sanjayite. I knew that if the Congress was returned to power (in New Delhi), it would mean the further rise of Sanjay Gandhi and that, I knew, would be too costly for the country. When I got to know that evening that the Congress was facing a rout in the north, I heaved a sigh of relief because the country was saved.

Urs had reasons to dislike Sanjay Gandhi. During the Emergency, he had become an extra-constitutional authority who, in some ways, was more powerful than Mrs Gandhi. Urs put a premium on experience and age and intensely disliked Sanjay's abrasive ways, but often had to stomach insults. He narrated one such experience:

> I had gone to Delhi for some work and, as was the custom, I called on Mrs Gandhi at her home. When I was coming out of her office, I found Sanjay sitting in the next room, all alone. I courteously greeted him and was getting out. Sanjay called out, 'Urs, come here'. There was no Mr Urs or Ursji, but just 'Urs, come here'. I felt like ignoring him, but could not, knowing the kind of clout he had. I went to him and he berated me for a while for no

reason at all, at the end of which he wanted me to give important positions in the cabinet to his Youth Congress friends. I felt miserable that I had to take this from an upstart, but I could not help it.

Urs claimed he was forced to promote Gundu Rao, a junior minister (and, ultimately, his successor), to cabinet rank because of Sanjay's insistence.

In the final tally, the Congress (R) won 26 out of 28 seats in Karnataka, conceding only two to the Janata Party. Compared to the previous election in 1971,[15] the margin of victory per constituency had been reduced. But this was still remarkable, since in north India the party had practically been wiped out. This impressive victory sent Urs's stock in the party soaring. Suddenly, he had real political weight at the national level. But the humiliation of the Congress (R) elsewhere also created acute troubles for Urs. They arose, predictably enough, from the opposition, but also from within his own party.

Post-Emergency Problems

For seven years, Mrs Gandhi's protection had enabled Urs to manage all manner of problems within the Congress (R) in Karnataka. Now she was gravely weakened. Partymen who had never mustered even a whimper of dissent now discovered their voice and began to carry tales against Urs to the party's national leaders, several of whom had begun to snipe at the supreme leader. A realignment of forces eventually occurred within the Congress (R) at the national level, and this inspired intensified in-fighting within Karnataka between the two factions.

K. H. Patil suddenly emerged as a serious rival to Urs. He was reinstalled as president of the state unit of the Congress (R) by Brahmananda Reddy, who had become president of the party at the national level. Patil gathered around him several important leaders who had felt slighted by Urs. All were ministers. While Patil challenged Urs within the party organisation, these other dissidents followed suit within the cabinet. Significantly, Gundu Rao was part of this group.

The opposition also started mounting attacks, even though it had fared badly in the parliamentary election. Detention during the Emergency

---

[15] Indian elections normally occur at five-year intervals, but Mrs Gandhi used the Emergency to postpone this one and to prolong her term in power.

had united most opposition groups into one party (in Karnataka as well as at the national level) just before the election. The new Janata Party welded together people who had been associated with the old Congress (O), the Hindu nationalist Jan Sangh, the Socialist Party and the Congress for Democracy (set up by Jagjivan Ram, the formidable Scheduled Caste leader who had served in Mrs Gandhi's cabinet during the Emergency, but broke with her when it was lifted). For the first time, the Congress (R) in Karnataka faced something approaching a single opposition party.[16]

A few weeks after the national election of 1977, the Congress (R) faced another round of crushing defeats in state elections across north India. This emboldened the opposition in Karnataka, since the Janata Party assumed, or at least hoped, that a similar fate awaited Urs and the Congress (R) in the long-overdue state election. It questioned the legitimacy of his government and did everything it could to destroy popular faith in the Chief Minister.

The government could easily be challenged on ethical grounds. The legislature, elected in 1972, should have completed its term in February 1977. But an objectionable constitutional amendment during the Emergency had extended the life of Parliament and all state legislatures by another year. Karnataka posed a dilemma for the central government which was now in the Janata Party's hands. It had dissolved the legislatures in the northern states through a presidential proclamation, on the grounds that the humiliation of the Congress (R) in the parliamentary election in these states had deprived it of the right to rule them at the state level. But in Karnataka, where the Congress (R) had won, this logic did not apply. Constitutionally, however dubious Mrs Gandhi's amendment had been, its state assembly would not end its term until March 1978.

For Urs, this extra year in power was a severe test of his fortitude and political skills. He had to deal with a bitterly hostile national government. Both national- and state-level Janata leaders saw as much evil in Urs as in Mrs Gandhi. They blindly seized upon a long list of complaints which dissident Karnataka Congress (R) leaders made, and prepared the ground for the central government to launch an investigation into their allegations of corruption, nepotism and misuse of office against Urs.

---

[16] The smaller Communist parties remained aloof from the Janata Party.

Urs knew that he could not escape scrutiny in these matters. The central government had swiftly launched several inquiries to examine abuses by Mrs Gandhi during the Emergency. He was certain that a similar inquiry would soon be mounted against him too, so he sought to pre-empt it by setting up a commission headed by a retired High Court judge, providing it with terms of reference that focused on administrative lapses, but which excluded other issues such as corruption and misuse of office. This ploy was all too obvious. Opposition leaders poured scorn on the terms of reference and the central government brushed it aside and announced its own commission of inquiry, headed by a retired Supreme Court justice, A. N. Grover, with a mandate to investigate the full range of allegations against Urs.

This was a serious blow and Urs's power appeared to be rapidly ebbing away. This persuaded K. H. Patil and his faction to strike at Urs from within his party. After a series of conclaves, five important ministers resigned from his cabinet, protesting against his arrogance. Gundu Rao, who was with this group and expected to resign, switched sides at the last minute and backed Urs.

This added up to a formidable challenge. For the first time in his tenure, Urs found the going exceedingly tough as adverse publicity mounted. The Grover Commission became a public court where his alleged misdeeds were examined almost every day. These included the allotment of sites by the Bangalore Development Authority to his daughters, the appointment of his loyalists to key non-official posts and grave charges of corruption. This was a time when all those associated with Mrs Gandhi were seen as villains, and Urs had to face the political onslaught from all sides.

A real taste of the public mood became available in November 1977. In the immediate aftermath of her election defeat, Mrs Gandhi had shut herself off from public life. But the new central government's attempts to bring her to book forced her to fight back, both legally and politically. After brief forays into states like Uttar Pradesh where she was reviled, she turned to the south, particularly Karnataka, to prove that she still had mass support. In November, she began a tour of the state from the northern district of Gulbarga. The turnout at her meetings and along her route was so unexpectedly large that both she and Urs were jubilant. At the end of the second day, Urs rang up a cabinet colleague and spoke at length about the massive response from the people in northern Karnataka. He asked him to spare no effort in organising a similar reception when she reached the southern districts. However, as soon as Mrs Gandhi crossed the Tungabhadra river and entered the old Mysore region, a nightmare began. She was scheduled to address meetings in every major town, but the opposition had organised protests that often turned extremely violent. In Shimoga and Hassan, for example, her entourage was heavily stoned. In small towns like Belur, people showered stones on her cavalcade and by the time she reached the outskirts of Hassan, it had become impossible to continue the tour. She had to travel in darkness to Bangalore. Her public meeting there the next day proved equally disastrous. Congress (R) and opposition activists clashed continuously at the venue and when she finally left the city, she had to travel to the airport in a police van, since it was feared that she would be attacked if she went by car.

This episode influenced the political strategies of the various contending groups. Congress (R) dissidents intensified their campaign against the Chief Minister on the assumption that a weakened Indira Gandhi implied a weakened Urs. For the Janata Party opposition in Karnataka, these incidents were suggestive of popular unrest against the Congress (R) which, they thought, might help carry them to victory in the state election due within a few weeks. Urs began to doubt his electoral prospects. But he saw no reason to ditch Mrs Gandhi. She was obviously unpopular south of the Tungabhadra, but the other national leaders in the Congress (R) with whom he might side, like Brahmananda Reddy (a rival to Mrs Gandhi), had no pulling power in the state. And since Urs's own rival, K. H. Patil, was in Reddy's camp, Urs could hardly join it.

Until mid-December 1977, the tension at the national level between Mrs Gandhi's faction and Reddy's remained high, but stopped short of splitting the party. But then swift developments in Karnataka in the last week of 1977 changed the course of politics at both the state and national levels. In the second half of December, the state cabinet scheduled a session of the legislature for the first week of January. Urs expected both Patil's faction and the Janata Party opposition to challenge him then, but Patil decided to strike even before the legislature met.

Patil knew that Janata Party leaders, particularly Deve Gowda (the then state-level, Janata Party president), wanted to oust Urs quickly so that he would not remain caretaker Chief Minister during the campaign for the state election expected in March. If Urs remained in office, he would be able to manipulate the administration to his advantage. The only way to remove Urs was the imposition of President's Rule, that is, direct rule from New Delhi. This, in turn, could happen only in politically volatile circumstances such as those created by defections from the Congress (R).

Since the Patil faction also wanted Urs out, it entered into an informal understanding with Janata Party leaders. They all knew that their combined strength — 20–25 for Patil, and just over 50 for Janata — would not deprive Urs of a majority. So they agreed to entice legislators from Urs's group, which was fraying at the edges since some legislators doubted Mrs Gandhi's capacity to help them win the election.

The Patil group managed to fool a lot of these doubters by making inflated claims about its strength. When it had attracted a sufficiently large number, it announced that it had lost confidence in Urs. The Janata Party then demanded that Urs's government be dismissed because it had lost its majority. Both groups met the Governor, Govind Narain, to argue their case forcefully. For the first time in the state's history, the Governor had to resort to a head count of legislators to determine whether Urs still retained a majority as he claimed. Urs demanded that this be tested on the floor of the assembly. His plea was ignored and Govind Narain, in his report to the President, concluded that there was serious instability in Karnataka and, in order to prevent horse-trading, the assembly should be dissolved.

When the report reached New Delhi, it posed a dilemma for Janata Party's national leaders who were empowered to determine the President's response. They were eager to oust Urs, but they also wanted to retain their democratic credentials. Dismissing a Chief Minister who had announced his readiness to face a vote in the legislature could damage their reputation, especially since they had consistently attacked Mrs Gandhi for resorting to such undemocratic means in the past. Nevertheless, they swallowed their doubts and at around midnight on 31 December 1977, Urs was thrown out of office by presidential proclamation. In Karnataka, Janata Party leaders were jubilant and Krishna, a leading light of K. H. Patil's faction, described the decision as a New Year gift to the state.

Urs, and practically all his followers, had left Bangalore for Delhi to take part in another political drama. Mrs Gandhi had called a convention of her supporters in Delhi to formalise a split in the party which had occurred, for all practical purposes, with Brahmananda Reddy's faction. Urs then returned to Bangalore, unhappy that he had lost power, but pleased that the party had split, since this gave him full control over the remains of the Congress (R) organisation as a state election loomed.

The State Election of 1978

The imposition of President's Rule meant that Urs would have to fight the election on an equal footing with the Janata Party, which had the advantage of solid support from a central government that was well-placed to raise funds for this campaign. It also meant that he would find it difficult to raise funds on his own for his party's election campaign from traditional sources (excise contractors, big businesses, etc.), since he could no longer apply subtle pressure from the apex of power.

It almost seemed as if he was starting again from scratch. He did not even have the premises to house his party's headquarters. The old Congress (R) office was in the possession of K. H. Patil's faction. To assemble his party machinery well in advance of the campaign, premises were rented on the outskirts of Bangalore, and Urs loyalist S. B. Nagaral, who had briefly been state party president, was reinstalled in this capacity.

Meanwhile, the Janata Party and Patil's version of the Congress (R) proceeded as if the days of an Indira-dominated Congress were over. The Janata Party had secured a respectable popular vote in the parliamentary election almost a year earlier, though it had won only two of the 28 seats from Karnataka. Since then, there appeared to be a ground-swell in its favour. Its president, Deve Gowda, was convinced it would soon be swept to power, and national leaders of the party apparently shared his view. To impress Karnataka's voters, the Janata Party's national executive met in Bangalore to select candidates for the state election slated for 25 February.

Patil fully expected that his faction of the Congress (R) would inherit most of the mass support that had always enabled the party to rule in the state. He engaged the Janata Party in informal negotiations on seat adjustments, to consolidate the anti-Indira vote. Negotiations fell through, largely because the Janata Party offered Patil so little that he finally decided to fight on his own.

The Janata Party had problems picking candidates for several reasons. Since almost everyone involved in politics believed that it would gain power, there was intense competition for its tickets. Various groups within it, for instance, the former Congress (O), the Jana Sangh and Socialist members, competed aggressively for shares of the Janata seats. And, there was also intense competition between the Lingayats and the Vokkaligas, who predominated within the Janata Party, for nominations.

Things went more smoothly within Patil's Congress. Most of the relatively small group that had either joined in the struggle against Urs or switched sides at the last minute were given tickets, as were their clients in other constituencies.

Urs should also have had an easy time of it. There was no one of substance in the party to challenge him and, after the split in the national party, Mrs Gandhi was thoroughly obliging. Yet, unexpectedly, Urs ended up facing greater problems than both the Janata Party and Patil's faction. He had retained the support of numerous sitting members, and they were renominated. But in the southern districts, most important leaders had left him. He was therefore forced to select far too many people with little or no experience of electoral politics. He also had huge problems in recruiting Lingayats and Vokkaligas, since these castes had been deeply alienated by his pro-poor policies. As if this was not enough, some party colleagues cut up rough. Nagaral was so unhappy about not being able to get tickets for men in the northern districts that he resigned the presidency of the state unit of the party and vanished. He holed up in a hotel and refused to return to the organisation, all of which demoralised Urs further.

Just before the election, close observers of the political scene got the distinct impression that Urs had begun behaving as if he were leader of the opposition. He used uncharacteristically strong words to criticise the administration run by the Governor. He appeared to be unsure of returning to power, and it later became clear that this perception was accurate.

His worries were compounded by his party's failure to obtain the use of the familiar Congress (R) election symbol. Both versions of the Congress had claimed it, so the Election Commission froze it. Urs's party lacked a symbol till as late as the deadline for filing the nominations. They were finally awarded the symbol of the hand, familiar today because the Gandhis' Congress has used it ever since, but a rather odd symbol at the time. The delay in awarding it inspired intense anxiety among Urs's candidates since they had little time to acquaint voters with it. Moreover, a couple of them did not receive the proper authorisation from the party, which was needed to secure the symbol, and at least one of them had to contest on an entirely different one.

Another problem for Urs was the Grover Commission. It had continued to proceed with its investigation of the various charges levelled against Urs, and issued an interim report indicting him for misuse of office. Although it was supposed to be an independent body, there has always been a suspicion that it was forced to come up with this report on the eve of the state election by the Janata Party government in New Delhi. Commissions of inquiry rarely produce interim reports. The timing was understandably unnerving for Urs.

Unlike in 1972, Urs chose to contest from his old constituency of Hunsur. His main rival, H. L. Thimme Gowda, was carefully chosen by the Janata Party. He lived locally and was a Vokkaliga from a constituency in which there was a numerical preponderance of his caste fellows. The Janata Party ran a high-pitched, lavishly funded campaign in Hunsur, forcing Urs to spend much more time in his constituency than he had originally intended.

Despite all these adversities, he did not lose heart. His government had, after all, achieved a great deal. He campaigned briskly all over the state and Mrs Gandhi also toured quite extensively, shuttling between Karnataka and Andhra Pradesh, where too a state election was under way. As expected, the Janata Party brought all its national leaders to tour the state, from Prime Minister Morarji Desai on down. K. H. Patil's version of the Congress was the poor cousin in the campaign, with no big names to exhibit.

This factionalism was expected to split the Congress vote. At any rate, it — and the new, unfamiliar symbols used by both Congresses — led most political observers to believe that the Janata Party would win. Urs shared this view at one point. He privately said that he was sure of about 60 or so seats, but would not hazard a guess about the rest. But then in mid-campaign, while on the road, he and D. B. Chandre Gowda, a Member of Parliament (MP), discussed trends in detail and concluded that the Congress (I) ('I' standing for Indira, as her faction now came to be called) might end up with about 115 to 120 seats in an assembly of 224. Urs's morale lifted to such an extent that he promised to make Chandre Gowda a minister in his cabinet if their assessment held good.

Their expectations were, in fact, surpassed. Urs's Congress (I) secured 149 seats (and a whopping 66.5 per cent of the votes), and the Janata Party won just 51. The other Congress was nearly wiped out. Only two of its candidates won, and its big guns, including K. H. Patil himself, were defeated.

This was impressive by any standard, and it was all the more remarkable given the difficulties Urs had faced. Several factors explained the result. His support base among the poor and the less privileged had indeed been consolidated. These mostly unlettered voters had had no difficulty in identifying the new symbol, and this vividly demonstrated their high level of political awareness on which Urs's entire strategy, in the years he was in power, had been predicated. His progressive policies — land reforms, reservations for the Backward Classes, free housing, the drive against indebtedness, etc. — had earned him a fresh mandate.

His party had also benefited from a squabble within the Janata Party before the election. When Janata leaders came to expect victory, they began strengthening their own individual factions to position themselves for the post-election division of the spoils. The party was substantially divided along caste lines between the Vokkaligas and the Lingayats, and more particularly between Deve Gowda and Veerendra Patil. When tickets were distributed, each group sought to maximise its share of the seats. This was quite normal, but then both factions made subtle attempts to sabotage the chances of the other in some (though not all) parts of the state. After their defeat, these leaders accused each other of these actions and of distributing funds selectively. Many in the Janata Party camp firmly believed that this conflict did serious damage. The over-confidence that caused it also explained the scuttling of the negotiations on seats with K. H. Patil's Congress. Had the Janata Party been more generous in those talks and more united, it might have run Urs very close. The fact that it lost nearly 50 seats by less than 5,000 votes, even when the anti-Urs Congress vote was split, supports this view.

What is certain is that for Urs, this unexpected victory was sweet. He had not only won a solid majority, but also cut to size many leaders and groups inimical to him. Most crucially, the once-dominant castes that had worked to defeat him had failed. The most astonishing defeat was that of the head of the immensely influential Sirigere *math*. Its *swamiji* (often a form of address for a Hindu religious instructor) had openly declared his support for the Janata Party and even toured areas where he commanded a strong following among the land-owning and numerically powerful Sadar Lingayats. In most of these constituencies, Urs's candidates won.

Implications

This victory, including those in the Sadar Lingayat heartland and in the southern districts of the state where Mrs Gandhi had encountered hostility, demonstrated that Urs's progressive policies were widely popular. His party had clearly sunk deep roots into the middle and lower reaches of society. As a result, there was no going back to Lingayat–Vokkaliga dominance. The worst that might happen would be an attempt by these castes to reassert control over the state government. But the changes in the political dynamics, and in the popular consciousness, that Urs had engineered meant that any attempt at such a comeback would be short-lived. After Urs, senior leaders who wanted to survive in office would be compelled to share power equitably among leaders of both prosperous and disadvantaged groups, in rainbow coalitions. And to sustain these coalitions, they would need to offer lower-status groups more than mere tokenism. Nearly all politicians in Karnataka in later years have been canny enough to recognise this, so no serious attempt at a dominant-caste comeback has ever occurred.

The changes that Urs triggered made Karnataka more genuinely democratic, but also more difficult to govern. Before he assumed power, dominant-caste ministers had already found it hard, with their limited resources, to respond adequately to the rising demands from their respective caste-clusters. By opening the system up to further demands from less prosperous groups, Urs made the problem of demand overload even worse, and in the 1990s, when fiscal constraints on the government became far tighter than in Urs's time, the problem would become excruciating. But Urs went ahead anyway, even though it meant that his task as Chief Minister would become more arduous. We shall see in Part III of this book that his successor Hegde faced a similar choice a decade later when a proposal to empower elected local councils arose. This, too, would encourage still more demands, but like Urs, he decided to proceed because, as with Urs, it served his political interests to do so, and because the deepening of democracy was the right thing to do.

The transition which Urs managed — from landed-caste dominance over state politics to a more open system in which less exalted groups could contest for power, and major parties were more deeply rooted in society — eventually occurred in almost all Indian states.[17] But he ensured that it happened sooner in Karnataka than in nearly all[18] other states, and that the transition was attended by less violence and spite between social groups than elsewhere.

While Urs often used rhetoric to depict himself as a man in great hurry to overturn practically everything in order to promote the interests of the have-nots, he privately admitted that he was a gradualist, because neither society in Karnataka nor the political apparatus that he controlled would accept drastic change. As he once told Raghavan when they discussed the limitations of his land reforms, 'I find it politically difficult to go the whole-hog no matter how keen I am to change things. I can only adopt an incremental policy in most cases.' But he pursued incremental change with such persistence and on so many fronts that the cumulative effect was immense.

The tradition of rainbow coalitions which he established at cabinet level contributed mightily to peaceable social and political relations in the state, since ministers now had to appeal to *all* sections of society. They thus avoided the poisonous politics that had emerged in some other states where leaders appealed only to *some* sections, fomenting division and conflict between them in the process.[19]

But despite Urs's revival of the reformist, accommodative brand of statecraft that had been established by old Mysore's maharajas, and despite the remarkable scale of his victory in the 1978 state election, he was soon to face major political troubles, which originated mainly from events at the national level.

---

[17] One notable and troubling exception is Orissa, where all major parties remain very shallowly rooted, and a tiny hyper-elite denies even land-owning groups substantial power.

[18] In this regard, a case comparable to Karnataka's is that of Maharashtra, where Y.B. Chavan and his successors followed a path similar to Urs's.

[19] Uttar Pradesh between 1990 and 2007 is a classic example of this kind of politics.

3

The End of the Urs Era

Urs's second innings commenced with a nominal challenge to his leadership from Basavalingappa. When the legislators met and, as the Congress (I) culture now required, sought a directive from Mrs Gandhi, she favoured Urs. Had she backed Basavalingappa or anyone else, the party would have been completely divided, but as we shall see, she now badly needed Urs. Nevertheless, there were rumours that this token challenge had been inspired by Mrs Gandhi, to indicate that she could not be taken for granted.

Urs's achievements in this second term were less impressive than in his first. He proposed no new policies of great substance and focused on completing the work begun earlier. Indeed, he appeared to be taking things easy. He now felt far less dependent on Mrs Gandhi. He reckoned, with some justice, that his re-election was the result of policies that had mostly been designed and implemented by him. He had done so without any prodding from Mrs Gandhi, in order to survive in the face of opposition from the Lingayats and Vokkaligas. Mrs Gandhi had permitted most other Congress Chief Ministers to get away with doing little to fulfil her earlier promises of pro-poor reform, which strongly suggested that she was not serious about them. Urs could not help noticing that nearly all these other, less reformist Chief Ministers had now been resoundingly rejected by the voters.

Some of his followers, adept in the art of flattery, told him that he was as formidable a leader as the lady herself. If Urs privately entertained such thoughts, he kept them to himself at this stage. But over time, he came to believe this idea, and this proved dangerous in the long run.

Politically, however, he was kept busy. The Grover Commission continued its sittings off and on in Bangalore. Its investigation of charges against Urs now appeared less threatening, since Urs had won a solid mandate despite them. After all, Congress (I) leaders argued, the people's court was vastly more important than any commission of inquiry. But it could not be ignored, and many hours were consumed in preparations to answer the accusations.

In the legislature too, Urs faced a formidable challenge. For the first time since independence, the opposition had enough members on its benches to make things difficult for the government. The Janata Party missed no opportunity to strike at Urs. He, however, carried on nonchalantly, even somewhat arrogantly. He became less interested in day-to-day administration and more preoccupied with politics at the national level in which his participation gradually increased. He was no longer just a Congress (I) Chief Minister. Mrs Gandhi now recognised his importance (she had very few other regional backers in power) and began consulting him on major issues. An opportunity soon arose for him to become the second-ranking leader in the party, and to make Mrs Gandhi feel more obliged to him than he was to her. He jumped at it, but this too carried grave risks.

The Chikmagalur By-Election

After her crushing election defeat in 1977, Mrs Gandhi kept a low profile for a time. The Janata Party government in New Delhi instituted numerous inquiries against her, and at one point she was even jailed briefly for the excesses committed during the Emergency. Her response was to go on the offensive, raising issues of popular concern and instructing her party colleagues in Parliament to mount attacks on the Janata Party regime. Her party's impressive victories in state elections in Karnataka and Andhra Pradesh convinced her that she still had mass appeal and that her party could not be written off. By mid-1978, she had decided that to defend herself effectively and to remain in the political limelight, she needed to return to Parliament.

This was easier said than done. Winning a seat from northern India was still out of the question and yet another electoral defeat might have finished her. Although Andhra and Karnataka were less risky, she was unsure of her prospects in these states too. The simplest and safest way back to power was to resort to indirect election to the Rajya Sabha, the Upper House of the Indian Parliament, from a state where her party had enough strength to make victory likely.[1] Karnataka seemed the ideal place. A couple of months after the state election here, she spent a few days resting at Nandi Hills, a quiet resort outside Bangalore. During this visit,

---

[1] Seats in the Rajya Sabha are filled by indirect elections in which legislators from the various Indian states constitute the electorate.

she quietly filed forms to register as a voter in Karnataka — a prerequisite for contesting from the state.

In May 1978, Urs had suggested that Mrs Gandhi seek a Rajya Sabha seat from Karnataka, which she declined. As Urs later told Raghavan:

> She thought the time was not opportune and that she had to wait a little longer before it would become acceptable to people. So we decided to field Sachidananda Swamy (Urs's political secretary) . . . He would have vacated the seat any time I asked him.

A few weeks later, Mrs Gandhi decided to seek a seat in the far more powerful Lower House, the Lok Sabha, which required her to face a direct election. She asked Urs to identify a safe constituency in Karnataka. After carefully examining all aspects of the problem, he chose Chikmagalur in the hilly southwest of the state. It was ideally suited for Mrs Gandhi in many ways. She wanted a completely rural constituency where the voters were less likely to be hostile to her. Chikmagalur fulfilled this criterion. It was a backward district, far from the kind of urban influences that had turned people against her after the Emergency. It contained a large number of poor people who could still be relied upon to vote for her, particularly since, during the Emergency, vulnerable groups in Karnataka had not experienced the kind of oppression faced by their counterparts in the north.

Ironically, Mrs Gandhi could count on a warm reception in Chikmagalur because during the Emergency Urs had secretly 'defied' her. He had quietly ignored pressure from her son Sanjay (and from the lady herself) to implement politically suicidal measures such as compulsory sterilisations and forcible evictions of poor people from their homes in the interests of 'beautification'. He had rightly believed that he could get away with this. The Gandhis had little good intelligence on states as far from New Delhi as Karnataka. And, by maintaining a constant flow of substantial tributary payments to the national leadership, he ensured that they remained content with him and not too inquisitive about what was actually happening in his state (Manor 1978).

Chikmagalur had also always been largely insulated from electoral swings. Not only had it returned Congressmen to the Lok Sabha at every previous election, but in 1971 and 1977 the party's candidate, Chandre Gowda, had won by handsome margins. The other consideration was the constituency's caste composition. Here, not only the Lingayats and

Vokkaligas but the Scheduled Castes, and Backward Classes such as the Billavas and Kurubas, also had considerable numerical strength. These three groups had traditionally lent strong backing to the Congress (I).

Urs, who was quite confident that he could get Mrs Gandhi elected from Chikmagalur, asked Chandre Gowda to resign, and he did so forthwith. Even then, Mrs Gandhi had nagging doubts. She was told by some Karnataka Congress (I) leaders that Urs would ditch her at the last minute. This put her off for a while. As Urs told Raghavan some months after the by-election:

> I had to convince her that I would take personal responsibility to get her elected from there. At this stage, Chenna Reddy [Andhra Pradesh Chief Minister] offered to get her elected to the Lok Sabha from Secunderabad. This was rejected because Secunderabad was not a rural constituency. Mrs Gandhi finally agreed with me, but wanted some more time to say yes.

When it became known that she was likely to contest from Karnataka, the Janata Party started looking for a formidable candidate to oppose her. It rightly believed that Rajkumar, a beloved Kannada film star, would offer a stiff challenge, and approached him. He was ideally suited because his popularity among the poorer groups all over the state equalled, and perhaps exceeded, that of Mrs Gandhi. He also had strong credentials for a contest specifically in Chikmagalur. He was an Idiga, the same caste as the Billavas, who were traditional Congress supporters and present in considerable numbers in two assembly segments in the constituency.

Rajkumar, however, was reluctant. Urs claimed that he applied a little pressure to deter the film star through important members of his caste, notably some excise contractors who were beholden to Urs. Subsequently, Rajkumar publicly declined the offer to stand as Janata Party's candidate against Mrs Gandhi.

Following this development, Urs's predecessor as Chief Minister, Veerendra Patil, was selected to oppose Mrs Gandhi. Several considerations influenced this choice. Since he was a prominent Lingayat, he was expected to outpoll her in the three assembly segments where his caste was dominant. The Vokkaligas, who had a strong presence in three other segments, could be trusted to vote for the Janata Party because the president of its state unit, the future Indian Prime Minister Deve Gowda, was a Vokkaliga. If the assumption that people would be reluctant to vote for Mrs Gandhi after they learnt about the atrocities in north India held good, there was a fair chance for Patil.

An important Vokkaliga leader told Raghavan during the campaign that Patil's name was proposed for one other reason. If he won from Chikmagalur, he would automatically find a place in Janata Party's cabinet in New Delhi, and this would take him out of the state political scene. If he lost, the party would still have to reward him in some way for taking on Mrs Gandhi. The reward one heard of at the time was a post as the Governor[2] of any state other than the one one belonged to. Either way, Patil would be out of state politics, an idea that was welcome to Vokkaliga leaders in the Janata Party.

It was only a day before she actually filed her nomination papers that Mrs Gandhi finally confirmed her intentions. On her way from Delhi to Chikmagalur, she made the announcement. She filed her papers amidst great enthusiasm among Congress (I) workers who took her out in a procession. The next day, Veerendra Patil filed his papers. At this stage, it was unlikely that either candidate anticipated the kind of blistering encounter that they faced over the next three weeks.

The Chikmagalur by-election turned out to be the most intense and arguably the bitterest electoral battle ever fought in India, before or since. It was so keen that at one stage it appeared that there was every chance that Mrs Gandhi would lose. Knowing fully well her and Urs's ability to sway the voters, the Janata Party mounted an immensely energetic campaign. The dynamic leader who headed the assault was George Fernandes. He had spent much of the Emergency in jail and had had to fight the 1977 Lok Sabha election from his prison cell. For him, Chikmagalur offered a chance to settle personal and political scores. He had been arrested during the Emergency on charges of attempted sabotage. Snehalata Reddy, a dear friend of his, who was locked up because of her closeness to Fernandes, died because of her imprisonment. His own brother was brutally maimed by the police. He had abundant personal reasons to treat Mrs Gandhi as an enemy. This was an opportunity to end her career.

Fernandes took charge of the campaign and during the three weeks before polling, it looked as if he, and not Veerendra Patil, was the candidate opposing Mrs Gandhi. Both she and Fernandes formally

---

[2] In the Indian federal system, Governors are largely ceremonial 'heads of state', performing roles akin to those of the President of India and the monarch in Britain.

opened the campaign in Karkala, a coastal town that formed part of the constituency. At that early stage, no one realised that this by-election would become the political equivalent of the Kumbh Mela.[3] However, that is how it turned out to be, as thousands of workers from all political parties descended on the constituency. The election was considered so important that hundreds of journalists representing the local, state, national, and international press turned up.

After the opening of the campaign, Urs and Mrs Gandhi almost never appeared together. This was deliberate. Urs wanted her to visit every nook and corner of the constituency, meeting as many people as she could. He had much more to do than she did. Besides addressing public meetings, he had to keep a constant eye on what the Janata Party camp was up to, deploy campaigners and funds adroitly and cultivate vote blocks through a network of local leaders.

During the two weeks or so that Mrs Gandhi spent in Chikmagalur, she visited almost every village and hamlet untiringly, often travelling to remote corners of the constituency. This was a strenuous task, as in terms of geographical area, this is one of the largest in Karnataka. It stretches for more than 150 kilometres from one end to the other. Two of its assembly segments are in the coastal region, three in the Malnad (hilly region), and another three in the sloping plains along the Western Ghats. Mrs Gandhi journeyed up and down the Ghats, spending nights in bungalows owned by coffee planters. On a typical day, she would set off early in the morning, making brief halts and speeches at every village, take a brief lunch break and continue campaigning until well past midnight. By prearrangement, Urs and Mrs Gandhi would meet at night once every two or three days to review the situation.

The Janata Party ran an even better campaign. Fernandes was all over the constituency, doing things that even Mrs Gandhi could not. Although he was a national-level cabinet minister, he would travel in private cars with a few of his followers, stopping at villages either to address a meeting or to go door-to-door. Being quite unassuming, he would stop by the wayside at tea shops. Other party leaders also went round the constituency, and a number of intellectuals and partisan mediamen also helped the party.

---

[3] The Kumbh Mela is a religious festival which attracts large numbers of people.

As campaigning picked up, the constituency witnessed great tension and some violence too. Early on, Janata Party campaigners were often roughed up by Congress (I) *goondas*. After a while, they returned this in good measure. Once, a couple of women Janata Party canvassers, including the daughter of Snehalata Reddy, were manhandled by the police when they tried to disrupt one of Mrs Gandhi's meetings. Yet another time, an attempt by Janata Party workers in a small village, Ujire, to seize a Congress (I) vehicle, allegedly carrying weapons and money, led to police firing in which an innocent college girl was killed and several journalists were beaten up by the police. These incidents made things difficult for Mrs Gandhi.

As if this was not enough, a Janata Party MP, Era Sezhiyan, dropped a bombshell at the very end of the campaign. He produced evidence to show that Mrs Gandhi had made a false declaration before the Election Commission. Although she had registered herself as a voter in Karnataka, her address, as mentioned in her nomination papers, was one of Delhi. This, he claimed, was a violation of election laws. Mrs Gandhi had no answer to this charge. She declined to comment because the matter was sub judice; a case had been filed by a Janata Party worker in the court at Doddaballapur, where Mrs Gandhi was said to have filed a declaration. Long after the election, when the case was heard in court, it was made out that the declaration filed in Doddaballapur had been a forgery and that Mrs Gandhi had never submitted it. However, according to Urs, she had. He told Raghavan after he had fallen out with her that Mrs Gandhi's original application was retrieved from the file before the case came up and a forgery was introduced in its place. Urs said:

> the original document was retrieved by Basavalingappa (the then Revenue Minister) a day after Era Sezhiyan disclosed that she had filed a false declaration. I was told by him that he personally handed over the original document to Mrs Gandhi, who destroyed it immediately.

As the campaign came to a close, there was so much tension in the constituency that Mrs Gandhi found it difficult to campaign in small towns. It looked like the Janata Party had made enough headway to defeat her. When she met the press a day after polling (but before the count), she did not sound confident when she said she would win. The margin of victory, she said, did not matter. If she sounded cautious, she had reason to. The large turnout and the enthusiasm of Janata Party supporters had made everyone believe that Veerendra Patil had a good chance. Some violence had also occurred on the day of polling and in one place Chandre Gowda, who had become well known for vacating the seat for Mrs Gandhi, had been physically assaulted.

On the day of the count, neither Mrs Gandhi nor Urs was in Chikmagalur. They monitored the trends from Delhi and Bangalore respectively. By night it had become clear that despite all the odds against her, Mrs Gandhi was emerging a clear victor. As it turned out, the margin was respectable, but similar to Chandre Gowda's in 1977. This raised an obvious problem. Despite being the best-known politician in the country, if she could not improve on the margin of a much more obscure can-didate, she had become less important in the public eye.

Urs was sure that but for his lavish last-minute payments to key sets of voters, Mrs Gandhi would not have won at all. 'How much money do you think I spent on the Chikmagalur election?', Urs asked Raghavan a few months later. The latter made a wild guess and suggested Rs 50 lakh.[4] Urs smiled and said, 'Twice that sum. I had to fund every bit that was spent on every party worker during those three weeks. That included, in many cases, air and train tickets too.' He added, 'I must tell you that the Janata Party spent more money than I did'.

Urs believed he had fulfilled his promise to Mrs Gandhi by getting her elected by fair means or foul:

> I cannot tell this to many. But I can tell you now that I consider I committed the biggest sin in my life in Chikmagalur by securing votes through large sums of money. If I had not distributed money in Kadur, Tarikere and Birur (three of the assembly segments), Mrs Gandhi would have lost.

Some readers may, understandably, view these comments with skepticism, since it is unusual in the extreme for elections to the Lok Sabha to be decided by money. There are so many voters in a parliamentary con-stituency that it is logistically difficult to reach and be able to influence enough people to change a result by this or any other dubious means. Besides, voters are accustomed to accepting money and then voting as they please. It is *rather* unusual for the result even of contests for the state assembly seats to be altered in this way. But we are less skeptical,

---

[4] Five million rupees.

for two reasons. This particular contest was quite close. And we have seen enough evidence of the high quality of Urs's intelligence gathering to regard his claim as plausible.

Mrs Gandhi's entry into Parliament from Karnataka was short-lived. Within a month of the by-election, she was unseated by the Lok Sabha for having committed contempt of the House in her time as Prime Minister. This decision, which entailed her being called to the bar of the House to hear the verdict, based on a report of the committee on privileges, triggered violence in many parts of the country. Her partymen in Karnataka were so angry that they indulged in unprecedented violence for three days. The state government, which was supposed to maintain law and order, did not lift a finger until it became too embarrassing to remain inactive. Urs, who was in Delhi for the first two days after violence broke out, went back to Bangalore to try and control the situation. It appears that he did so after the Governor, Govind Narain, cautioned him against being indifferent and negligent of his duties as Chief Minister.

Urs and Indira Gandhi: The Unravelling

Curiously, the Chikmagalur by-election sowed the seeds of distrust between Urs and Mrs Gandhi. He believed that his exertions had won the seat for her and expected her to feel obliged to him for her political rehabilitation. She was aware of the contribution that he had made but, characteristically, did not respond with gratitude.

The election had enhanced Urs's stature to such an extent that he came to be regarded within the Congress (I) hierarchy as next in importance only to Mrs Gandhi. He felt cheated when she declined to acknowledge how much his work as Chief Minister, and — more specifically and crucially — during the by-election, had mattered.

It was this that impelled Urs to try to steal some of the limelight from Mrs Gandhi within the party. He started dropping hints, both privately and in public, that he was responsible for her victory in Chikmagalur. When this went on for a while, some of his party colleagues from Karnataka once again began carrying tales against Urs to her. She was told that Urs was out to belittle her and that he could not be trusted any longer.

Typical of her, Mrs Gandhi chose a convenient issue with which to strike at Urs. She asked him to give up the presidency of the state unit of the party, which he had held from January 1978. He was told that the principle of one-man–one-post should apply to him and that he should resign forthwith.

Urs was patently angry. He had, however, no excuse whatsoever for continuing as both Chief Minister and state party president. The chosen issue was acutely sensitive. It was argued that he would face a conflict of interest whenever the party launched an agitation. As party president he would have to organise it. But as Chief Minister he was responsible for law and order and would have to put it down. Urs accepted this argument but privately decided to settle scores in his own way. He insisted that a successor to head the state unit of the party could be found only through a proper election and not by an appointment from on high. On this, he was on a strong wicket. After all, he reminded Mrs Gandhi and her minions, it was his opposition to the imposition of K. H. Patil the previous year that had enabled her to engineer the second split in the Congress Party.

By March 1979, it appeared as if Urs was keen on leaving Mrs Gandhi. For this, she was responsible in many ways: not only had she refused to acknowledge his strength, but she also used two ministers in his cabinet as guardians of her interests. Their task was to put a spoke in everything that Urs attempted. One of them, once a loyal protégé of Urs, was Gundu Rao. He and some of his associates worked to widen the rift between Urs and Mrs Gandhi. He had shifted his loyalty from Urs to Sanjay Gandhi in a largely successful attempt to become the latter's man in Karnataka. His ties to Sanjay had enabled him to win a promotion to the state cabinet in 1977, and then in 1978, to secure an important money-spinning portfolio. Gundu Rao apparently sought to project himself as Urs's equal at least as far as influence with Mrs Gandhi and her younger son was concerned.

When Urs realised that Mrs Gandhi was out to belittle him, he more or less made up his mind to break with her as honourably as he could. But he found this a painful and risky decision. Even in private conversation he found it difficult to admit this and would launch into a tirade against her without ever answering whether he was keen on leaving her. Once, when Raghavan caught him in a pleasant mood and began to discuss his differences with Mrs Gandhi, Urs explained:

> My difficulty is that I shouldn't precipitate things and be seen as wanting to leave her. After all these years that I have been with her, it will be difficult for me to explain to the people why I left her. On the other hand, if it is seen as her throwing me out, people would be sympathetic to me.

It was this calculation that made him adopt a posture which finally left Mrs Gandhi with two options. Either she had to concede what Urs wanted — a proper election to replace him in the party organisation — or throw him out of the party. If she conceded defeat, Urs would emerge stronger. But throwing him out also posed serious risks.

For the next few weeks the uneasy relationship between them continued. Urs met Mrs Gandhi for the last time just before he fell ill in June 1979. It was early in the morning when he called on her at her Willingdon Crescent residence in Delhi. The two had not spent even 10 minutes together before both emerged from the house. Mrs Gandhi was being courteous in seeing Urs off, but it was evident from the expressions on their faces that they had had an argument. Both looked sullen and when Raghavan asked Urs, as he was getting into his car, what had transpired between the two, he angrily shot back, 'Ask her', and left. As soon as the car left, Margaret Alva, a member of the Rajya Sabha from Karnataka, went up to Mrs Gandhi and suggested she do something to save the situation. Mrs Gandhi raised her voice and said, 'What can I do if some people want to leave?'

A few days after he returned to Bangalore, Urs had an attack of herpes and was bed-ridden for a few weeks. Political developments, however, continued apace towards what appeared to be a further split in the Congress, limited, in this instance, to Karnataka alone.

After hesitating for a while, Mrs Gandhi finally struck. She got her party's Working Committee to dissolve the organisational set-up in Karnataka and appointed Bangarappa, a minister in the state cabinet, as president of the Pradesh Congress (state unit of the party). Urs, who was still recovering, hit back by asking Bangarappa and Gundu Rao to resign from his cabinet. Gundu Rao did so. When Bangarappa declined, he was dismissed. At a press conference, Urs also attacked the central leadership for its arbitrary action. This caused the Working Committee to issue a show cause notice to him for indiscipline. Urs wrote a long letter, authored not by him but by a highly imaginative north Indian journalist who was hired as his press advisor, joining issue with Mrs Gandhi. The tone and content of the letter gave a convenient handle to the Working Committee to throw Urs out of the party. He was not sorry. This letter was only the last in a series of actions inviting such a response. It left Mrs Gandhi with no choice but to oblige him.

When we consider this episode in the context of Mrs Gandhi's actions over the preceding few years, it becomes unimaginable that she could have given Urs the kind of prominence within the party which he believed, with good reason, that he had earned. Arguably from the time since she first split the Congress in 1970, and certainly since 1971, she had been unwilling to tolerate not just equals within her party, but formidable regional lieutenants too. She saw the latter as threats rather than as what they actually were: invaluable allies in managing such a huge, complex polity. She had worked relentlessly to centralise power in order to ensure her personal dominance over the party and the political system. The Emergency had dramatised this, but it had been evident well before it was imposed in mid-1975 (see Kochanek 1976; Manor 1981). Her drive for personal control had been apparent even when she had been most secure after the landslide election victory of 1971. But by the time the conflict with Urs arose, she had become much less secure and thus even more inclined to dominate. Her expulsion from Parliament after the Chikmagalur by-election lent credence to her belief that she was surrounded by enemies. In his efforts to trigger his expulsion from the party, Urs was, as he understood with characteristic shrewdness, pushing at an open door.

Urs in Opposition

Urs's expulsion from the party which he had served loyally since 1970 was not without its minor drama. To prepare himself for the inevitable, he had gathered his legislators together and announced that he was forming a separate party. When this happened, a small number of them, led by Gundu Rao, pledged their support to Mrs Gandhi and stayed with the Congress (I), forming a separate block in the state assembly. On the night the Working Committee met to expel Urs, Basavalingappa attended the meeting and endorsed the decision. But he seemed to be wavering over whether to remain with Mrs Gandhi or go with Urs, who still held power in the state. The next day when he took the flight to Bangalore, Mrs Gandhi drove with him to the airport to persuade him to stay on with her. He, it appears, wanted to be named the leader of the Congress (I) group in the legislature. Mrs Gandhi did not make any such announcement because she was still not sure whether to trust him. He, however, pledged that he would remain with her. When he reached Bangalore airport, Urs's supporters, who had been waiting for

Basavalingappa, drove him straight to the Chief Minister. After some gentle persuasion by Urs, he announced he would remain with Urs. Basavalingappa's prevarication helped ensure that Gundu Rao was made leader of the Congress (I).

Within a couple of days, Urs held a convention of his supporters and converted his group into the Karnataka Congress, a regional party. This outfit, however, did not last long because of unexpected developments at the national level.

A few days later, the Janata Party government in New Delhi fell as Charan Singh, Deputy Prime Minister, walked out of the party with his supporters. As a consequence, Prime Minister Morarji Desai was forced to resign, since he had lost his majority. Charan Singh could not muster a majority either. He therefore began negotiating with the Congress (S) — the group of Congressmen in Parliament opposed to Mrs Gandhi and led by Swaran Singh (hence the 'S').

By offering to share power, Charan Singh was able to secure the support of the Congress (S) to form a government. Mrs Gandhi also declared that she would back Charan Singh. After Desai's resignation, India's President, N. Sanjiva Reddy, invited Charan Singh to form a government provided he could demonstrate his majority on the floor of the Lok Sabha. When the House met a few weeks later, the latter failed in his attempt and was forced to resign. This time around, the President did not offer a chance to Jagjivan Ram, who had become leader of the Janata Party, and who appeared to have majority support. Instead, he took the highly controversial decision (Manor 1988) to dissolve the Lok Sabha, and asked Charan Singh to continue as caretaker Prime Minister.

With an election to the Lok Sabha due within six months, some leaders of the Congress (S) appeared keen on handing over the reins of the party to someone who could find the financial resources to fight the election. They turned to Urs, and he obligingly took on the responsibility.

His calculations, carefully charted over months, went awry in July 1979. When he had forced the break with Mrs Gandhi, he had reckoned that he would have at least four years as Chief Minister to consolidate his position in Karnataka before facing an election to the state assembly. This would have offered him sufficient time to come up with a few more progressive programmes, to establish his own political identity (separate from Mrs Gandhi's) in the minds of the voters, and to convince them that he was more trustworthy than she was. However the fall of the Janata Party government in New Delhi upset these calculations, and the political adjustments he then had to make left him little room for manoeuvre. When he accepted the presidency of the Congress (S), which then became the Congress (U) ('U' for Urs), he took on a responsibility that kept him away from Karnataka. Between July and December of 1979 he had to spend a lot of time in New Delhi, trying to keep the party afloat and preparing for the election. Consequently, he neglected the state.

Urs could never manage the Congress (U) efficiently. The office-bearers he had to work with had neither loyalty nor respect for him, and were constantly pestering him for funds (mostly raised illicitly within Karnataka) for the day-to-day management of the organisation. He was spending more time and resources on being party president than as Chief Minister of the state, at a time when winning the next state election was politically vital to him.

The neglect of the state's affairs stemmed from his over-confidence. Urs had begun to think that he was invincible in Karnataka. He was proved wrong in January 1980 when, in the mid-term election to the Lok Sabha, Mrs Gandhi's Congress won 27 of the 28 seats. The 28th seat, Bangalore South, went to the Janata Party. Congress (U) candidates fared miserably, finishing third behind even the demoralised Janata Party. In many constituencies, Urs's candidates lost their deposits, as they failed to secure one-sixth of the votes polled. Urs had known that his party would do badly across the country. But the results in Karnataka, where he had hoped to win at least half the seats, completely shattered him.

By the evening of the day the votes were counted, the trends from the 28 constituencies in Karnataka were so clear that a large number of legislators who had been with Urs decided to desert him. They gathered under the leadership of H. C. Srikantaiah, a powerful Vokkaliga minister, to negotiate rejoining Mrs Gandhi's party. That night Urs knew that the game was up, and he called on the Governor to submit his resignation. The very next evening, he addressed a public meeting in Bangalore to thank the people for having supported him. It was a rare gesture for a politician who was stepping down. The turnout was so large that Urs was astonished. He came to believe that although his party had fared badly in the Lok Sabha election, his personal popularity had not suffered. He also firmly believed that most voters in the state did not fully grasp that he had broken away from the Congress (I), and that people mistakenly voted for Mrs Gandhi's party in the belief that in doing so they were voting for Urs too.

A couple of days after he resigned, a Congress (I) ministry was installed under Gundu Rao's leadership. Its strength in the state assembly had gone up overnight from 42 to 127 (out of 224) because of large-scale defections.

After the swift change of guard, Urs sat in the opposition as its leader. At the national level, he found his Congress (U) colleagues increasingly critical, which finally led him to resign from the party presidency. Thereafter he tried to concentrate on affairs in Karnataka. He made political capital out of the misrule of the Congress (I) (see Chapter 4), but found in the course of the next few months that many of his supporters, whose careers he had personally nurtured, were deserting him and joining Mrs Gandhi. This left him traumatised. His sense of his own dignity, however, prevented him from asking any of them to remain with him. It was during this lean patch that he suffered personally too. One of his three daughters, Nagarathna, died under somewhat mysterious circumstances. This deeply saddened him, and he suffered a heart attack.

Despite all this, Urs was quite confident he would return to power. Whenever he seemed to be less than enthusiastic about openly criticising or opposing the actions of the Gundu Rao government, and was asked about it, he would tell friends (the few that were left, that is):

> I am not interested in correcting this government. Let them commit mistakes so that people are disgusted. I will strike then and win back power. I have no doubt in my mind that in the next assembly election, whichever party I am in will come to power in Karnataka.

After giving up the presidency of the Congress (U), Urs toyed for a while with the idea of joining the Janata Party. Some honest brokers tried to bring him together with Chandra Shekhar, the Janata Party president. But it did not work. Towards the end of 1981, Urs was forced to convert his party in Karnataka into a regional outfit, since the Congress (U), then led by Sharad Pawar, effectively wound itself up and joined the Congress (I). Urs christened his party the Karnataka Kranti Ranga. By then, the number of his supporters in the state assembly had reduced to a handful. But he did not lose hope. A deeply religious person, he firmly believed that he was destined to rule the country one day. He thought not only that he had the ability to do so but that he was fated to do so. He once explained why:

Once, a friend of mine took me to a *math* [monastery] in Hassan district. The *math* had a palm-leaf manuscript which was supposed to contain astrological predictions. At that stage, I had no faith in these things, but out of curiosity I asked the person who could read and intrepret the palm leaf to find out what was in store for the country. This must have been sometime in 1961 or 1962. Those days many of us Congressmen were preoccupied with the question, 'After Nehru, who?' Mind you, Nehru was still alive.

After offering pooja, the scholar picked up a particular portion from the palm leaf manuscript and read out a very cryptic prediction. It ran like this: 'This country will be ruled by a widow, after which the country will go through troubled times. After that, it will be ruled by an Arasu (the maharajas' sub-caste to which Urs also belonged, and when transliterated differently, is rendered as Urs).

I dismissed the whole thing as a joke then. I could not imagine a woman ruling this country, let alone a widow. To my surprise, a few years later the first part of the prediction came true. Mrs Gandhi became Prime Minister, and she was a widow. At this stage I thought maybe there is some truth in what the chap read from the palm-leaf manuscript. Then I thought Jayachamaraja Wadiyar (former Maharaja of Mysore) would probably become President of the country. Those days, there was some talk of this. He died. During the Emergency the country went through troubled times, and it was then that I thought, perhaps, there was some truth in the prediction. I think I am destined to rule the country because I belong to the Arasu (princely) community.

This, however, was not to be. In July 1982, on a Sunday evening, Urs died following a heart attack — ironically, at the house of an astrologer which he used as something of a private hideout.

But perhaps the prediction at the *math* in Hassan was not incorrect. After all, V. P. Singh, a raja, became Prime Minister in 1989.

Part II

R. Gundu Rao, 1980–83

4

An Inept, Insensitive, Brutish Government

Devaraj Urs was always going to be a hard act to follow, no matter who succeeded him. Even an adroit, effective Chief Minister would have looked ordinary by comparison. Urs was a perceptive analyst of the complexities that faced him, and a brilliant and tough tactician in crafting responses which disarmed or isolated opponents and turned problems to his advantage. He was a fine administrator, who made good use of the considerable strengths of the state's best bureaucrats.

He was also remarkably effective at acquiring financial and human resources for his party. Most of the funds were raised illicitly, but he disbursed them cannily and constructively, in ways that would earn his government broad popular support. For instance, he used a large part of the illicitly raised money to finance penniless candidates and caste associations for low-status groups. He developed his party's human resources that had been at a low ebb, by recruiting promising political talent from social groups that had long been excluded from politics, shielding them from the hostility of the formerly dominant groups, and promoting those who performed well.

He reinforced all this with an array of programmes, both substantive and symbolic, that addressed inequality, exclusion and disadvantage. These conveyed a consistent message: the land-owning elite's control over the state government had been broken. The less-privileged majority would at last receive its fair share. He developed a set of policies that did more to fulfil Mrs Gandhi's anti-poverty promises (which she had made in the 1971 national election) than any other Congress Chief Minister or the lady herself at the national level. His contribution to the state's politics was more remarkable than that of any of his predecessors in Karnataka, even though most of them had performed admirably. Indeed, his achievements surpassed those of all but a small handful of Chief Ministers in other states in the years since Indian independence.[1]

---

[1] This handful, in the years before Urs left office in 1980, included Y. B. Chavan of Maharashtra, Mohanlal Sukhadia of Rajasthan and Jyoti Basu of West Bengal. But Chavan and particularly Basu had strong party organisations available to them which Urs at first had lacked and had had to create from scratch. Only two or three other names might be added to this short list.

Urs was not a 'charismatic' leader (a word used too often in discussions of Indian politics). But he had a powerful presence on the public platform, delighting audiences with wry jokes and reassuring them with serious displays of his commitment to the disadvantaged majority. As a result of this, and of the concrete benefits that his policies provided, he achieved an unlikely combination of qualities. He was a determinedly adversarial political operator. But as Governor Govind Narain, a shrewd, dispassionate observer, put it in private, 'the people loved him'.[2]

So, any successor, however splendid he might be, faced a daunting challenge to measure up to Urs. And as we shall see, the man who came next was far from splendid.

Finding a New Chief Minister

In the first week of January 1980, hundreds of newly elected Congress MPs had gathered in their party's headquarters at 24 Akbar Road, New Delhi for a get-together that the party had organised for them. Mrs Gandhi (who had staged a spectacular return to power) spoke to them briefly and went into the office for a meeting of the Congress Working Committee.[3]

This meeting was a mere formality. Its purpose was to review the performance of the party in the recently held national election, which was scarcely necessary since the Congress (I) had exceeded even its own expectations, trouncing every opposition outfit in the country except the Communists in West Bengal. It was, however, customary to hold such a meeting after every election, among other things, to formally thank the people for reposing their faith in the party. The meeting soon ended, but while many Working Committee members trooped out, Gundu Rao took quite some time to emerge. He was huddled with Mrs Gandhi, discussing a question that was of paramount importance to their party's affairs in Karnataka. Eventually, he rushed out and told Raghavan, 'I am meeting the Governor tomorrow', while wading through the crowd to his car. The latter asked, 'Who else will be sworn in along with you?' Gundu Rao thought for a while and said, 'Moily and Bangarappa. Rest, after I

---

[2] Govind Narain, interview by James Manor, Bangalore, 10 August 1981.

[3] The standing executive committee of the Congress Party.

have had sufficient time to consult Mrs Gandhi. I have to rush to catch a flight to Madras and from there to Bangalore', before he left.

Gundu Rao was so preoccupied with the desire to rush back to Bangalore that he forgot to inform Bangarappa, who had also attended the Working Committee meeting in his capacity as president of the state unit of the party, that Mrs Gandhi had decided that their party would stake a claim to form a government with the help of the 85 legislators who had defected overnight from Urs's party.

This was not an attempt by Gundu Rao to keep Bangarappa in the dark. It was simply his style: shooting from the hip, overlooking details and acting with little or no prior calculation. What mattered to him were his close ties to Mrs Gandhi and her son, Sanjay. The niceties of his links to others, even his state party president, were not of much consequence.

He met the Governor, Govind Narain, the next day. Without any hesitation, the latter invited him to form the government, and a day later Gundu Rao was sworn in along with Bangarappa and Moily.

He had gone prepared to Delhi. In Bangalore, he had won over Srikantaiah and, with him, 84 other legislators who had been with Urs until the results of the Lok Sabha election were declared. What had persuaded the defectors to desert Urs was the threat that the assembly would be dissolved if they did not switch sides. None of those who had backed Urs was prepared for an immediate election, since they feared losing. They had seen Urs's party fail to win even one Lok Sabha seat. He had brought them to prominence, but their instinct for political survival forced them to abandon him.

On the evening that the results of the Lok Sabha election were trickling in, Urs had got wind of a large gathering of legislators at Srikantaiah's house, which was next to his official residence. They were weighing their options. Urs made one last bid to stop the Congress (I) (as Mrs Gandhi's party was now known) from coming to power. Knowing full well that Srikantaiah could carry legislators with him, Urs decided to offer him the leadership of his own Karnataka Congress legislature party, and thus the chance to try to form a government after Urs resigned. He tried to telephone Srikantaiah. Although the latter was very much at home, he declined to take the call. Had he done so, politics in Karnataka might have taken a different shape.

As soon as Gundu Rao arrived in Delhi with a signed statement by the 85 legislators, pledging their loyalty to Mrs Gandhi, he set about convincing her and Sanjay that the Congress (I) should form the government even though it would do so solely on the strength of the defectors. It could not hope to govern without them, since it had only 42 legislators in a House of 224.

Raghavan asked Gundu Rao if he had not thought it better to allow a dissolution of the state assembly, so that fresh elections could be held, than rely on legislators who, only a few days before, had been campaigning against the Congress (I) in the Lok Sabha election. Gundu Rao thought not, and explained his reasoning thus:

> We would like to start with a fresh mandate, but we are not sure whether out of sheer sympathy people would vote for Urs, if an election to the assembly is held within a month or two. After all, we cannot ignore his strength. My intention is that we should form the government now with the help of defectors, come up with some good programme, and after three months go to polls and win a mandate on our own. Three months is long enough for us to do some good work, and for people to lose sympathy for Urs.

Even as he was advancing this argument with national Congress (I) leaders who mattered, Srikantaiah arrived in Delhi. As the leader of a group of 84 legislators, Srikantaiah was in a politically strong position. However, F. M. Khan, a close friend and political ally of Gundu Rao, literally kept him captive for the next two days, to prevent him from meeting either Mrs Gandhi or other leaders to bargain for an important position in the government. Mrs Gandhi found Gundu Rao's argument in favour of forming a government with the help of the defectors convincing.

The decision rested entirely with her and her son Sanjay. Although Sanjay's gross misjudgements had dislodged the Congress (I) from power for three years, the party and its leader still depended heavily on him.

When Gundu Rao was sworn in two days later, he was the youngest Chief Minister the state had seen, and relatively inexperienced. Unlike his predecessors, he had received only a rudimentary education. Most significant was the fact that he was a Brahmin. In Karnataka, Brahmins were economically and numerically weak (only 3.5 per cent of the population) — vastly less formidable than the Lingayats and Vokkaligas, and far removed from the numerically powerful Backward Classes, who stood further down the traditional caste hierarchy. Until this time, a Brahmin Chief Minister had been an unthinkable proposition. Brahmins had been reduced to a secondary political role in Karnataka nearly a decade before independence in 1947, so that they had had very little political influence thereafter. Gundu Rao would have to be exceedingly adroit to win mass popularity. Unfortunately, as we shall see, he was anything but adroit.

Nonetheless, given Gundu Rao's proximity to Mrs Gandhi and, more importantly, to Sanjay, it was inevitable that he would become Chief Minister when Urs resigned. On the day he was chosen, caste was not considered.

Politicians in the state knew that during the Emergency, Gundu Rao had gone out of his way to cultivate Sanjay Gandhi, who was then seen as the emerging leader of the next generation within Mrs Gandhi's Congress. When Urs and Mrs Gandhi had begun to distrust each other, Gundu Rao had acted as Mrs Gandhi's gate-keeper in Karnataka, funnelling information both upwards and downwards. If visible proof was needed of his being in Mrs Gandhi's good books, it was provided by the lady herself. On the day she was to be sworn in as Prime Minister in 1980, she chose to ride to the Rashtrapati Bhavan[4] in Gundu Rao's official car. This public manifestation of Mrs Gandhi's faith in him was enough for partymen in the state to accept Gundu Rao, disregarding his caste, his lack of education, his devil-may-care approach to tasks, and his earlier reputation of being Urs's 'muscleman'. The fear of his influence with the mother and son persuaded the Lingayats and Vokkaligas, who would otherwise never have tolerated a Brahmin Chief Minister, to meekly accept his leadership. For someone who had virtually no accomplishments to mark him out, Gundu Rao had come a long way.

The Curious Rise of Gundu Rao

The son of a school teacher, Gundu Rao did not complete his higher education, and his economic difficulties forced him to work as a bus agent in Kushalnagar, a town in Kodagu district that sits on the bank of river Cauvery, adjacent to Mysore district. 'Bus agent' was a dignified description. The work such agents performed was to usher passengers

---

[4] The official residence of India's President, where the swearing-in occurs.

into a bus and receive payment for this service. The more passengers a bus agent managed to get into the buses, the higher the wages he received.

After a couple of years at the bus stand, Gundu Rao found employment in a co-operative bank as a clerk. He got into serious trouble when he allegedly replaced gold ornaments, pledged by customers against a loan, with brass imitations. Another politician from Coorg, who was Gundu Rao's political opponent, told Raghavan several years later that someone else had committed the offence. Gundu Rao, it appears, had been made a scapegoat.

His involvement in politics started a few years later. In a local municipal election, he was fielded by a group of youngsters as an Independent and won. He went on to become president of the town municipality. By this time he and F. M. Khan, a relatively well-off planter, had become close friends. The two of them decided to dabble in party politics.

The Congress split in 1970 brought both of them to Bangalore for good. They decided that their future lay in the Congress (R) (as Mrs Gandhi's party was then known) because it afforded better opportunities for the young. Urs, who was setting up the organisation and recruiting allies, put them to good use. They brought to politics what were then considered crude and uncouth methods. They provided 'muscle' for the party by enlisting the support of a number of youngsters who were willing to do their dirty work. These included, picketing, agitations and, quite often, physically intimidating opponents, not excluding those within the party.

Urs, who had faced many adversaries in his early days as ad hoc president of the state's Congress (R) committee, faced a severe shortage of low-level leaders or activists on whom he could rely. Gundu Rao and Khan won his trust and, in his battles with Siddaveerappa and others, they served him well.

When Urs made Gundu Rao the president of the state's Youth Congress, the latter packed this outfit with youngsters (including many college students) who were seeking opportunities to make their mark in politics, often by deploying coercive force against people who were deemed to be adversaries.

Gundu Rao had no difficulty in securing a party ticket in the election to the state assembly in 1972. Urs had been finding it hard to locate men of stature to fight on behalf of the Congress (R) and was finally forced to pick anyone who offered to contest. Moreover, in Gundu Rao's case, his selection as a Congress (R) candidate was also a reward for services rendered. When he filed his nomination papers from Somwarpet in Coorg district, even the otherwise ever hopeful Gundu Rao may have felt that he had little chance of winning. This constituency had a sizeable Vokkaliga and Kodava[5] vote, and a significant Lingayat vote too. It also had a large number of migrant plantation labourers. Being a Brahmin, Gundu Rao could not bank on the support of any of these sizeable castes.

In Somwarpet, Gundu Rao had earned little respect. He was generally seen as an upstart and, by the refined standards of the Kodavas, a rowdy. Nevertheless, he surprised many in the district by winning the seat without much effort. This was a testament to the popularity of Mrs Gandhi's Congress (R) after her triumph in the parliamentary election the previous year.

With this victory, he became a reasonably important politician and, thanks to his links with Urs, began to acquire substantial influence. However, he had to wait for a considerable time to become a minister. Even before he was made a junior minister,[6] Gundu Rao and his crony, Khan, had acquired a degree of notoriety and were seen in the party and in the public eye as politicians who were unscrupulous and of low moral standards. This did not change after he gained promotion. During his stint as junior Minister for Information, Gundu Rao did nothing to enhance his image.

Gundu Rao's alter ego, Khan, did not lag behind in politics either. Though very young, he won Urs's support for a seat in the Rajya Sabha. Urs's intention was to use him as a reliable junior to run political errands in New Delhi. This task enabled Khan to cultivate a large number of middle-level leaders from other states, and in less than two years, he and Gundu Rao were able to attract the attention of Mrs Gandhi herself.

Gundu Rao's ascent in politics accelerated during the Emergency. Only days after Mrs Gandhi imposed it to stifle opposition, he realised that Sanjay Gandhi was becoming an important political actor, and went out of his way to cultivate him. This eventually blossomed into a reasonably close relationship — close enough for Gundu Rao to share breakfasts with Sanjay almost every time he visited Delhi. Sanjay, who

---

[5] A prosperous and accomplished tribal group, sometimes also referred to as 'Coorgs'.

[6] That is, 'Minister of State' rather than 'Minister'.

utterly disregarded politicians of the older generation, found himself at home with youngsters like Gundu Rao and started promoting them. Gundu Rao's close ties to Sanjay helped him gain still more importance. It was Sanjay who forced Urs, during the Emergency, to promote Gundu Rao from a junior ministerial post to the state cabinet. This was the result not of a quid pro quo between Sanjay and Gundu Rao, but of a genuine friendship between them. This closeness also ensured that Gundu Rao became the Gandhis' informant in Karnataka. He was, however, a distinctly inept, inattentive spy. He never grasped, for example, that Urs was giving Mrs Gandhi inflated figures for the number of forced sterilisations in Karnataka during the Emergency.

Gundu Rao remained loyal to Mrs Gandhi and Sanjay even after the Emergency when many in the party were increasingly wary of, if not averse to, them. Both mother and son desperately needed such unswerving support in the states at a time when the entire country looked down on them. Gundu Rao's extremely close links with the Gandhis at the national level made him suspect in Urs's eyes. But either because Gundu Rao had Mrs Gandhi to protect him, or because Urs looked on Gundu Rao with affection, or both, he did nothing to cut Gundu Rao to size, as he had done with some others.

In 1977 when Urs completely fell out with the powerful Congress leader K. H. Patil, Gundu Rao appeared to flirt for a while with the dissidents in the state cabinet. He remained in their company for some time. But when he was expected to resign as a minister, along with Patil and the others, he surprisingly stayed on. Urs tolerated this indiscretion. When a friend asked Gundu Rao why he had switched sides at the last minute, he explained, 'Within the party I sensed that Urs was a winning horse and that Mrs Gandhi would support him and not the dissidents. I did not want to be on the wrong side.' For all his crudity, Gundu Rao had a simple political doctrine of his own to guide him. He once explained it to Raghavan:

> This is a country of idol worshippers. A majority of people look for an idol even in politics. That is why people treated Mahatma Gandhi or Nehru as gods. By the same token, Mrs Gandhi is also an immensely popular figure though, for the present, she is out of power. She will return to power one day because there is no other political idol available for the people. After her, it will be Sanjay Gandhi because there is no family other than the Nehru

family that can win votes. If I remain faithful and close to him, I am sure you will agree, I will benefit too.

Many may consider this long-term opportunism. But Gundu Rao was also genuinely devoted to Mrs Gandhi and Sanjay. It was this sense of loyalty that made him stay with them when Urs was expelled from Mrs Gandhi's Congress and set up his own regional party. After Urs was expelled, for tactical reasons the leadership of the state unit of the Congress (I) was entrusted to Bangarappa although, logically, the job should have gone to Gundu Rao. Mrs Gandhi was aware of Urs's popularity with the Backward Classes. In order to demonstrate that she was as concerned as Urs about safeguarding their interests, she made Bangarappa, an Idiga (an important Backward Classes group), state president. Interestingly, she took this step in consultation with Gundu Rao. The leadership of the party in the legislature, however, went to Gundu Rao. For the first time since he had become a legislator, he had to sit on the opposition benches, leading a group of 41 legislators.

It now fell to him to create an organisation for Mrs Gandhi, a task that Urs had successfully performed twice before, in 1970 and 1978. This was no easy task, and matters became more complicated as differences cropped up between leaders within the party even before an executive for the party unit could be named. Within a couple of days Bangarappa insisted that as party president he, and not Gundu Rao, had the right to sit on the party's national Working Committee. Gundu Rao thought otherwise. He was senior to Bangarappa in the party and also more important. Moreover, he felt that Bangarappa had only been made party president for reasons of political expediency.

The differences between the two men became acute and embarrassing. Mrs Gandhi finally had to step in to resolve the issue. She conceded Bangarappa's point that he should sit on the Working Committee, but appeased Gundu Rao too by making him a member of the party's Central Parliamentary Board. By doing this, she had elevated Gundu Rao since in theory, the Parliamentary Board was the more important decision-making body, though in effect, like all other party institutions, it was a mere rubber stamp for Mrs Gandhi. Its membership, nevertheless, con-ferred importance on a leader and placed him very high in the hierarchy at the national level.

This did not, however, ensure lasting harmony in the state unit of the party. Factionalism reared its head much faster than anyone had expected. Bangarappa (who often overplayed his hand throughout his political career) and Moily — both belonging to the Backward Classes — joined forces against Gundu Rao. While it was true that his position was unassailable because of the Gandhis' blessings, the squabble proved to be a nuisance for him.

Between July and December 1979, Gundu Rao's main objective was to recruit more leaders and party workers to the Congress (I). By the end of July it was known that a national parliamentary election was due in the first week of 1980. Events at the national level had their impact on Karnataka. The Janata Party was breaking up in the state as it had at the national level. Some legislators and party workers chose to join Urs on the assumption that he was electorally invincible in Karnataka. A few others, who were personally opposed to him but thought it imprudent to remain in the Janata Party, joined Mrs Gandhi's Congress (I). These included Veerendra Patil (her opponent in the Chikmagalur by-election and a Lingayat) and C. M. Ibrahim (one of the few Muslim leaders in the Janata Party in a state in which 12 per cent of the population was Muslim). K. H. Patil (a prominent Vokkaliga) and his followers, who could not work with Urs, rejoined Mrs Gandhi when Urs became president of the anti-Indira Congress (U).

For about six months until the Lok Sabha election in 1980, the political scene in the state was utterly confusing, largely because of uncertainties at the national level. Until the election was over, most of the political observers in Karnataka did not take Mrs Gandhi's outfit very seriously. The leaders of her party appeared to be little more than politicians who had missed the bus. Urs, on the other hand, was riding high as leader of the Congress (U), despite being preoccupied with national politics.

In the run-up to the election, even the shattered and demoralised Janata Party was rated second best in Karnataka after Urs's party, while most observers did not see good prospects for the Congress (I). Mrs Gandhi had no difficulty in picking candidates from the state. Many veteran MPs like Shankaranand and Jaffer Sharief were automatically chosen. In constituencies where newcomers had to be selected, she mostly relied on Gundu Rao's advice.

During the campaign, Mrs Gandhi had to take Karnataka more seriously than she had done before, since neither Gundu Rao nor Bangarappa were the kind of campaigners that Urs had been while he was with her. Moreover, Urs was now ranged against her on his home turf. He also commanded abundant financial resources. Mrs Gandhi, on the other hand, had to channel money to the state, where she was determined to end Urs's political career.

During her tour of the state, it was evident that she still commanded respect, since she drew large crowds. This was proved far more resoundingly when the results were declared. She won 27 out of 28 seats, pushing Urs's Congress (U), astonishingly, into third place behind the Janata Party.

This victory did not alter Mrs Gandhi's anxieties about Urs. She thought, perhaps rightly, that given a choice between her nominee and Urs in a state election, voters would prefer Urs as Chief Minister. It was Urs's resignation as Chief Minister which gave her the idea that her party should stake a claim to form a government with the help of defectors. At least as far as Karnataka was concerned, this marked a significant change in Mrs Gandhi's much-feared daring. In 1972, when her party was in a similar position, she had not been afraid of a fresh election in the state. Eight years later, she was, because she feared a contest with Urs in which he was the local issue.

Gundu Rao in Power

An ominous incident occurred on the day Gundu Rao and his colleagues were sworn in as ministers. A group of Urs's supporters had gathered near the scene of the swearing-in to register a peaceful protest. They were set upon by a group of Congress[7] thugs bearing clubs and, in some cases, razors. Several protestors were left gravely wounded, while the police standing close by refused to intervene.[8] Karnataka was heading towards difficult times.

Gundu Rao began his stint in power with enormous goodwill, but soon frittered it away. He had an uncanny ability to make a mess of things. He never recruited sound political advisors. The ones he relied

---

[7] Here and subsequently, for the sake of simplicity, we use the term 'Congress' to refer to the party led by Indira Gandhi and, in Karnataka, by Gundu Rao. We do so because Urs's party changed its name to 'Kranti Ranga', so that only one Congress remained.

[8] James Manor witnessed this incident at close quarters.

on were more interested in exploiting him for personal and political gains than in offering him good advice. His biggest problem was that his party in the legislature was wracked by constant factional strife. An arbiter was needed, but Gundu Rao proved seriously inept in this role.

From the very beginning, a number of Congress politicians who had long been attacked by Urs's followers resented the induction of these very people as defectors into the party. 'Only the other day', some of them said, 'we were fighting each other. How can we be expected to get along with those who opposed us not even a week ago?'

Excluding the defectors from ministerial posts was a convenient way of keeping the lid on the faction-ridden legislative party. Since over 80 late comers (those who had defected from Urs's party) among his legislators were barred on the grounds that they must wait and prove their loyalty, most long-term loyalists (because they were few in number) found ministerial berths. The loyalists thus had good reason to support him, and the defectors could be kept under control by the prospect of eventual inclusion in the ministry. So, Gundu Rao continued for over a year without drawing in the latecomers.

However, another conflict, this time between the party organisation and the government, soon surfaced. This was largely rooted in the personal rivalry between Gundu Rao and Bangarappa. For a few months after he became Gundu Rao's number two in the cabinet, Bangarappa continued to head the state unit of the Congress. However, he found it impossible to develop adequate communication channels with the Chief Minister, so he soon began operating as a parallel power centre within the government. Gundu Rao hit back by getting Mrs Gandhi to remove him from his party post and replacing him by K. T. Rathod.

Gundu Rao continued to ride high. His sense of euphoria persisted for quite some time and, as a result, he began to behave in disconcerting ways. He became both recklessly generous and extremely patronising. He granted virtually anything that any individual or organisation asked for, as long as he received the obeisance he thought he merited. This was enthusiastically exploited by so-called followers who organised functions to felicitate him and used these occasions to extract promises and political spoils from him. They continued to celebrate his elevation to the Chief Minister's post till six months after the event.

Gundu Rao was so recklessly obliging that sometimes even those who sought patronage were taken aback with his generosity. A senior politician who had set up several educational institutions in his constituency wanted to start a polytechnic. He invited the Chief Minister to take part in a function and politely asked for official permission for the new institution. Gundu Rao turned around and proposed that he start an engineering college. This was a much bigger undertaking, for which permission had, until then, been next to impossible.

There were many such instances. Unlike most Indian Chief Ministers, who err on the side of caution and prevaricate, Gundu Rao wanted to be seen as a man of action. On numerous occasions he announced policy decisions without prior consultation and warning, off the cuff and by himself, leaving officials to work out the details later.

When a spate of such actions was criticised in the press, he began to attack newspapers, and called journalists names.

The Politics of Muscle and Menace

While Gundu Rao merely used words, his followers believed in drastic action. Some ardent Youth Congress members laid siege to the *Deccan Herald* and *Indian Express* newspaper groups' offices one night. It seems they were provoked into doing this because some newspapers, notably these two, had begun to write articles on Gundu Rao's leadership that were not entirely to his liking. Peeved by the newspapermen's criticism of his rash and arbitrary ways, Gundu Rao voiced his displeasure. In one of his public meetings, he said that journalists who do not report facts (he obviously meant facts as he saw them) should be drowned in the Arabian Sea. This public harangue prompted his minions to lay siege to the newspaper offices to prevent printed copies of the papers from being moved out. The siege was only lifted the next morning, and the fact that the police did little thereafter to deal with the perpetrators was attributed to the fact that they had the Chief Minister's support. Nothing remotely like this had happened in the state before, and it drew nationwide attention to the brutish side of the regime.

Rowdy elements who passed themselves off as Youth Congress workers, or certainly had the support of some Youth Congress leaders, also began indulging in gang wars and extortion in Bangalore on an unprecedented scale. For instance, on the flimsy pretext of organising programmes, they would collect money from petty shopkeepers. Some government agencies, such as the Department of Commercial Taxes, were unofficially used to persuade traders and businessmen to contribute to such 'programmes'. Those who resisted would be dealt with by hoodlums protected by Youth Congress leaders.

For many such shady characters, F. M. Khan became a godfather. They could always be seen hanging around his residence and office. In fact, he started functioning as a de facto Chief Minister. Not only party functionaries and legislators, but even bureaucrats began to fear offending him because doing so would have been tantamount to offending Gundu Rao. The latter made no attempt to dissuade his friend from interfering in government work. As Khan's importance became well-known, civil servants began taking orders from him without qualms. Some of them bent over backwards to curry favour with him. He was considered to have become so influential that whenever he chanced to walk into the legislature lobby, every Congressman, no matter how senior and important himself, would stand up in a show of deference. Many disregarded their own status and unashamedly fawned on Khan. Gundu Rao encouraged such sycophancy. Those who were close either to him or to Khan could get away with anything. Many of the courtiers of these two men walked around with a swagger, instilling in Congressmen and others a sense not of respect but of fear.

Insulating the Government from the Citizens and Their Representatives

As Gundu Rao was fond of saying time and again, he was only a minor player in a drama directed by Mrs Gandhi. He owed his position as Chief Minister entirely to her and not to the Congress Party's legislators, as, he believed, did the latter. They held their posts only because she had brought them votes. So, he saw himself as being accountable only upward, and not downward to legislators. He felt they held legislative posts only to fulfil a quaint constitutional requirement. It might have been argued that representing their constituents' interests was part of this requirement, and that their exclusion from any meaningful influence prevented them from fulfilling it. But this is not how Gundu Rao saw things. In his view, they had no business interfering in the administration.

In theory, he should have acquired vast administrative powers from the exclusion of the legislators. But in practice, he was extremely bored by the policy process and (as we shall see) utterly incapable of dealing with it. His overwhelming preoccupation was with the distribution of patronage. As such, he left the job of administering the state almost entirely to civil servants. His government can be described as 'civil-servant raj'. It resembled regimes that existed under the British rule more closely than any other Indian state government since independence. Most policy decisions were made by bureaucrats; the Chief Minister merely endorsed them.[9]

Legislators found it impossible to obtain appointments even with middle-ranking civil servants. This was a radical change that weakened the government by depriving it of useful information that legislators brought from their constituencies. The Chief Minister also barred them from interfering in the process of governmental transfers. In theory, this was an excellent idea. In the past, many legislators had made ob-noxious amounts of illicit profits from official postings. In practice, it failed because those who were in the good books of the Chief Minister could still get what they wanted. Worse, bureaucrats had a field day: favouritism and corruption — in which legislators had previously had a share — persisted, but now as the exclusive domain of civil servants.

Another politically unsound measure of Gundu Rao's was his decision to abolish the over-80 statutory boards and corporations created during Urs's regime, largely to find positions for Congress activists outside the government. By taking away these positions from politicians, Gundu Rao not only alienated them, but once again strengthened the hands of civil servants who were entrusted with the responsibilities of the old boards and corporations. They performed poorly because there was no political machinery to keep an eye on their work.

Not surprisingly, Karnataka's civil servants look back to the Gundu Rao years as a golden era. They were, for the only time in their careers, freed from the troublesome task of dealing with the elected represen-tatives of the people. The Chief Minister was also oblivious to commu-nications from legislators on policy issues that affected their constituents. While the civil servants found the diminished power of the legislators advantageous, such a situation severely undermined democratic prin-ciples, and produced one of the least responsive and insensitive state governments ever seen in India.

---

[9] This and several other themes in this chapter are discussed in more detail in Manor (1984).

One startling example of Gundu Rao's insensitive regime is worth noting. He wanted to be known as a forceful man of action who moved with lightning speed to tackle problems. This and his devil-may-care approach to possible consequences led him into a course of action which every other Chief Minister of the state, before or since, would have rightly seen as politically insane. Early in his time in office, he discovered that farmers who had benefited from the construction of irrigation facilities owed the government large sums of money as a 'betterment levy'. This was something that any semi-accomplished politician should have known, since farmers were a crucial interest group. They had immense numerical strength and, thanks to their control of land, had long exercised potent leverage over legislators and some influence over other rural groups at election time. But Gundu Rao's knowledge of such matters was sketchy at best. Arrears in the payment of the betterment levy had piled up over the years as successive governments had been deliberately lax in collecting dues, lest they alienate farmers. Gundu Rao, however, decided that the arrears should be collected aggressively, and all at once, to demonstrate that his government meant business.

He ordered that debts should be collected by force, and that moveable property should be seized where cash payments were not forthcoming. This triggered an agitation by farmers in Dharwad district. It turned violent and, when the Chief Minister insisted that the police respond robustly (another exceedingly unwise act), several farmers were shot down. This was deeply shocking in a state that had seen next to no deaths from police firings, and virtually none among farmers, during the 20th century.

Gundu Rao then set up an official committee, headed by Revenue Minister Bangarappa, to look into farmers' grievances. Even before it had finalised its report, he announced, without consulting Bangarappa, a large package of concessions amounting to Rs 85 crore.[10] However, to compound the problem further, the announcement remained just that — a mere announcement; the concessions never reached the farmers.

As his months in power passed, it became apparent that this blunder was not merely an early slip by an inexperienced young leader. His casual approach to administration — vintage Gundu Rao — could be expected over the long term. This was perhaps inevitable, given his intellectual

---

[10] 850 million rupees.

limitations and remarkably short attention span. Karnataka's then Governor, a distinguished retired civil servant, had spotted the problem at an early stage and attempted to tutor the Chief Minister in how to read and process government files. But he found that his pupil had great difficulty reading more than a few lines of text without losing focus, and that he struggled to write even two lines in the margins.[11]

To make matters worse, Gundu Rao kept several important portfolios for himself, in order to maximise his power. Since he was decidedly uninterested in the proposals and files that were sent to him, huge backlogs and delays developed. It was said that on one occasion during his tenure, several thousand files had piled up in his office, awaiting clearance. Senior bureaucrats could have made all the decisions themselves, but they would not have been implemented until Gundu Rao had provided his signature. Early in his term in office, Gundu Rao had announced in grandiose terms that he was shutting off the main secretariat building for a couple of days in order to achieve a clearance of all government files. He ordered all to be cleared within a stipulated period and, when this process had ended, he proudly claimed that all files had been disposed of. In reality, the files had only been moved up or down a level within the administrative hierarchy. This exercise did not lead to any improvement and, as a result of the Chief Minister's dilatory habits with files, things only deteriorated thereafter.

Gundu Rao was also in the habit of spontaneously announcing policies without consulting the files or the ministers and officials concerned. Even cabinet meetings were taken lightly. It had long been customary for reporters to be briefed immediately after cabinet meetings on the decisions taken. Under Gundu Rao, they sometimes had to wait indefinitely, only to be told that only routine administrative decisions had been taken and that there was nothing worthwhile for the government to explain. When the press complained, the Chief Minister promised to brief journalists at a fixed time. But then he over-corrected.

On one occasion, a cabinet meeting started very late and had not even been in session ten minutes when Gundu Rao realised that he had agreed to meet reporters in the next couple of minutes. He asked his colleagues to wait, went out of the cabinet hall, met the press, and announced several decisions that the cabinet was 'supposed' to have taken. When the

---

[11] Govind Narain, interview by James Manor, Bangalore, 17 January 1981.

Chief Minister said he had to go back to the cabinet meeting, a puzzled reporter asked how he could have announced decisions even before they had been made by the cabinet. Gundu Rao was, as usual, candid. He said, 'I did not want to keep you waiting, so I have told you the decisions the cabinet will make. After all', he smiled smugly, 'can the cabinet say it will not agree with what I want?' He was not wrong. None of his colleagues, except Bangarappa in the initial phase, had the courage to oppose him.

In 1981, the Chief Minister's habit of taking precipitate action with little thought about the consequences led to an appalling disaster. Gundu Rao placed one of the state's most able and energetic civil servants in charge of the Excise Department, which oversaw the production and sale of alcoholic drinks. His purpose was to bring to heel both the producers of legal liquor who had been crucial allies of Urs's, and those who made illicit and thus untaxed, cheap drink consumed by the poor. These producers of illicit liquor often had close ties with other politicians who, in turn, were Gundu Rao's rivals. The civil servant in question proved to be so effective in curtailing supplies of potable alcohol to the manufacturers of illicit liquor that they mistakenly imported a shipment of methanol, a deadly poison. When they mixed it with other ingredients and sold it in July of that year in Bangalore, over 300 poor people died agonising deaths and many more suffered severe neurological damage. India has witnessed numerous liquor poisonings over the years, but this was by far the worst in its history (Manor 1993b).

One of the few things that rivalled patronage distribution as a preoccupation in Gundu Rao's regime was illicit fund-raising. He focused on this partly because it provided him with patronage to bestow, and partly because he needed to make huge tributary payments to Mrs Gandhi in New Delhi. Even at its very least, corruption under Gundu Rao's regime remained at the peak levels it had reached under Urs. Probably it had even gone up and, more importantly, it was now radically centralised. The ruling party's legislators, who had been permitted to line their pockets in Urs's day, now found themselves without influence to peddle. Most of the money flowed to the apex of the system, now controlled by Gundu Rao. Many suspected that he had lined his own pockets as well.

A Chief Minister — Inept, Corrupt, Complacent — on an Extended Holiday

A flurry of cosmetic changes which Gundu Rao had announced soon after taking power rapidly lost momentum. The rest of his tenure was essentially a fire-fighting operation. Unfortunately for him, there were too many fires, many of which were of his own making. As the following example will illustrate, an important cause of it was his tendency to take action abruptly, sometimes for dubious reasons, and with little regard for important issues that arose as a result.

A few days after he took the reins, the government found that water levels in hydel reservoirs were extremely low, and that stiff power cuts had to be imposed to tide over the water scarcity until the onset of the monsoon. After a quick consultation with some officials, probably those who made a habit of misleading him, Gundu Rao announced that within a few days of a specified date, the power supply to all industries in the state would be completely shut off. This announcement, which was typical of his penchant for summary but ill-considered action, was nat-urally alarming as it would affect the entire economy. However, within twenty four hours, even before the state could recover from the shock, he withdrew the decision and imposed marginal cuts in power instead. There were rumours later that this astonishing set of decisions had been very profitable personally to the Chief Minister, since private indus-trialists hurriedly made huge contributions to persuade him to reverse his decision. Such talk continued throughout his tenure. Some officers privately admitted that the Chief Minister and certain key min-isters regularly got a cut from every deal the government made. Charges of corruption became so commonplace that after a time ministers stopped rebutting them.

For almost a year Gundu Rao had to deal with an inimical number two in his cabinet. Bangarappa, who never saw eye to eye with the Chief Minister, was a constant irritant. Finally, thanks largely to Mrs Gandhi's realisation of the fact that she needed Gundu Rao more than Bangarappa, he was able to ask his Revenue Minister to resign. Bangarappa did not oblige easily. In order to demonstrate that he owed his job to Mrs Gandhi and not Gundu Rao, he sent his resignation letter to the Prime Minister. She, in turn, forwarded it to Gundu Rao for acceptance.

Meanwhile, Gundu Rao lost his mentor. When Sanjay Gandhi crashed a plane doing aerobatics at low altitude over New Delhi, the Chief Minister was politically orphaned for a while. But, he quickly made up for it by being more ingratiating to the mother. He made weekly visits to Delhi, and once told Raghavan that Mrs Gandhi had asked him to be available in Delhi on weekends for consultation on political matters. For a couple of months he made it a point to meet her every week. Later, however, his visits became infrequent, because over time Mrs Gandhi partially recovered from the shock of her son's death and, more crucially, she came to realise Gundu Rao's limitations as a political counsellor (something that should have been obvious from the start).

By this time, what little esteem his administration possessed had been completely lost. During the time he remained in office, the state government was clearly adrift and without purpose. Having forced Bangarappa from the ministry, Gundu Rao had the entire cabinet under his thumb, and most ministers functioned as his courtiers.

He began to pay less and less attention to his duties, allowing himself to indulge in activities which he enjoyed but which distracted him from his work. He cultivated a particular fondness for helicopter-hopping from one place to another, making pronouncements that he could not fulfil, stirring up controversies where there were none, and generally giving an impression that he was out to have fun — a Chief Minister on an extended holiday.

He used to privately say that good work did not matter in elections. Urs, he would point out, had done enormous work but failed in the 1980 election. What was required, he believed very strongly, was a link to a vote winner, and that as long as Mrs Gandhi was by his side, he need not worry. The voters would follow her blindly.

Gundu Rao's firm belief in this perverse logic explains why he did not think there was any need to apply his mind to governing the state. While in Bangalore, he spent little time in the office. Bureaucrats who needed to meet him urgently for crucial discussions often had to wait indefinitely for an appointment, even as the Chief Minister would be at home doing nothing. Officers claimed that they had found that he kept himself busy watching video films during the day and attending parties in the evening. Not all parties were formal. Many were private drinking sessions, where he would gather a few friends and admirers around him and polish off a bottle of champagne all by himself. He obviously thought every day was worth celebrating.

A civil servant, who had served as one of his secretaries, gives us yet another example of Gundu Rao's casual approach to work. He recalls that the Chief Minister often started his day with a swim in the pool at Bangalore's Hotel Ashok because, as the official explained, he liked to show off his physique to the foreign women who were guests at the hotel. The secretary often had great difficulty persuading the Chief Minister to leave the pool and come to the office.[12]

It is perhaps to Gundu Rao's credit that he was neither ashamed of what he was doing, nor did he try to hide it. He truly believed that good times were to be savoured. Moreover, since his position and influence brought with them a host of attendants ready to offer any service, life was truly enjoyable. He knew that his good fortune was unexpected and achieved against great odds. With little education, to rise to such high office at 43 was not a small feat. Simply *being* Chief Minister was enough for him. He used to say, 'No matter what happens to me politically later, no one on earth can snatch away the title "former Chief Minister" from me.'

Since he treated his tenure as an opportunity for extended revelry, his colleagues could not be expected to do better. Most of them thought that they too were on a binge. It was, therefore, no wonder that several politicians close to him found themselves ensnared in some controversy or other. His friend Khan took the cake. He appeared to have a finger in every pie. Though he held no office in the state, his interference in the administration became widely known — almost an accepted fact — within the bureaucracy. Politically, he seemed as powerful as Gundu Rao himself. It was quite natural for all and sundry in the Congress to court him. In fact, soon after the government came to power, a massive public reception was organised for him in recognition of his services to the country. It did not matter that his service was limited to being a member of the Rajya Sabha in New Delhi and an abjectly loyal follower of Mrs Gandhi and her son Sanjay. Khan's followers set up a committee of hosts consisting mainly of industrialists and businessmen keen on cultivating good contacts in the ruling party. Through this committee, and through indirect official pressure, a large sum of money was collected to fund the reception. A procession, consisting mainly of party workers and hired slum dwellers, was taken out. Finally, as a token of appreciation, Khan was presented a brand-new imported car.

---

[12] Interview with a civil servant, by James Manor, Bangalore, 27 September 2000.

A few months later in July 1981, Khan got involved in an ugly incident with senior police officers. Although an official inquiry later set up by the Chief Minister failed to bring out the truth, Khan had evidently had an altercation with the officers. While driving home one night, he got into an argument with a truck driver on the outskirts of Bangalore, dragged the driver to the nearest police station and threw a tantrum. Two senior police officers went to the station around midnight. There are two versions of what transpired next. According to the first, in the course of a further argument with these officers, Khan allegedly slapped one of them. According to the other, given by a top police official, when Khan misbehaved with them, one of the officers, enraged with his behaviour, slapped him. Khan was so shocked that he nearly broke down. He then walked to his home, several kilometres away, instead of accepting a lift from another senior officer.

He also bought a company which had staked a claim for over 3,000 acres of forest land in nearby Tamil Nadu, allegedly with an eye on timber estimated to be worth several crores[13] of rupees. Khan never denied the charge. His friend, R. Y. Ghorpade, Gundu Rao's associate in Coorg, was also accused of attempting to grab forest land worth crores. Another close supporter, K. M. Ibrahim, whom Gundu Rao had appointed as general secretary of the state unit of the Congress, was allegedly involved in similar attempts to grab forest land with an eye to exploiting timber.

There were other murky scandals too. Several involved C. M. Ibrahim who, along with Veerendra Patil, had joined the Congress before the parliamentary election of 1980. In his earlier days in political parties opposed to Mrs Gandhi, Ibrahim had earned a reputation for being an extraordinarily fine speaker. He could hold an audience in rapt attention while he spoke in chaste Kannada, considered surprising for a member of the Muslim minority, many of whom mainly spoke Urdu. Ibrahim had spent the Emergency in jail and had been with the Janata Party until 1979. He had lost in the Lok Sabha election of 1977 when he had contested on a Janata Party ticket, but a few months later got elected to the state assembly from Shivajinagar in Bangalore city, again on a Janata Party ticket.

In one of his vituperative speeches, he had described Mrs Gandhi as an 'international prostitute'. Yet, Gundu Rao had thought it fit to make

---

[13] Tens of millions.

him a minister, entrusting him with the food portfolio. (The Chief Minister's ability to persuade Mrs Gandhi to accept this indicates the influence which his extravagant pledges of loyalty to her had won him.) It did not take long for the opposition in the state to mount an attack on Ibrahim for alleged misuse of office. They alleged that in a single day he had issued licenses to 32 flour mills to lift large stocks of wheat, in defiance of specific directives from the central government to not do so. He did this in response to bribes offered to him. The controversy produced enough heat to compel the Chief Minister to order an inquiry by the Central Bureau of Investigation, though nothing came of it.

Two of Ibrahim's brothers in Bhadravati, an industrial town, had acquired such notoriety that they had proved to be an embarrassment even for him. At one point, they were accused by the police of alleged involvement in the murder of an RSS worker. They also allegedly led a gang in the town which indulged in violence and extortion. In a gang war, one of them was murdered in broad daylight.

Meanwhile, Ibrahim himself got embroiled in another controversy. On one of his visits to the Gulf countries, he accepted a Rolex watch as a gift, but failed to notify the government as he was expected to. He later boasted at a public reception that the watch, bearing the emblem of a falcon, gave him free entry into the United Arab Emirates. At this, some opposition leaders accused him of acting as a spy.

Ibrahim was forced to resign from the ministry on an issue involving his surviving brother. This brother had abducted a middle-aged woman, allegedly after she failed to send her daughter to sleep with him. She was forcibly brought to Bangalore. She testified in court that she was kept prisoner at Ibrahim's official residence. When she filed a complaint to this effect before a magistrate who, in turn, ordered an inquiry, Ibrahim resigned from the government. It is also worth noting that the Chief Minister, given his closeness with Ibrahim, had delayed insisting on the inquiry for quite some time, despite protest marches by outraged women's groups.

Another colleague of Gundu Rao, Renuka Rajendran, also had to resign when the Corps of Detectives[14] filed a case against her allegedly for cheating a youth. According to the case filed in court, she had accepted a bribe from an unemployed youth on the promise of getting him a job in

---

[14] A branch of the state police which specialises in investigations.

the police department. When she could not deliver, she returned part of the money and gave a cheque for the rest. The cheque bounced and the youth made a formal complaint. This was while she was just a legislator. By the time the police completed its inquiry and filed a chargesheet, she had become a minister. When charges were filed, Gundu Rao had no choice but to ask her to quit.

There were also numerous allegations of corruption against the Chief Minister himself. It was the Public Accounts Committee of the state assembly that finally unearthed hard evidence of misuse of office by Gundu Rao. In the course of a routine inquiry into the working of the Irrigation Department, the Committee discovered that officers involved in various projects had come up with uniform complaints about projects being delayed for want of adequate supply of cement. The Committee decided to investigate what had happened to the distribution of cement by the government. It found out that the Karnataka government had sought and received a special quota of cement from the central government, specifically to speed up public works. But practically all of it had been diverted to private high-rise apartment builders in Bangalore city. The diversion had been ordered by the Chief Minister, even though the civil servants concerned had advised him against it. The Committee, suspecting a quid pro quo in the deal, indicted Gundu Rao and his minister for civil supplies. In another report, the same committee held the Chief Minister's order, suspending seigniorage rates for forest produce, to be illegal.

Gundu Rao brushed aside these findings. In the case of the cement scandal, he adopted the unusual approach of holding a debate in the state assembly and rejecting the report. He could get away with this arbitrary action thanks to the majority that he commanded in the House.

Amid scandals and maladministration, the Chief Minister created further difficulties for himself by repeatedly mishandling problems that were entirely manageable. The issue of the farmers' 'betterment levy' was not the only one Gundu Rao bungled. He created similar confusion where industrial workers were concerned. Workers in public-sector industries in Bangalore, numbering almost 100,000, were agitating for better wages as well as for parity in wages between the various public sector units. The central government, which controlled these units, did not want to accept the principle of parity and this led to a long strike by workers, mainly in Bangalore. The state government had little control over the negotiations between the workers and the central authorities. Gundu Rao, as in his earlier dealing with the farmers' protest, ineptly treated the issue as a law and order problem. He authorised the state police to wield the stick, and the trigger-happy force ended up killing as many as 130 people during his tenure. By doing this, Gundu Rao's government managed to set a ghastly record. In less than three years, the police directly in his charge had killed more people than they had over several decades, including several before independence. Indeed, the last time carnage on this scale had occurred in Karnataka was during the Poligar Uprising during the 1830s. Citizens of the state were naturally left dismayed and astounded by the turn of events.

If further proof of his inability to come to grips with a problem was required, he provided it while handling the issue of the language to be taught in schools. In the course of a year, he made decisions on this matter, scrapped them, then revised them, and finally came up with a fresh set of decisions. This happened so often that many wondered whether the Chief Minister was capable of understanding a problem at all.

For a number of years until 1979, students in secondary schools could choose from among Kannada (the majority language in the state), Hindi or Sanskrit as their first language. In schools meant for minority communities, students could choose their mother tongue. Although there was nothing wrong with the scheme, students taking Sanskrit as their first language were found to have a certain advantage in that they invariably ended up scoring more marks than students who had taken Kannada. This led to the demand that Kannada alone should be the first language. In 1979, Urs had accepted this and had had appropriate government orders issued.

However, as soon as he assumed power, Gundu Rao yielded to the demands of one group and restored first-language status to Sanskrit, along with Kannada. However, when pro-Kannada activists and students of Kannada protested, he set up a committee headed by a noted Kannada writer. It recommended that Kannada should be the sole first language, and that all other languages should be in a list of second languages. It went even further, suggesting that teaching of other languages should occur only at a later stage.

Without pausing to consider the consequences, Gundu Rao had the recommendations approved in full at a cabinet meeting. His friend Khan then led a procession on behalf of the minorities a few days later, opposing the decision, at which Gundu Rao promptly withdrew the government order. This led to a sustained counter-agitation by pro-Kannada activists all over the state. Many learned scholars and Kannada writers joined it, and Rajkumar, the vastly popular Kannada film actor, also lent his voice. Gundu Rao, who initially refused to invite leaders of the agitation for talks, was finally forced to accept a formula that was acceptable to both the pro-Kannada activists and the linguistic minorities. Had he had the wisdom to consult the various groups before unilaterally adopting the committee's recommendations, several lives would have been saved from yet more police firings during the agitation.

An Oblivious Chief Minister Amid Popular Disgust

By the end of his tenure, the government had become so unpopular that for the first time in over 30 years, ministers could not travel around the state without an armed police escort. Gundu Rao himself had a siren-blaring police escort car piloting his bullet-proof Mercedes-Benz, specially bought by the government after he took office.

In one of its flights of fancy, Gundu Rao's government bought a single-engine Cessna aircraft, presumably for the use of ministers. As usual, no thought was given before the purchase was made. After the plane was bought, it was discovered that ministers were barred by security rules from flying in it because single-engine aircraft were considered too risky.

If Gundu Rao's government appeared blindly meandering and confused, the party organisation over which he had total control was no different. It was as crippled as the government was. The state Congress president, Rathod, a timid man, was a mere figurehead. He had to wait upon the Chief Minister both for resources and directions in running the organisation. Any attempt by partymen to voice dissent was utterly thwarted by Gundu Rao's men, often by force. A striking example of this was provided at a meeting of the party executive Rathod had called in Bangalore. As the Chief Minister was also expected, the police were present in large numbers. So were party hangers-on. When a party legislator, I. P. D. Salappa, a camp follower of Jaffer Sharief (a central government minister), reached the office, he was brutally roughed up by goons who were shouting slogans hailing Gundu Rao, Khan and the Youth Congress president (another ardent follower of Gundu Rao).

Salappa's clothes were torn and he was pushed to the ground. As he was lying on the pavement, one of the goons threw a non-poisonous snake on him and Salappa was threatened with dire consequences if he continued to oppose the Chief Minister. Salappa's only offence was that he had criticised the Chief Minister in a meeting of the Congress legislature party. While this disgusting incident occurred, party workers remained mute spectators, with no one going to Salappa's aid. Nor did several ministers who were in the office and could easily hear the commotion outside. The police also remained uninvolved.

Such strong-arm methods became the order of the day, with goons passing themselves off as Youth Congress workers. They freely indulged in gang wars, and these spilled over into educational institutions; colleges became centres for political parties to recruit raw muscle.

While such ugly incidents and unsavoury politics took centre stage, the state's developmental efforts took a back seat. The government's finances, always stretched to breaking point, worsened, and the authorities often had to resort to overdrafts from India's central bank. Even though a shrewd politician, Veerappa Moily, managed the Finance Department, things were never rosy. Even politically crucial social-welfare measures that had been initiated by Urs slowed down. Programmes intended for the poor — for instance, the housing programme for the economically weaker sections — suffered grievously. The distribution of free houses and sites for the poorest of the poor and the Scheduled Castes failed to match the work done in this regard during Urs's time. On every front, the state slid down from the position it had earlier occupied in the country. If every previous regime in Karnataka had considerable achievements to its credit, Gundu Rao's tenure was marked for near-complete failure in every respect.

The Chief Minister, however, thought otherwise and genuinely believed he was doing wonderfully well. To substantiate his claim, he would cite examples of Congress victories in by-elections in the state during his tenure. It was true that of four by-elections since 1980 (one to the Lok Sabha and three to the state assembly), the Congress had won three. Only Basavanagudi in Bangalore, considered a stronghold of the Janata Party, proved impossible to win. The other three victories made Gundu Rao confident, indeed over-confident. He had some reason to bask in the glory of these victories. By-elections in Karnataka, at least since the 1970s, have been intensely fought. Quite often, during the stewardship of Urs, the opposition had won. In two by-elections under Gundu Rao, the campaign was one-sided in favour of his Congress. The opposition, in these cases the combined forces of Urs and the Janata Party, did not even put up a good fight. Gundu Rao naturally thought that people continued to prefer his party. Eventually, however, things began to unravel.

When Urs died suddenly in July 1982, the last remnant of any opposition to Mrs Gandhi's Congress in the state seemed to have been removed. Though a fallen giant, he had still been capable of rising for a major fight for which he was preparing himself. He had by then tried to develop accommodations with the Janata Party in the state legislature, and was preparing for an electoral understanding with them for later. His death appeared to have left a vacuum in the opposition ranks, but this impression did not last long, and the credit for that largely goes to Gundu Rao himself.

5

The Destruction of Congress Dominance

Alternatives Emerge

Even before Urs's death, Gundu Rao had begun to hound his opponents within the Congress out of the party. And there was no dearth of MPs who had turned against him. Sharief, a Bangalore-based Muslim who was a junior minister in the national government, was not afraid of criticising the Chief Minister. Within the party in the state legislature, Bangarappa had also become the focal point of a small group of dissidents. They had long pinned their hopes on Mrs Gandhi, and expected her to discipline Gundu Rao.

Bangarappa had been biding his time from the moment he was asked to resign as party president in early 1981. He had made frequent trips to Delhi to meet Mrs Gandhi and others, to complain about Gundu Rao. For a while at least, he thought that he received a sympathetic hearing, partly as a result of Mrs Gandhi's initiation into politics of her son Rajiv after the death of his brother Sanjay. Rajiv treated Bangarappa with the same courtesy that he showed to most people. Besides, it soon became apparent that Rajiv found Gundu Rao distasteful.

For Rajiv Gandhi, an airline pilot who had studiously avoided any direct contact with the murky business of party politics, it was a difficult transition. When he became a member of the Lok Sabha from the constituency his brother had represented, he still held no important position in the party, although Congressmen from all over the country had begun to court him as Mrs Gandhi's successor. Rajiv tried to bring some sophistication into politics, as opposed to the crude and vulgar displays of power by his late brother. Unlike Sanjay, he did not rely on boisterous members of the Youth Congress, but chose his own friends as advisors. For many of them, with more experience in corporate strategies than in the politics of bargaining, dealing with men like Gundu Rao was quite distasteful.

Despite this, Mrs Gandhi chose Gundu Rao to preside over the formal anointment of Rajiv as her heir. He was asked to organise a national Youth Congress convention in Bangalore at which Rajiv was to be formally elected president of the organisation. For Gundu Rao, who was out of tune with Rajiv's low-key, urbane style, this was a golden opportunity to curry favour with the new leader. He worked overtime to make the convention a gala event.

He virtually handed over the city to Youth Congress activists who plastered walls with posters carrying portraits of a beaming Mrs Gandhi, Rajiv and, of course, Gundu Rao. Not satisfied with this alone, F.M. Khan and his cronies dug up every important road in the city to erect welcome arches for the leader-to-be. At the conference venue too, no effort was spared. Senior ministers scurried about taking care of arrangements. The horticulture minister was seen personally supervising the placement of flower pots by gardeners from his department — a job they could have done better without him breathing down their necks! The show cost a vast sum. It was as ostentatious as it could be.

On the day Rajiv arrived from Delhi, Gundu Rao and his minions had arranged a massive reception for him. People (mostly hired) had been lined up all along the route from the airport to the state guest-house, where Rajiv was to stay. At the airport, hundreds of party leaders and workers waited to greet the heir apparent. Khan had even arranged for an airplane look-alike float, fully covered with jasmine flowers, in which Rajiv was to ride into town.

Some of the dissidents thought that if Rajiv rode in this vehicle, it would be suggestive of his favouring the Gundu Rao–Khan clique. As soon as Rajiv's plane landed, a few members of the anti-Gundu Rao camp complained to Arun Nehru, Rajiv's confidant, who took one look at the ugly float and decided that his friend would not ride in it. Khan was crestfallen. This incident sums up how political equations in the Congress of that day often hinged on trivia. The importance of a leader in the party was not gauged on the strength of his popularity or his hold over a constituency, but on his proximity to Mrs Gandhi and later, Rajiv.

It did not take long for Bangarappa to realise, however, that no matter how much Rajiv disliked Gundu Rao, there was no way the latter would be disciplined. The Chief Minister continued to behave as before and had utter contempt for the dissidents. Two important members of the party in the state's Upper House, Abdul Nazirsab and M. Raghupathy, were denied renomination because they were critical of Gundu Rao and had aligned themselves with the Bangarappa group. Both of them, incidentally, had remained loyal to the Congress before the 1980 parliamentary election. This convinced the dissidents that no matter how disastrous Gundu Rao was for the party, Mrs Gandhi would keep backing him to the hilt. The only option was to quit the party, and they did so.

Urs's death made it easy for Bangarappa to decide his future course of action. While Urs was alive, Bangarappa could not have joined his party since Urs held him in contempt. Urs believed that he had given Bangarappa a major boost in politics when, in 1977, he had inducted him into the Congress and made him a junior minister. He had turned bitter towards Bangarappa in 1980, when the latter had decided to remain with Mrs Gandhi. Whenever his close followers raised the issue of opposition groups in Karnataka joining hands, Urs would say that he was willing to deal with anyone but Bangarappa. After Urs's death, his Kranti Ranga party, which was left with hardly 10 legislators, sought to recruit important leaders, particularly from the Backward Classes. In spite of an open invitation from the Kranti Ranga, Bangarappa, a Backward Classes leader, did not join it right away. Instead, he organised a convention to demonstrate his popularity, so that he could bargain from a position of strength.

Opposition parties in the state had long been carefully coordinating their activities. Many issues, such as the problems of farmers and industrial workers, had brought them together (often on the same platform), as their small numbers in the legislature forced them into a united front. Gundu Rao's bungling provided them with abundant opportunities to collaborate on other issues too. They mounted agitations regarding the issues of law and order and primacy to Kannada. Not only the Janata Party and the Kranti Ranga but also, for the first time in Karnataka (and possibly India), the two Communist parties — the CPI and the CPI (M)[1] — and the BJP shared a platform.

So a degree of understanding, if not unity, among the various opposition parties already existed by the time Bangarappa and his group exited the Congress. All these groups worked keeping in mind the election to the state assembly due in about seven months.

Throughout his career, Bangarappa tended to operate aggressively in a winner-takes-all spirit. Although this sometimes enabled him to

---

[1] Communist Party of India and Communist Party of India-Marxist, respectively.

make short-term gains, it damaged his long-term interests, those of the various parties that he, as a serial defector, joined and, ultimately when he became Chief Minister in the 1990s, those of the state. When he finally decided to join the Kranti Ranga, he created complications by insisting that the presidency of the party should go to him. He exploited differences within the party in an effort to hijack it. At a meeting of the Kranti Ranga convened by J. H. Patel after Bangarappa had joined it, the latter's supporters prevented Patel from beginning the proceedings by loudly insisting that he hand over the presidency to Bangarappa then and there. An exasperated Patel refused, but left the venue in disgust and later declared that Bangarappa's actions violated party rules. Neither man was willing to climb down so that, ironically, the Kranti Ranga, at this moment of 'unification', was threatened with a split.

It required enormous effort by some of its leaders to prevent the split. They and some Janata Party leaders came up with a compromise formula. Neither Patel nor Bangarappa would head the Kranti Ranga. Abdul Nazirsab became party president and B. Rachaiah, a veteran Scheduled Caste leader, was made chairman of its parliamentary board.

The State Election of 1983: Rejection for the Congress

Amidst all these developments, Gundu Rao continued to ride high. He too had begun to prepare for the election due in or before March 1983. However, in November 1982 Mrs Gandhi surprised everyone, including Gundu Rao, by announcing that elections to three states, including Karnataka, would be advanced by two months to January.

While Andhra Pradesh's Chief Minister, Vijayabhaskar Reddy had learned in advance of Mrs Gandhi's intentions, Gundu Rao had not. Just two days earlier, he had told a meeting of the Congress legislature party that the election would be in February. The day the *Indian Express* broke the story, he refused to believe it. On the same morning, he was to participate in a public function in Bangalore. Several reporters, anxious to get his comments, were told not to take the story of an early election seriously. It was mere speculation. Even as he spoke, an aide whispered in his ear that the Election Commission had just formally declared January to be the date. Two hours later, Gundu Rao, characteristically brushing aside embarrassment, told the state assembly that the surprise announcement was advantageous to everyone. When the House adjourned, he tried to dispel the impression that he had no prior knowledge of the announcement, but not even his partymen believed him.

An hour before the assembly had convened, legislators from both the Congress and the opposition had trooped into the lobbies with anxiety writ large on their faces. The prospect of an immediate election was unappealing to all. As the assembly was going through the motions of the day's business, most members went into huddles in the lobbies, weighing the pros and cons of an early election. After the House adjourned, Gundu Rao stayed in his seat to have a word with party colleagues. When some reporters approached him, he greeted them with his usual bonhomie and answered questions amidst murmurs of sycophantic approval from his colleagues. 'I assure you, we will win at least 160 seats' (out of 224), he began. 'There is no question of the Congress faring badly because people have faith in Mrs Gandhi.' He reminded them that of the four by-elections, the Congress had won three. People would not vote for the opposition.

The next few days before parties began selecting candidates were utterly chaotic. At the Congress office, thousands of aspirants for tickets filed applications. The state party president was constantly besieged by party workers keen on obtaining nominations. However, the more serious aspirants, including all sitting legislators, completely ignored him and hovered around Gundu Rao and other senior leaders. Some of the latter, including Moily,[2] were drawing up lists of their own supporters in the hope that the high command in New Delhi would not completely yield to Gundu Rao as it finalised the list.

Unmindful of all this, Gundu Rao went about drawing up his own list. For the sake of formality, an election committee was set up by the party high command, consisting of prominent state leaders. Mrs Gandhi even sent Dr Shankar Dayal Sharma,[3] a national-level Congress leader who served as a central observer, to assist this committee in Bangalore. Gundu Rao did not believe in such tedious formal meetings so, he asked all committee members to join him in Delhi to finalise the list. When Dr Sharma arrived in Bangalore, he found that the committee had shifted base and returned to the capital. In Delhi, the committee met once or twice, but left the final decision about candidates almost entirely to Gundu Rao. He, in turn, adopted a very unusual procedure to finalise the list.

---

[2] A leader belonging to the Backward Classes, and future Chief Minister of Karnataka.

[3] Future President of India (1992–97).

As soon as the committee left for Delhi, practically every serious aspirant for a party ticket also rushed to the capital city to lobby the Chief Minister. Sitting in Karnataka Bhavan, Gundu Rao interviewed one after another. Present during these meetings was the chief of the state's police intelligence, D. R. Kartikeyan. Months before, Gundu Rao had asked the Intelligence Department, which reported directly to him, to make an assessment of the party's chances in each constituency, including those which the Congress had won in 1978. Armed with dossiers on every sitting legislator and other aspirants, Kartikeyan assisted in making the selection. This was naturally resented by several senior party leaders. After all, Kartikeyan was an officer of the Indian Police Service, and was expected to serve not the ruling party but the government. Although the Intelligence Department carried out work of a political nature, it was expected to keep its distance from party politics. Kartikeyan's presence at these meetings was seen as transgressing this limit.

It also did little to ensure a shrewd selection of candidates. On this and other occasions across India, when intelligence services have assisted with candidate selection, the quality of their advice has usually been poor. Party organisations are far better equipped than policemen to gather political intelligence. But Gundu Rao (like his leader Indira Gandhi at the national level) had, in the pursuit of personal dominance, presided over the weakening of the Congress's organisational capacity. So, it was now far less effective at information gathering than it was a few years before. And in any case, Gundu Rao, again like Mrs Gandhi, was disinclined to accept much advice from the party.

Worse was to follow. When the selected candidates in far-flung constituencies had to be asked to file nomination papers, Gundu Rao had Kartikeyan send them wireless messages over the police communications network. This was an even more flagrant case of misuse of office, and the Election Commission, to which a formal complaint was made, held a hurried inquiry and passed an order barring the over-zealous Kartikeyan[4] from election duty. This generated enormous adverse publicity that damaged the Congress's chances in the election.

---

[4] He was later the principal investigator into the assassination of Rajiv Gandhi in 1991.

In Delhi, Gundu Rao was able to finalise his own list with ease. He made some concessions to other leaders by including some of their protégés. He had trouble reconciling differences between the loyalist and defector groups of legislators. The loyalists opposed the automatic re-nomination of all defectors. The defectors, on the other hand, mustered enough courage to demand that their interests should not suffer merely because they had joined the party after the 1980 Lok Sabha election.

Gundu Rao used only one yardstick in reaching his decisions. He chose as candidates those whose loyalty to him was beyond question. Many competent partymen (including several sitting legislators), capable of winning, were denied tickets simply because they had independent minds and refused to be his toadies. Once he had finalised the list, he had little trouble getting the approval of the party's central parliamentary board. He flew back to Bangalore two days before nominations closed and released the list.

It contained more candidates from the dominant castes of the Lingayats and Vokkaligas than the Backward Classes. This was to be expected since Gundu Rao had increasingly come to rely on Lingayat leaders from northern Karnataka, though this did not necessarily mean that ordinary Lingayat voters were with him. The net result was that the Congress, which had pursued a policy of preferment to the Backward Classes and other, still lower-status groups after Urs assumed power in 1972, was now seen to have jettisoned this policy. This was fully exploited by Bangarappa, a Backward Classes leader himself, during the campaign.

The opposition parties, meanwhile, were getting their act together so quietly that many overlooked a significant development. A day after the announcement of the election, Hegde, national-level general secretary of the Janata Party, convened party leaders and convinced them that there was a pressing need to hammer out an electoral understanding with other opposition groups, to avoid a split in the anti-Congress vote. On his own initiative, he called in the Kranti Ranga leaders and the two groups agreed that they should avoid a contest against each other.

Although Hegde took this initiative, he tried to remain in the background throughout the talks between the various opposition groups. This helped a great deal since, by holding back from direct involvement in the bargaining, he could arbitrate between the groups. To start with, he decided that talks on seat adjustments would be between the Janata Party and the Kranti Ranga to begin with. Discussions with the Bharatiya

Janata Party (BJP) and the two Communist parties would be held separately after the initial negotiations had made sufficient progress.

In the meetings, held at Hegde's house, the Janata Party was represented by S. R. Bommai,[5] president of the state unit of the party, and Deve Gowda[6]. Other leaders like M. S. Gurupadaswamy, a former central government minister, joined later. On behalf of the Kranti Ranga, Nazirsab[7] as president, Rachaiah[8] as chairman of the parliamentary board, Bangarappa,[9] and J. H. Patel[10] took part. Since these talks were held quite informally, many other leaders from both sides occasionally participated too.

To avoid getting bogged down in the numbers game, that is, in the relative shares of tickets for the Janata Party and the Kranti Ranga, the leaders adopted a shrewd approach. First, the constituencies held by the two parties respectively were cleared, and in all but one case, sitting legislators were chosen. Then a list of constituencies where the Janata Party or a Kranti Ranga aspirant had finished closely behind the Congress in the previous election was drawn up, and after some bargaining, this list was also finalised. Within days, the two parties had more or less agreed to candidates in about 120 of the 224 constituencies. There was hard bargaining for the remaining constituencies, and Hegde often had to step in to resolve the differences.

Even as this process was unfolding, the leaders from the two parties had begun to consider other issues. They decided that they would form a common front and run a joint campaign. After some hesitation, the Kranti Ranga agreed to adopt the election symbol of the Janata Party, since it did not have a reserved symbol of its own.[11] It was also decided that they would have a joint manifesto.

---

[5] A Lingayat and future Chief Minister of the state.

[6] A Vokkaliga and future Chief Minister of Karnataka and later, Prime Minister of India.

[7] A Muslim who would go on to become one of the most imaginative state-level ministers of India during the 1980s.

[8] A Scheduled Caste leader, a formidable Education Minister of Karnataka and later, Governor of Kerala.

[9] A Backward Class (Idiga) leader and future Chief Minister of the state.

[10] A Lingayat and future Chief Minister of the state.

[11] In Indian elections, ballots give the names of candidates but also their pictorial symbols, so that illiterate voters are able to indicate their preferences.

Once the talks between the Janata Party and the Kranti Ranga were progressing smoothly, Hegde invited the BJP and the two Communist parties for similar discussions. As expected, these parties pitched their demands quite high, but eventually the CPI and the CPI(M) agreed to five seats each. Negotiations with the BJP, however, proved difficult. At first, the BJP president, A. K. Subbaiah, and others demanded over 100 seats, but later reduced their claim to around 40. The difficulty arose over the choice of constituencies. The BJP wanted almost all the seats in Bangalore city. These included some that the Janata Party had won in 1978. BJP leaders were not prepared to accept the basic principle that a constituency that had been won by a party in the previous election should automatically go to it. In spite of these problems, talks between the Janata Party and the BJP continued for several days, but finally broke down. The BJP then decided to field its candidates in about 125 of the 224 constituencies.

Between them, the Janata Party, the Kranti Ranga, the CPI and the CPI(M) fielded 220 candidates and left four seats to Independents. With the BJP fielding 125, it was still possible for the opposition to ensure a straight fight with the Congress in nearly half of the constituencies in the state.

Meanwhile, Gundu Rao surprised many when he filed nomination papers from two constituencies: Somwarpet, his home town, and Chitapur in Gulbarga district. This led to obvious suspicions that he no longer considered Somwarpet safe. Subbaiah, the sharp-tongued leader who had focused all his attention on unearthing scandals during the Gundu Rao regime, had announced beforehand that he would fight Gundu Rao in this constituency. The Chief Minister appears to have taken this threat seriously, since one morning, he hopped into the government helicopter and flew to Chitapur to file his nomination papers.

This led to a minor drama for a couple of days. It left Gundu Rao open to one of two damaging charges. He could be accused of the misuse of office under election laws for taking the official helicopter to Chitapur. On the other hand, if he offered to pay the cost of the trip, he could be accused of exceeding tight campaign-spending limits. Eventually, because his decision to contest from two constituencies was seen as a sign of weakness, Gundu Rao decided to withdraw from Chitapur.

On the night that he released the list of Congress candidates, Gundu Rao prophesied that his party would win 200 of the 224 seats. It was a characteristically tall claim from a person who never showed signs of modesty. No one took him seriously, but then at that early stage, no one believed that the Congress could be defeated in a state where it had always won.

As the campaign began, Gundu Rao and his men seemed to have a head start over the opposition. The Chief Minister faced no shortage of funds, and he organised publicity for his party in style. In sharp contrast, the Janata–Kranti Ranga combine did not even have enough posters to display. It was not short of enthusiastic workers or supporters, but it certainly lacked money. In almost every constituency, its candidates had to fend for themselves, either spending out of their own pockets or raising funds through local donations.

Despite these severe handicaps, the opposition campaigned hard. Bangarappa, for one, travelled all over the state for two weeks to support other candidates. So confident was he of his own victory from Sorab in Shimoga district that he decided he would spend just one day there on the eve of polling. He made this decision despite the fact that Gundu Rao had chosen to field Kagodu Thimmappa, an Idiga and an ex-socialist like Bangarappa, from the same constituency. Thimmappa had been brought into the Congress and made a minister by Gundu Rao in 1981 solely to counter Bangarappa.

Two other opposition leaders also toured the entire state, campaigning from dawn to midnight. Hegde, who had been instrumental in fashioning the opposition alliance, and Nazirsab, president of the Kranti Ranga, were not seeking seats themselves, so unlike other opposition leaders, they were not tied down to a constituency. Rather surprisingly, most national-level leaders of the opposition stayed out of Karnataka. Except for Chandra Shekhar, who made a brief visit (breaking his long march from Kanyakumari to Delhi), and Madhu Dandavate, no other national leader visited the state. But for the Congress, Mrs Gandhi, as in the past, was there to criss-cross the state as often as she could. Both she and Rajiv Gandhi, by now the general secretary of the party, divided their time between Andhra Pradesh and Karnataka.

At first glance, the 1983 campaign looked rather dull compared to that of 1978. But beneath the surface, there were subtle hints of a polarisation of votes. Few observers fathomed this, however, simply because they approached the election with the pre-conceived notion that the Congress would win no matter what.

In most constituencies, it gradually became apparent that voters were determined to express their displeasure with the Congress. Many civic groups and organised interests adopted anti-Congress stands for a diversity of reasons. These included some which had initially preferred to keep their distance from all political parties, but now felt they must make their displeasure with the Congress known. For example, the influential Raitha Sangha,[12] which represented farmers, had reasons to be unhappy with the Gundu Rao regime. It had pursued anti-farmer policies which no sensible Chief Minister would have adopted, given the numerical strength and economic power of the cultivators. These had hardened the attitudes of well-to-do farmers in districts like Mandya, Shimoga, Hassan and Chikmagalur to such an extent that the Raitha Sangha was able to organise some resistance to government efforts to collect overdue loans.

The leading lights in the Sangha had long kept aloof from political parties in order to build an independent movement of farmers. When the state election was announced, the association decided to boycott the election, as a token of its disapproval of government policies. Its members were also barred from either contesting or campaigning on behalf of parties. But this apolitical stance did not last long, because the rank and file in the movement thought that they should do everything to defeat a government that had done them great harm. Some leaders and workers in the association disregarded the call for boycott and got involved in the campaign. A couple of them, including H. G. Govinde Gowda, a highly respected Vokkaliga from Chikmagalur district, contested on the Janata Party ticket.

The increasing demand from its members, and the disregard shown by some for the boycott of elections, forced the association to revise its decision and allow participation in the campaign. Even this stance was too moderate for many farmers, and after pressure from some leaders in Mandya, a centre of farmer power, the association finally asked its members to vote against the Congress.

An organisation at the opposite extreme of the socio-economic hierarchy, the Dalit Sangarsh Samiti, a body fighting for the uplift of the Scheduled Castes[13], also decided to work against the Congress all over the state. This was astounding, since the Scheduled Castes had

---

[12] Raitha Sangha means 'farmers' association'.

[13] Ex-untouchables.

long been a crucial element of Mrs Gandhi's social base. Other informal groups, like those of the pro-Kannada intellectuals and writers, also supported the opposition.

Gundu Rao had clearly alienated an extraordinarily diverse array of interests. Nothing like this broad-based discontent has arisen in any other Karnataka election — before or since. Indeed, in its breadth, it has had few parallels anywhere in India, apart from the massive revulsion with the Emergency which became evident in the 1977 parliamentary election.

As so many diverse interests coalesced against him, even the usually oblivious Gundu Rao began to see, half-way through the campaign, that things were not proceeding as smoothly as they had at the start. In his own constituency, Somwarpet, he suddenly found the going quite tough as many groups that had traditionally supported him proved lukewarm this time. The large vote bank of plantation workers, mostly migrants from across the border in Kerala and Tamil Nadu, were no longer as enthusiastic as before. He also realised that a small but influential segment of Lingayat voters, tucked away in one corner of his constituency, were against him.

Khan, encountered mid-campaign in Somwarpet, looked worried and after some prodding by Raghavan, admitted that his friend was in a spot. He was anxious despite the fact that Gundu Rao was spending a large amount of money on his campaign. Hundreds of cars with party workers were criss-crossing the constituency, appealing to people to vote for the Chief Minister. Every tree, wall and lamppost carried election posters of the Congress. Gundu Rao himself spent more time in the constituency than he had earlier planned, riding around in an imported car. He and Khan even brought in some Tamil film stars to urge Tamil plantation labourers to vote for the Congress.

Gundu Rao's publicity blitz placed his Janata Party opponent, Jivijaya, at a severe disadvantage. To make matters worse, the latter faced severe psychological stress born of the fear that Congress goons would cause him harm. As the campaign wound to its close, there were also worries that one of the Independent candidates in the fray might be killed, so that the election could be countermanded. At least one candidate, a Muslim, went into hiding a few days before polling, fearing a violent attack. Surprisingly, a large section of Muslims in the constituency had turned against the Chief Minister, despite his well-known ties to

Muslims such as Khan and Ibrahim, and despite the Muslims' traditional preference for the Congress. Popular alienation from the government appeared to know no limits, reaching into core sectors of Congress support.

It was not just Gundu Rao who was in trouble. Many of his ministerial colleagues also faced difficulties. And yet, because the campaign still 'appeared' to be so one-sidedly in favour of the Congress, no one thought that a uniform pattern was emerging across the state. Gundu Rao clearly faced unprecedented difficulties because he had alienated so many interests, but at this early stage it was not seen as a sign of his party's likely defeat.

Except for some stray incidents of violence, polling passed off peacefully on 6 January. Gundu Rao, who got feedback on the pattern of polling through the Intelligence Department and his party network, still thought he had no reason to worry. He was, however, no longer confident of winning as many seats as he had expected at the outset.

When the counting of votes was begun the next day and the trends began to pour in the afternoon, everyone was in for a shock. The Congress was losing quite badly in every region of the state. By the end of the day it appeared that it would fall short of 100 seats out of 224. The combined opposition was set to secure enough seats to muster a majority. Indeed, by night many Congress heads had rolled and the biggest was that of Gundu Rao himself. He had lost in Somwarpet by over 2,000 votes to Jivijaya.

Next morning, when practically all the results were in, it was evident that the Congress was out, though the opposition was not exactly in. The outcome was so shocking to the Congress that it was unable to react to the new situation. It was so thoroughly demoralised that the best efforts of its troubleshooter, Buta Singh, sent specially by Mrs Gandhi in the last few days of the campaign to salvage the situation, were in vain.

For the first time in the post-independence history of the state, the Congress had been rejected — and comprehensively at that. It seemed a genuine political miracle. Also for the first time, it was apparent that Mrs Gandhi was no longer a charismatic leader who could conjure victories for her candidates under any circumstances. In most of the constituencies that she and Rajiv had visited, Congress candidates had *lost*.

The party ended up with 81 seats out of 224. The Janata–Kranti Ranga combine had secured 95, and its electoral allies, the CPI and the CPI(M), got three seats each. The BJP got 18 and the Independents, a few of them Congress rebels, got 23. So while the verdict was damning for the Congress, it was somewhat uncertain for its opponents. The Janata–Kranti Ranga combine was 28 seats short of an absolute majority. This triggered another political drama that lasted for months.

Gundu Rao took his and his party's defeat in his stride. A day after the results were out, he told Raghavan:

> It is perhaps fate that intervened. After all, if I had remained in the contest in Chitapur, I would have continued to be a member of the assembly. Perhaps, I was destined to lose and so was my party. We must, in good faith, accept the verdict of the people. They have shown that they do not want a Congress government. We must respect that sentiment and sit in the opposition.

There were not many hangers-on at his house that morning. Although there was a tinge of sadness in his eyes, Gundu Rao retained some of his old good humour. He said that no one could take away the title of 'ex-Chief Minister' from him. For a person who had started out as a ticket tout 20 years back, it was a great achievement. There were few others that he could point to.

Gundu Rao's 'Contribution' to Political Transformation

After the long litany of Gundu Rao's mistakes set out in the preceding sections, readers might justifiably ask why we have discussed his case in such detail. Why give space to such a completely inept politician, in a study that also deals with the two highly accomplished and constructive Chief Ministers who came before and after him?

A key argument in this book is that senior politicians, Chief Ministers in this case, have a huge impact on politics, institutions, state–society relations and the pursuit of development. This may be obvious to readers, but the academic literature on these topics in less developed countries largely omits these crucial actors. Chief Ministers' influence can be mightily constructive, as Devaraj Urs and, later, Hegde vividly demonstrated. But they can also do vast damage. Gundu Rao did little else, although, as we shall see presently, the very ghastliness of his performance made ironic and unintended contributions to all the positive changes examined in this book.

Our account of Gundu Rao's politics shows that Indira Gandhi's decisions could throw up not just brilliant innovators like Urs, but appalling bunglers too. By tracing the explanation for his astonishing survival in office through three long years of surpassing incompetence to his being a part of Mrs Gandhi's inner circle, we also remind ourselves of how destructive her last premiership was, not just to India and the democratic process, but also to her party and herself.

Gundu Rao was a man of limited intelligence and little education. His attention span could be measured in seconds rather than minutes. He was, however, not as monumentally incapable as another of Mrs Gandhi's choices for Chief Minister, Baba Saheb Bhosale of Maharashtra. A leader who belonged to Bhosale's caste told Manor that 'he was so stupid that his eyes did not focus when he looked at you, and the brain behind the eyes was even worse'.[14] The story of his selection as Chief Minister is revealing. Mrs Gandhi had so thoroughly centralised power that she had very little time for the vast number of issues referred to her for decision making. For instance, when a decision for the choice of a Chief Minister for a crucial state like Maharashtra had to be made, she called for a list of the Congress legislators from the state. She had got only as far as the 'B's in the alphabetically arranged list when she spotted Bhosale's name, which she recognised. She told her aides that she had once dined with a relative of his, and that he would do.[15]

Where Gundu Rao was concerned, Indira Gandhi had at least become acquainted with him. But she clearly failed to pay close attention to the selection of such a woefully inept man, and her failure to dismiss him when his bungling became apparent was an even more appalling mistake. It indicates how much damage was being done to, among other things, Mrs Gandhi's own interests by her reliance on the extravagant pledges of loyalty by leaders such as he, and on the influential but spectacularly flawed advice of her son Sanjay.[16]

In assessing Gundu Rao's record as Chief Minister, we need to note several damaging actions which he did *not* take. What does not happen

---

[14] Interview with a Maratha leader, by James Manor, Mumbai, 30 January 1992.

[15] Interview with a member of Mrs Gandhi's staff, by James Manor, New Delhi, 17 January 1998.

[16] For evidence of the great extent to which Sanjay Gandhi influenced Mrs Gandhi after 1974, see Tandon (2006).

is often as important as what does. He did not insert the most corrupt and pliable civil servants into key posts, as Bangarappa — Karnataka's only other decidedly destructive Chief Minister — later did, between 1990 and 1992. Instead, he drew some of the best of them into key posts, but then gave them perverse tasks to fulfil, something that the illicit-liquor tragedy most vividly illustrates.

Nor did he browbeat, humiliate and wreck the morale of the civil service, as many north Indian Chief Ministers have done. On the contrary, he indulged them to a degree never seen before in independent India, and this led to an extremely unresponsive government. Thus, he did not undermine the institutional strength of the administration, although he certainly undermined the role of representative institutions, since legislators had virtually no influence over bureaucrats.

He also did not attempt to inspire antipathy between different social groups as Chief Ministers have done along caste lines in Uttar Pradesh and Bihar, and as another has done along religious lines in Gujarat. So there were limits on the damage done by Gundu Rao, but he was still mightily destructive.

But how can we claim that he made unwitting 'contributions' to the three constructive changes that are the main themes of this book? To reiterate, the three changes were as follows:

- The control which the land-owning Lingayats and Vokkaligas had exercised over state politics until 1972 was broken, and replaced by a system in which power was widely shared within rainbow coalitions of interest groups, thereby making democracy broad-based.
- The dominance which the Congress Party had enjoyed over Karnataka's politics until 1983 was replaced by a competitive party system, giving voters a choice of plausible alternatives in every subsequent election.
- The highly centralised political system in which immense powers were concentrated in the hands of ministers at the state level was fundamentally changed after 1983, as substantial powers were transferred to elected councils at lower levels, deepening democracy in the process.

Gundu Rao made an unintended contribution to the survival of the first of these changes – the installation of rainbow coalitions at the apex of power – which Urs had introduced. He abandoned Urs's strategy, but the precise way in which he did so ensured that it would swiftly be revived. Here again, things that he did *not* do were crucial. Despite some reliance on dominant-caste leaders, especially the Lingayats, he had not effectively cultivated support from a *narrow* set of social groups. Instead, his ineptitude meant that he failed to cultivate *any* – despite erratic spasms of excessive generosity. As a result, he alienated them all. Politicians who represented every important interest group therefore gravitated towards the opposition, which thus became a rainbow coalition. As we shall see in Chapter 6, this enabled (indeed, required) his successor to reinstate such a broad coalition when he constructed his government. So Gundu Rao, who wrought immense damage to institutions (the authority of the legislative assembly, the integrity of the police and the civil service, the organisational strength and reputation of the Congress Party, among other things), ironically also enabled rainbow coalitions to become institutionalised as standard practice for at least the next quarter century.

The forces arrayed against him in the 1983 state election may have included leaders from every important section of society, but they were still only loosely organised on election day. However (as we shall see in the next chapter), once they had an opportunity to govern, they evolved into a coalition capable of surviving grave threats to its survival. It contained a remarkable diversity of talents. It included formidable representatives of Vokkaligas (Deve Gowda), Lingayats (Patel and Bommai), Brahmins (Hegde), the Backward Classes (Bangarappa), the Scheduled Castes (Rachaiah), and Muslims (Abdul Nazirsab). This is a complete list of the key social groups in Karnataka's politics. The strength of this team is apparent from the fact that it included five men who would go on to become Chief Ministers of the state, one future Prime Minister of India, and a future governor of Kerala. And the one man who did not achieve a high office because he died young, Abdul Nazirsab, was arguably the most constructive figure in the impressive government which came to power in 1983.

Gundu Rao also made a decisive contribution to the destruction of Congress dominance. He gathered such vast powers unto himself that he became the face of the Congress in Karnataka. As such, when he turned out to be inept (and at times brutish) the Congress, which the state's voters had always supported because it had provided reasonably good government, paid the price. The opposition may have lacked cohesion and a clear leader, but in 1983 anything was better than Gundu Rao's wretched regime. So it was not the opposition but the Chief Minister himself and Mrs Gandhi, who stuck with him despite the succession of colossal mistakes he made, who deserve most of the blame (or credit) for the destruction of the Congress dominance in Karnataka.

Gundu Rao also made an ironic contribution on the third front. By radically over-centralising power and then misusing it, he inspired a strong need for decentralisation, to which the next government responded very generously and constructively.

We see, then, that Gundu Rao played a key role in deepening democracy in Karnataka, and in making it more competitive, accommodative and inclusive despite, or rather because of, the fact that he stood for just the opposite.

Finally, his rejection in the 1983 state election demonstrates that the democratic process in Karnataka had become remarkably resourceful and resilient, in that it was able to provide a corrective to his ghastly regime. Several leaders now represented quite a few well-mobilised social groups to provide an alternative. And the people of the state, whom Gundu Rao had assumed to be docile, unsophisticated and incapable of looking beyond Mrs Gandhi, seized upon this opportunity.

Part III

Ramakrishna Hegde, 1983–88

6

Constructing the First Non-Congress Government

When political institutions in developing countries suffer serious damage, it is often extremely difficult, at times even impossible, to repair and revive them. But India is, for the most part, different. Here, both at the national as well as at the state level, when institutions or democratic processes have been severely undermined, it has often been possible to regenerate them or to replace them with alternatives (Manor 1994: 230–41). Gundu Rao had wrought havoc in Karnataka, but because voters valued the institutions and norms that he had ignored, and sometimes wrecked, they threw him out and turned to others who were committed to rebuilding. The government that succeeded him (the victors of the state election of 1983) fulfilled this mandate, and then went further, creating (as we shall see, briefly here and in more detail in Chapter 10) new institutions that deepened the democratic process. But before they could make much headway with these tasks, they had to organise themselves and consolidate their grip on power. This was hardly an easy assignment.

Finding a Chief Minister

Around noon on 7 January, Hegde telephoned Raghavan, who had begun pulling together counting trends in the election from various sources. Hegde wanted to crosscheck the initial information that had reached him from different districts. Before the conversation ended, they tried to estimate the final tally in the 223 constituencies where polling had occurred. It was difficult since the trends had not yet begun to present a clear picture, but they eventually concluded that the Janata–Kranti Ranga front was likely to finish with about a hundred seats. There were also many Independents who were leading. The Congress was in for a shock.

Hegde had chosen the same afternoon to travel to Mangalore to keep a private engagement. 'How can you be away from Bangalore when there is a possibility of your party putting together a government?', Raghavan asked him. 'I will be back tomorrow', he replied.

An hour later, he called Raghavan again from the airport, as his flight was delayed. This time Raghavan had something more concrete to share.

It had more or less become clear that the Congress, which had entered the fray with a clear advantage, was losing quite badly, and that Chief Minister Gundu Rao and many of his cabinet colleagues were trailing their rivals in the count. This news enthused Hegde, and he said he would leave a statement for the press with his daughter.

A short while later, Abdul Nazirsab, president of the Kranti Ranga, dropped in to share his happiness over the outcome. He had a broad grin on his face, having had a lot to do with forging a combined opposition. The inevitable next question was: who will lead the Janata–Kranti Ranga legislature party? Nazirsab winced at this question. He had reasons to. If defeating the Congress was difficult, putting together a government was similarly daunting, since it was tough to reconcile the claims of the two partners in the front. Between them, the Janata Party and the Kranti Ranga had at least three aspirants for the leadership.

That night, there was great jubilation in the non-Congress parties as, for the first time since independence, the Congress was clearly heading for a defeat. By rejecting the Congress in this election, the voters had made a conscious decision to pick the non-Congress alliance to preside over their destinies. The question which now arose was whether such a newly formed combination would operate coherently.

When Hegde returned from Mangalore the next afternoon, the process of consultation among the leaders of the Janata Party and the Kranti Ranga had still not commenced because most leaders had not returned from their constituencies. A day later, Bangarappa, who had left the Congress a few months before the election to join the Kranti Ranga, arrived after having won by a handsome margin. The minute he landed in Bangalore, his followers besieged him. They assumed he would be the natural choice to head the government, so much so that the proprietor of a local newspaper (an ardent supporter of Bangarappa), anticipating that Bangarappa would become Chief Minister, placed around his neck a huge garland of roses, specially flown in from Madras.

Bangarappa himself remained non-committal. 'It is', he told Raghavan, 'for the party to elect the leader.' But he appeared quite confident that the party would not look beyond him. Indeed, he thought he should be the natural choice, since he was convinced that he was singularly responsible for the defeat of the Congress. It was this assumption that made him behave intractably, and proved his undoing.

Bommai, state-level president of the Janata Party, returned the next day from Hubli, from where he had won with some difficulty. 'I am ready for the job if the party asks me to form the ministry,' he told newsmen. The Janata Party had emerged as the senior partner, having won 63 of the front's 99 seats. He considered it natural that the chief ministership should go to the Janata Party and, as its state president, to him.

The third aspirant, Deve Gowda, a seasoned politician from the old Mysore region, began lobbying, but more quietly than the other two leaders. He reached out to fellow Vokkaliga legislators from both the Janata Party and the Kranti Ranga, to size up his strength.

Before another 24 hours had elapsed, uncertainty had given way to confusion. To start with, some in the Janata Party thought Hegde would make a better Chief Minister in a situation that demanded extraordinary agility to manage a minority government. His subtlety and guile in constructing a largely united front against the Congress made him an eminently qualified candidate. Hegde himself was unwilling. He had not been elected to the assembly, and had not manoeuvred himself into a position of importance. He thought that three aspirants was more than enough, and that the new leader should be chosen from among them.

Hegde rued the fact that the Janata–Kranti Ranga combine had fallen short of the required majority, although it had emerged as the single largest group ahead of the Congress. The latter had 86 seats, as against 99 (after the realignment of a few legislators)[1] for his combine. But it was still 17 short of a majority (after the support of other parties for it is taken into account). 'If we had had more resources, we would have done better', Hegde told Raghavan. However, if money had been a deciding factor in this election, Gundu Rao's Congress, which had funds that were at least a 100 times more than what the Janata–Kranti Ranga had at its disposal, would have swept the state. Nor would Gundu Rao himself have lost in Somwarpet.

There was, however, some truth in what Hegde said. To put up a decent fight in any constituency, a bare minimum of funds was required. There were posters to put up, vehicles needed to tour the constituencies, and election workers to pay. None of this comes free, and even volunteers

---

[1] A few members of the legislative assembly had aligned themselves with the Janata–Kranti Ranga after the election result became known. This explains why the figures cited here are different from those mentioned in the previous chapter.

had to be moved around and fed. In many constituencies, Janata–Kranti Ranga candidates lacked even the most minimal resources. More funds would probably have turned results in several constituencies where they had lost by narrow margins.

The Congress was too shell-shocked to do anything to upset the popular verdict. But like many others, Hegde was unsure about who should be chosen as the Janata–Kranti Ranga leader. He wondered aloud in the presence of a couple of confidants:

> It finally boils down to three names: Bangarappa (from the Backward Classes), Bommai (a Lingayat) and Deve Gowda (a Vokkaliga). If the choice of the leader is to be made from the major communities (Lingayats and Vokkaligas), I think Deve Gowda would make a better Chief Minister. He is dynamic and hardworking.

Hegde had reservations about Bommai. He more or less ruled out Bangarappa, since the Kranti Ranga (to which the latter belonged) had won fewer seats than the Janata Party. Hegde thought at this stage that he had no stake in this exercise.

He knew that, up to a point, his word carried some weight since he had been pivotal in the victory. 'Personally, if I am asked to make a choice, I would certainly like to see Nazirsab as Chief Minister', he said. This was an amazing statement to make. While everyone respected Nazirsab as a well-read, committed, even lovable, individual, no one took him seriously as a politician. He appeared to lack guile and was not manipulative. Hegde explained that he preferred Nazirsab because in the last few weeks, he had discovered in him well-concealed skills and a strong attachment to issues that were dear to Hegde himself:

> He might appear to be naive. He is not. If we had a majority, I would work hard to make Nazir the Chief Minister. In the situation in which we find ourselves, I do not think others will accept it. But I will try to persuade them.

This was impossible. Other leaders were unwilling even to listen, since they were eager for the mantle to fall on them. When Raghavan asked Hegde about his own candidacy, he ruled it out. He thought there was no place at the top for a Brahmin like him. If Gundu Rao had become Chief Minister despite being a Brahmin, it was because he had the blessings of Mrs Gandhi, and no one dared oppose her. Several months before the 1983 state election, when Raghavan asked him why he was reluctant to return to state politics, Hegde had recalled that way back in 1967, when Chief Minister Nijalingappa had decided to serve as full-time national president of the Congress, he had chosen Veerendra Patil (a fellow Lingayat) as his successor in Karnataka, though he (Hegde) was more experienced and better equipped for the chief ministership.

> I thought that Nijalingappa would at least sound me out . . . Had he, I would have suggested Veerendra Patil's name. The fact is that in the politics of dominant castes, people like me have no place . . . I no longer have such intentions.

Meanwhile, the three aspirants for the chief ministership continued hectic lobbying. By the evening of 8 January, two conclusions had begun to emerge. Bangarappa's chances had dimmed considerably because of the political arithmetic. His group, with 36 members, could not dictate terms to a larger group of 63. Besides, members of the Janata Party distrusted him. Many were upset because during the election, he had distributed resources selectively and had not helped all candidates. They suspected that he would be narrowly partisan, interested only in promoting the faction useful to him. Even within the Kranti Ranga, several leaders who had initially been enthusiastic about him had now become disillusioned. But within the Janata Party, neither Bommai nor Deve Gowda was able to enlarge his support base. This meant that none of the three aspirants was in a position to win the contest.

The Congress saw an opportunity here. They assumed that the Janata–Kranti Ranga combine would split over the choice of a leader, as had other non-Congress formulations in the past. There was a remote possibility that amid this confusion, the Congress might increase its strength, if necessary by devious means, so as to stake a claim for power. The party's central observer, Buta Singh, who had been stunned by the verdict for a couple of days, became active. He and the only recognisable Congress leader to win a seat, Moily, hoped that the Governor would be forced to call upon the Congress to form the government. To acquire additional support, they began to work on several Independents who had won seats, some of whom were actually Congress rebels who had been denied tickets. It was thought that they could be won (or bought) over. However, most Independents were afraid of going against public opinion which, at this point, was extremely hostile to the Congress.

Karnataka's voters had a reputation for quiescence, but their anger on this occasion was apparent from more than the election result. *Thousands* of ordinary citizens continuously monitored developments by hanging around the offices of opposition parties.

The national-level president of the Janata Party, Chandra Shekhar, sent Biju Patnaik, a senior party figure, to observe the election of the legislature party's leader. Patnaik unwittingly added to the prevailing confusion. Among the first to call on him was Bangarappa. He took along with him Khadri Shamanna, a reputed journalist. Shamanna, a socialist and an out-and-out anti-Congressman, had appointed himself an advisor to the Janata–Kranti Ranga leaders during the campaign. He had decided to project Bangarappa (also a former socialist) as a chief ministerial candidate. He believed that Bangarappa's efforts had been crucial to the anti-Congress campaign. At the meeting with Patnaik, Shamanna argued for a dynamic 'Backward Class' leader as Chief Minister. Patnaik, it appears, made the customary courteous remarks in response. He also suggested that the Janata Party and the Kranti Ranga should merge forthwith, to deny the Governor an opportunity for mischief at the behest of the Congress. This was mistaken by Bangarappa and Shamanna to mean that the Janata Party high command favoured Bangarappa. Both of them rushed from this meeting, gathered members of the Kranti Ranga, and informed them that Bangarappa's election was now only a formality. They hurriedly convened a formal meeting of their party's legislators and passed a resolution merging the Kranti Ranga with the Janata Party.

Next evening, when the Janata Party and Kranti Ranga legislators finally met, Bangarappa's followers sensed that all was not well. They expected the automatic selection of their leader, but no such decision was made. Amidst the prevailing confusion, Bommai and Nazirsab, state-level presidents of the Janata Party and the Kranti Ranga respectively, merely announced to waiting journalists that the merger under the 'Janata Party' label had been completed. They then rushed to the Raj Bhavan[2] to inform the Governor, Govind Narain, that he was duty-bound to invite the newly united party to form the government.

---

[2] The official residence of the state Governor, who is empowered to play the role of referee in the parliamentary system at the state level. For instance, he can decide whom to summon to form the government.

As both were anxiously pacing the corridor, waiting to be ushered into the Governor's office, Bommai told Raghavan that there was no way he would back out of the leadership contest. He was obviously worried that, apart from Bangarappa and Deve Gowda, there was now also talk of Hegde emerging as a compromise candidate. Nazirsab had different ideas. A man not given to hiding his emotions, he was glum. He categorically ruled out the possibility of members of his former Kranti Ranga[3] backing either Bommai or Deve Gowda, but members of the original Janata Party (that is, the Janata Party before its merger with the Kranti Ranga) were unlikely to back Bangarappa. He said, 'Let us be realistic; it is not fair to expect the senior partner in the front to accept someone from the ranks of the junior partner'. He added, 'Let me tell you in confidence, many Kranti Ranga members are not in favour of Bangarappa either'. He thought that these people were likely to accept Hegde over Bangarappa.

These developments were followed by a long night in which each leader did his best to win fresh support. Bommai had a head start since the big guns among fellow Lingayats were working overtime for him. Even Nijalingappa, a veteran who had stayed away from active politics, was busy canvassing support to get power back in Lingayat hands. Deve Gowda worked, as he always did, by contacting individual legislators.

Late that night, Nazirsab, Patel and Chandre Gowda met at the latter's house to consider their options. They found that there was no change in their perceptions of the situation. They did not want either Bommai or Deve Gowda, since both represented the dominant castes whose control over the state's politics had been brought to an end by Urs. But they were also disillusioned with Bangarappa. Patel, who had had a bitter tussle with Bangarappa over the presidency of the Kranti Ranga after Urs's death, detested him. Nazirsab and Chandre Gowda, too, had their share of grievances against Bangarappa, as they had been alienated by his narrowly partisan behaviour during the election campaign.

Once the three had decided whom they would 'not' support, Patel proposed Nazirsab as their choice. Nazirsab thought that the idea was downright stupid. He was a Muslim with poor manipulative skills and a distaste for 'fund-raising'. He thought he would last no more than six

---

[3] Hereafter, the term 'Kranti Ranga' will refer to this party prior to its merger with the Janata Party under the latter party's banner.

months, and dismissed the suggestion. Patel persisted but finally agreed that if Nazirsab's candidature was not acceptable to others, they would then propose Hegde. In their view, Hegde was acceptable because he was not swayed by casteism.

When Bangarappa learnt that leaders from his own side had deserted him and that there was no way that the Janata Party high command would back him, he began to sulk, feeling he had been cheated of the position that was rightfully his. He literally shut himself in and refused to talk to anyone other than close supporters. He did not realise it, but by cloistering himself he probably lost an opportunity to become Chief Minister, courtesy of Deve Gowda.

Once he saw that he had no hope of majority support, Deve Gowda made one last bid to prevent Bommai from becoming Chief Minister. He met H.R. Basavaraj, a leading excise contractor who was thought to have influence over Bangarappa, since both of them belonged to the same community. It appears that Deve Gowda offered to support Bangarappa, provided that the latter agreed to make him Deputy Chief Minister. Bangarappa was then telephoned with a request that he speak to Deve Gowda. But Bangarappa was so angry at the turn of events that he refused to speak to anyone. It was after this that Deve Gowda decided to back Hegde in order to thwart Bommai.

By the time the legislators gathered in the conference hall in the Vidhana Souda[4] on 9 January, two things had become clear. First, there would be a contest for the leadership. This was remarkable, given recent experience under Congress rule when Chief Ministers were 'chosen' by Mrs Gandhi. Second, the BJP (with its 18 seats) had decided to support the Janata Party's bid to form the government. The local unit of the BJP still felt aggrieved over the breakdown of talks on seat adjustments with the Janata Party before the election. But the then BJP president, Atal Behari Vajpayee, announced in Delhi that his party would extend unconditional support. The two Left parties, each of which had won three seats in an alliance with the Janata Party, also naturally offered their support since they too were eager to end the Congress dominance which was all that the state had ever known.

There was, however, yet another tantalising possibility. If Bangarappa and a sizeable section of the Kranti Ranga members opted out, it would

---

[4] The Karnataka state assembly building.

be impossible for any leader to obtain a majority in the assembly. Such a move would throw things into utter disarray. Bangarappa called a meeting of all erstwhile Kranti Ranga legislators at his home early in the morning before the legislature party was to meet at 9 a.m. He obviously wanted to find out if all of them would support him if he decided to throw a spanner in the works. However, things did not work out as he had expected.

Not all 36 of the former Kranti Ranga members attended the meeting. Many of them had made up their minds the previous night to go along with Nazirsab, Patel and Chandre Gowda in their decision to not back Bangarappa. These three were among those who did not go to Bangarappa's house. Even among those who did, not all were as bitter as some of the ardent supporters of the sulking leader. Many attended in the belief that it was a meeting to discuss the strategy for the legislature party. The minute some of them learnt that Bangarappa was trying to use them as bargaining chips, they quietly left.

The meeting of the full legislative party was delayed for a considerable time, because of last-minute efforts to persuade Bangarappa to attend. A delegation of three leaders from the erstwhile Kranti Ranga rushed to his house to ask him to reconsider his decision. Their effort was in vain and one of the three, Azeez Sait, who knew Bangarappa from his days in the Socialist Party, returned, angrily muttering that Bangarappa was stupid. Sait had been asked to convey to Bangarappa that he would be offered the post of Deputy Chief Minister if he did not spoil the occasion by his non-attendance. Bangarappa declined this offer.

Finally, when the central observers decided to go ahead with the meeting, only two people — Bangarappa and an Independent he had supported — stayed away. Bangarappa had asked several close followers to take part. Their arrival put an end to the intense anxiety of the leaders gathered there. However, the delay had allowed time for the intense lobbying to reach a consensus. At the meeting, two things swiftly became clear. First, Bangarappa would not enter the fray. When someone meekly suggested his name at the meeting, there was no one to back him. Second, Deve Gowda had also decided to back out in favour of Hegde. But Hegde himself was still undecided, since he was not a member of the legislature, and had been away from state politics for six years. He was unfamiliar with those who had come into politics during his absence, as also with the changed political context.

With Bommai still pitching in strongly, two others — A. Laxmisagar, the opposition leader in the previous assembly, and M. S. Gurupadaswamy, former Union[5] Minister — also showed interest in the chief ministerial post. Inside the hall, Bommai, Nijalingappa and some others were busy trying to rope in Kranti Ranga members to support Bommai's candidacy. Since a contest appeared a distinct possibility, ballot boxes were carried inside. Meanwhile, a sizeable crowd, notably youngsters, had gathered outside the Vidhana Souda, anxious to know what had transpired within.

When Patnaik opened the meeting, it was agreed that since unanimity could not be reached on a single name, the opinions of legislators would be sought individually, and the leader with the widest support would be chosen. Once this was settled, Bommai's supporters volunteered his name for the chief ministerial post. Nazirsab's name was proposed by some members of the erstwhile Kranti Ranga. He demurred and said he would support Hegde. Laxmisagar declared that he would also stake a claim. Individual opinions were then collected.

At one extremity of the large conference hall, Patnaik and another central observer sat along with Nazirsab. A large screen partition separated them from the rest. It was agreed that the three would keep a score card and that once the consultations were completed, they would merely announce the winner without disclosing the number of votes that the three candidates had secured. At the end of the process, Hegde emerged as the one with the greatest support. While the actual number of votes secured was never announced, Nazirsab, who had kept the score sheet, told Raghavan that Laxmisagar had secured only one vote (probably his own), Bommai 34, and the rest (63) were Hegde's.

Hegde was thus formally elected leader. Many made the customary felicitation speeches, which Hegde promptly accepted. A resolution was signed by all those present, and this was hurriedly submitted to the Governor.

Setting up a Minority Government

The announcement of Hegde's election was wildly cheered by the crowd outside, which by then had swelled considerably. While the Janata Party had managed to choose a leader with scarcely a hitch and little bickering, there was still widespread concern over the future. Ordinary

---

[5] National government.

citizens who had gathered outside the Vidhana Souda were worried that the voters' preference for a non-Congress government might be thwarted by the Congress's manipulation of the Governor. Such things had happened in other states. People in Bangalore were particularly anxious since they had jettisoned every Congress candidate.

As soon as the election meeting concluded, Hegde got into a car with Deve Gowda and Bommai and drove straight to Bangarappa's house to placate him by offering him the post of Deputy Chief Minister. A huge milling crowd of his supporters, who were by then aware of the outcome and as angry as Bangarappa, barred their way. Some banged on the bonnet of the car and shouted abuse, and as Deve Gowda tried to get out of the car, they tore his *kurta* (shirt). The three leaders then departed, quite shaken by this rowdyism.

Hegde later drove to Raj Bhavan where important leaders and a large posse of mediamen had gathered. He met Governor Govind Narain and staked a claim to form the government. He explained that besides the members of the now united Janata Party, the BJP with 18 members, the CPI, the CPI (M) and several Independents were also supporting him. To substantiate this claim, legislators of these three smaller parties spoke to the Governor in separate groups, and several Independents also met him individually to pledge their support. In the overwhelming anti-Congress atmosphere, the only way these smaller parties could ensure that the Congress did not manipulate its way back to power was by supporting the Janata Party's bid to form the government. But the Independents still needed to be looked after, lest they succumbed to temptations that the Congress might offer. So two Janata legislators took them into their 'protective care' to ensure that they did not stray.

It was evident that while the Janata Party held only a minority of seats, it could muster a legislative majority. In any case, since it was the single largest party, the Governor was bound to call upon its leader to form the government. Narain, however, sought time to make up his mind. This naturally added to the anxiety. Even though Narain had impeccable credentials, and was known to be a non-partisan Governor, there was wild speculation that the electoral verdict might be negated through manipulation.

His hesitation was largely on account of the line the Congress had adopted. Buta Singh, the party's central observer who was still in Bangalore, called on him along with Moily (Gundu Rao's Finance

Minister who had retained his seat), and submitted a memorandum asking him not to invite Hegde to form the government. The Congress leaders argued that the merger of the Janata Party and the Kranti Ranga was, in reality, no such thing, particularly since Bangarappa had more or less dissociated himself from it. If the merger was not taken into account, then the Congress with 86 seats (against 63 for the Janata Party and 36 for the Kranti Ranga) was the single largest party, entitled to a summons from the Governor.

Narain would have been correct in rejecting this argument, but he decided to give the Congress an opportunity to prove its claim within 24 hours. Frantic efforts by Congressmen to entice members of what was formerly the Kranti Ranga to switch sides failed. The offers made by the Congress were tempting, but potential defectors feared the electorate, which was in no mood to accept a reversal of the anti-Congress verdict.

Meanwhile, efforts to placate Bangarappa resumed in earnest. Two former Kranti Ranga leaders who were close to him were finally able to persuade him to accompany them to Hegde's residence. It was by then fairly clear that the Governor would formally invite Hegde to form the government, though this was not yet official. The shocking incident of Deve Gowda being roughed up by Bangarappa's supporters led many, including key leaders who had worked with Bangarappa earlier, to argue that the offer of the number two post should be withdrawn from him.

Hegde and Bangarappa spent 30 minutes together. The latter opened the discussion by accepting the offer of the post of Deputy Chief Minister. Hegde explained that several other leaders were opposed to the idea, but Bangarappa said he would accept nothing less than this post. Hegde then asked him to wait for some time so that he could consult senior leaders in another room. All of them, including Deve Gowda, Bommai, Nazirsab and Patel, were firmly opposed to Bangarappa being offered the number two post. Hegde later told Raghavan that Deve Gowda had turned emotional. Teary-eyed, he had said that if Bangarappa was made Deputy Chief Minister, he would opt out of the ministry.

Subsequently, Hegde informed Bangarappa of the others' opposition. He pleaded with him to join the cabinet, and promised to make him Deputy Chief Minister in two months' time. Bangarappa declined this arrangement. After he left, Hegde received a call from Raj Bhavan.

Narain, whom he met soon after, formally invited him to form the government. The swearing-in ceremony was fixed for 4 p.m. When Hegde spoke to waiting journalists at the Raj Bhavan after meeting the Governor, he looked worried. Nervously puffing on a cigarette, he dodged several questions on who would be in his cabinet, probably because he himself was unclear at that stage about the composition of his government.

Deve Gowda and a respected Janata Party leader were again dispatched to Bangarappa's house to make a final effort to appease him. Deve Gowda pleaded with him to accept the number two position in importance in the ministry without officially being designated Deputy Chief Minister, but Bangarappa again refused. Hegde finally decided to induct a small team with him that afternoon, and to enlarge it later to make it broad-based.

The swearing-in ceremony on the lawns of the Raj Bhavan was a simple affair, but there was enormous excitement as ordinary party workers and curious citizens gate crashed. There was so much jostling on the dais that no one could sit. Enthusiasm replaced the solemnity that one usually finds on such occasions.

Deve Gowda was angry at the last-minute inclusion of Laxmisagar (for whom he had no liking) in the cabinet. It was evident that he had not been consulted by Hegde on this. To express his displeasure, instead of turning up at the first meeting of the cabinet, Deve Gowda appeared to go home. Hegde delayed the meeting until he turned up. A close confidant of Deve Gowda later told Raghavan that though Deve Gowda was upset over Laxmisagar, the real reason for his late arrival was that he had gone to a temple to offer thanks on having become a minister.

The only significant decision the cabinet took that evening was to place Karthikeyan, Gundu Rao's hyper-active intelligence chief, under suspension. Hegde, who stepped onto the third floor of the Vidhana Souda (on which senior ministers' offices are located) after, as he put it, '13 years of *vanavas*',[6] promised a clean government. He also declared that he would unhesitatingly continue various policies and programmes started by Urs, including those of preferential treatment to the Backward Classes.

---

[6] Literally, living in a forest; figuratively, banishment, of the kind that the Pandavas in the *Mahabharata* and Rama in the *Ramayana* were forced to undertake.

Given the hectic pace at which events had unfolded since the election results were announced, many failed to realise the full import of the dramatic change that had occurred that day. But anyone who had the faintest idea of politics realised that the Congress, which had ruled the state since 1947, had finally been ousted out of power. For the Congress rule to give way to another party in Karnataka — its strongest bastion in India, as the following statistical details will show — was nothing short of a watershed development.

In the parliamentary election of 1977, when the party had suffered a crushing defeat all over the country, it still won 26 of the 28 seats in this state. In 1978, despite an impressive showing by the Janata Party, the Congress had retained power in the Karnataka state election. A massive and, by the standards of those days, extravagantly expensive campaign against Mrs Gandhi had not stopped her from winning a by-election in Chikmagalur later that year. In 1980, the Congress had won 27 of the 28 seats in the parliamentary election, despite opposition from Urs, who had by then fallen out with Mrs Gandhi. And yet now, only three years later, it had lost control of the state. With this defeat, Congress dominance in every part of India had come to an end.

The new regime that replaced the Congress was entirely novel in Karnataka's political history, not just because of the change of parties, but in two other senses as well. One, it was a minority government, and two, it was essentially an experiment with coalition politics. In India during the 1980s, minority governments had often proved short-lived, and coalitions were despised because — allegedly — they never worked. They had failed in several northern states in the late 1960s, and another at the national level after 1977 had been a disaster. Hegde had no choice but to carry with him not only the two factions within the ruling party (the Janata Party and the erstwhile Kranti Ranga), which was tantamount to a coalition, but also to attend to the three parties that supported his minority government from outside (two from the Communist Left and one from the Hindu Right), as well as potentially unruly Independents. And if this hair-raising prospect did not pose enough risks, he also had to deal with the alienated, truculent Bangarappa.

This was hardly an easy task. Efforts resumed, yet again, to bring him into the ministry. Talks with him through intermediaries went on for several days at two levels: private and public. In private, though Hegde had withdrawn the earlier offer of the number two slot in the cabinet, he sent word that Bangarappa was still welcome to join. As Hegde explained in confidence to Raghavan, 'We cannot be making one offer after another for him to spurn.' Publicly, however, he still expressed the pious hope that Bangarappa would come on board. In a letter, Bangarappa offered to join the ministry as an ordinary cabinet minister if the merger of the Janata Party and the Kranti Ranga was reversed. This was naturally unacceptable to Hegde and, for that matter, to everyone else, including those from the erstwhile Kranti Ranga.

Bangarappa then made a trip to Kerala to meet Chandra Shekhar, national president of the Janata Party. He insisted, characteristically exaggerating in his own interests, that the latter had made a pre-election commitment that he would be Chief Minister. In reality, an aide had only suggested to Chandra Shekhar that the post should necessarily go to a Backward Classes leader. Chandra Shekhar himself told Raghavan that he had made no commitment to Bangarappa:

> When this suggestion was made to me in the presence of Bangarappa, how could I say the idea was ridiculous? I could not be uncivil, so I told them it is not a bad idea; we will see after the election. How could I make a commitment before the election and expect newly elected members to honour that? Surely, you do not think I am that stupid.

A week after his Kerala meeting with Chandra Shekhar, Bangarappa was still undecided about joining the cabinet. Hegde decided to wait no longer. He added several new faces to the ministry. While many leaders who deserved berths got in, several newcomers were also included to maintain the balance between the Janata Party and the Kranti Ranga, as also between the dominant castes on the one hand and the Backward Classes, the Scheduled Castes and the minorities on the other. The tradition of rainbow coalitions that had prevailed since Urs had broken the control of the Lingayats and Vokkaligas over state-level politics in 1972 was thus sustained.

The ministry-making exercise was not without its minor dramas. M. Raghupathy, who had heard that he might be offered a junior post as Minister of State, lobbied hard for a cabinet berth. Eventually, Hegde put him in the list of cabinet ministers. At the swearing-in, where cabinet ministers are administered oaths before Ministers of State, Raghupathy's name was the last among cabinet ministers to be called. When he was summoned, he rose from his seat and took a few tentative steps towards the dais. However, he was suddenly seized by doubts about whether he had been called to be sworn in as the last cabinet minister or the first Minister of State. Uncertain, he resumed his seat, refusing to be sworn in. Sensing this confusion, Hegde asked the Chief Secretary,[7] Naik, who was conducting the ceremony, to repeat Raghupathy's name. Naik called out Raghupathy's name again, adding 'cabinet minister' by way of clarification this time. A beaming Raghupathy then took the oath.

A New Kind of Government: Democratic Decentralisation and Rural Development

Roughly two-thirds of the people of Karnataka live in villages. Elections are, effectively, won and lost here. So, we might expect state governments to focus intensely on the needs of villagers, and to seek to discern and respond to their preferences. Urs had done more than most in this vein with his tenancy reforms. But all governments in Karnataka (and, indeed, in nearly[8] all of India) before 1983, including Urs's, were guilty of two serious sins of omission. First, they failed to devote enough attention and resources to small-scale projects at the local level — minor roads, school buildings, tubewells for clean drinking water, and the like — for which villagers had a strong appetite. Second, they failed to empower and fund elected councils at lower levels, which would have enabled villagers' preferences to matter in decisions about development projects.

Hegde was determined to change things on both these fronts. Even before the expansion of the ministry, he had decided to implement election promises related to these two issues, without delay. The more important of these was democratic decentralisation: the transfer of power to elected councils or panchayats at lower levels. This was a subject dear to Hegde. Way back in the 1960s, as Minister for Co-operation and Panchayati Raj, he had tried in vain to introduce a strong and viable decentralised system in the state. His efforts were thwarted by Congress legislators who (like legislators in all countries) were opposed to decentralisation, since it diminished their power. Hegde had even considered resigning over the issue, but the then Chief Minister, Nijalingappa, dissuaded him and soon changed his portfolio.

---

[7] The head of the state's civil service.
[8] The sole exception was the West Bengal government after 1977.

In 1983, Hegde had close at hand a colleague who was as committed to Panchayati Raj as he was, if not more so. This was Abdul Nazirsab. Their shared enthusiasm provided a strong bond between these two men who were otherwise from very different backgrounds. Nazirsab, however, had been reluctant to become a minister. On the morning before Hegde was sworn in, he told a few friends in private: 'My job is over. We have put together a non-Congress government and I will be happy to work in the party organisation ...'[9] This is something many politicians say publicly, without meaning it. But Nazirsab had spoken in confidence, and he was serious.

Eventually, however, friends persuaded him to join the cabinet if asked, since he refused to lobby for a post. He also indicated that he would prefer the Rural Development and Panchayati Raj portfolio to anything else. This was surprising because these departments usually went to a junior minister. They lacked large budgets and had little potential for patronage distribution. It was a 'dry' ministry that could not be milked for party funds and personal enrichment, and most leaders sought 'wet' postings. But Nazirsab was a rarity among Indian politicians. He lived simply, had no interest in profiteering and was deeply committed to bringing about constructive change that would enable ordinary, not least poor and socially excluded, people to have some influence over their own destinies.

When Hegde invited Nazirsab to join his team, he was surprised when the latter insisted that he would accept only if he was given the rural development charge. Hegde told Raghavan, 'He could have asked for and got any portfolio. But I understood his desire. He chose rural development because of the immense potential it had for any one who was committed to work. And no one could dispute Nazirsab's commitment.'

Within his first few days as a minister, Nazirsab raised the issue of decentralisation, promised in the manifesto, at a cabinet meeting. Some senior ministers, including Deve Gowda and Bommai, were lukewarm to this issue, rooted as they were in traditional politics which entailed efforts to centralise power. Nazirsab told Raghavan:

> When I pointed out that it was a promise we had made to the people, both of them said: 'No government can keep all the promises it makes, and in any case we are not bound to implement promises soon after taking office. We

---

[9] E. Raghavan was among those present.

have five years to fulfil the promise.' I said if this promise was to be broken, then I would rather resign forthwith. Hegde, who did not butt in until then, put his foot down and gave me virtually a blanket permission to go ahead and draft a bill for decentralisation of power through panchayat bodies.

Nazirsab began in earnest within 24 hours, and eventually produced a fundamental change in the character of Karnataka's politics, thereby deepening democracy. We shall return to this pivotal topic shortly, but we must first consider an even more urgent issue which he tackled with similar determination and speed. And as we shall see in due course, it proved crucial in political terms.

Karnataka's villagers had been suffering from a prolonged drought. It had not only damaged agricultural productivity, but left many areas severely short of drinking water. This made the drought life threatening. Within days of assuming office, Hegde and Nazirsab were horrified to discover that the Gundu Rao government had done precious little to address this crisis. As soon as it sees that seasonal rains have failed, a state government must send a memorandum to the authorities in New Delhi to trigger the release of money for relief operations. Astonishingly, no such step had been taken by the previous government. The Janata Party government, thus, had a major emergency on its hands.

Nazirsab was painfully aware of the problems that people living in rural areas face in a year of scanty rainfall. He came from Gundlupet which is particularly vulnerable to droughts, and had worked as an organiser among rural labourers, the very people who suffered the most. He recognised that he had to prioritise drought-relief operations as his first task. He set about organising the sinking of borewells on a war footing, and saw to it that the bureaucrats, who are generally apathetic to such needs, never rested for a minute. Nazirsab had 60,000 sunk in his first few months in office, which rivalled the total sunk between independence (in 1947) and 1983. He personally toured the districts constantly to monitor progress. It was a period when drilling rigs, deployed in large numbers in all problematic areas, notably in northern Karnataka, worked non-stop.

The urban elite could not comprehend the significance of this programme. But in rural areas, where women had to trudge miles to a water source to fill and carry several pots, a clean, unpolluted source close at hand was a godsend. The programme, which was actually an old one that Nazirsab had merely galvanised, seized the imagination of rural dwellers. It continued even after the drought had passed, and later became a model for the rest of the country.

In less than two years from 1983, he could justifiably claim that he had provided one drinking water source for every 200 persons in drought-hit rural areas. It was an immense achievement. Nazirsab, who had not been taken seriously by political leaders until then, acquired legendary status among the majority living on the land. Villagers coined a nickname for him: 'Neersab' (*neeru* in Kannada means water, and *sab* is a corrupted variant of the Urdu word *saheb*).

He then turned his mind to democratic decentralisation, where he would provide an even more monumental and lasting contribution. S. K. De, author of the community-development programme at the national level during Jawaharlal Nehru's time, was brought in for consultations. Hegde personally monitored the drafting of the law. It took a great deal of compromise, extraordinary skill and a bit of bluff and bluster to fashion and ram the legislation on new panchayat institutions through the cabinet and then the legislature. When the new bill was sent to New Delhi for the President's assent, it was delayed for an inordinate period. At one stage, Nazirsab publicly threatened to undertake a hunger strike in front of the Rashtrapati Bhavan (the President's residence). The threat seemed to work and the bill was approved, making it an official act.

Nazirsab's original draft of the bill had been watered down a little before being sent to the President. An entire section on Nyaya Panchayats (village councils to settle petty disputes) had to be kept in abeyance. Reservation of seats for women,[10] originally intended to be 50 per cent, had to be scaled down to 25 per cent. Opposition to this provision was strong because the concept was entirely new; it had never been tried before anywhere in India, and scarcely anywhere in the world.[11] Legislators, who had been excluded from the panchayats in the original draft, were given non-voting roles. But despite these changes, the new act empowered the panchayats to a degree matched only in the state of West Bengal, and

---

[10] In reserved constituencies, people from every section of society can vote, but candidates must come from the reserved category.

[11] Mainly as a result of the innovation in Karnataka, such reservations — 30 per cent — were made national policy when a constitutional amendment on panchayats became law in 1993.

in one or two other countries in Asia, Africa and Latin America. This new initiative of democratic decentralisation begun in Karnataka helped spur a major international trend in subsequent years.[12]

The government then had to decide on the subjects or development sectors that could be transferred to the new elected councils at the district and local levels, called Zilla Parishads and Mandal Panchayats[13] respectively. Despite general bureaucratic reluctance to part with power, the new Chief Secretary, T. R. Satish Chandran, managed to transfer nearly all development activities to the elected councils at lower levels. Co-operative societies, an important subject, was taken away from the new councils by a decision the cabinet took after Nazirsab had left the meeting.[14] But this was the only significant concession that was made.

Next, panchayat elections, which had not been held for over ten years (even though this was illegal), had to be conducted. The delimitation of constituencies and updating of electoral rolls delayed this until 1987. But once the elections had occurred, the number of elected offices in the state rose from just 224 (seats in the legislature) to over 55,000. Large numbers of people who had become alienated from the democratic process, because they saw little chance of serving in public office, suddenly found official roles.

Another promise the government fulfilled was to restore elected urban bodies throughout the state. Urs had given bureaucrats control of urban government in the early 1970s because he felt that urban voters were anti-Congress. For this reason he had put off civic elections indefinitely. The result was urban bodies which were insensitive to popular demands, and which, therefore, gradually became dysfunctional.

Within six months of taking office, the Janata Party government ordered civic elections all over the state. It also enlarged the electoral base by lowering the voting age from 21 to 18. More significantly, it earmarked 30 per cent of the seats for women. This was unprecedented in India, and it inspired extremely favourable political and popular responses, first in Karnataka and later elsewhere in the country.

---

[12] For a more detailed account, see Crook and Manor (1998: Chapter 2) and Manor (1999).

[13] An intermediate tier (Taluk Panchayat Samitis) existed at the sub-district level, but they had far less power than the tiers above and below them.

[14] Interview with S. S. Meenakshisundaram (a long-time close aide to Nazirsab), by James Manor, Bangalore, 7 January 2007.

In theory, every elective office in India had been open to women since the first general election in 1952. But in practice, only token representation had been given to women in the local bodies, state assemblies and Parliament. The innovation adopted in Karnataka was later incorporated at lower levels throughout the country. It was arguably as significant as the principle of positive discrimination in favour of the Backward Classes that Urs had pioneered a decade earlier. The Hegde government thus broadened democracy further by ensuring a participatory role for women. Also significant was the decision to set apart one seat in each council, rural and urban, for a woman from the Scheduled Castes and Scheduled Tribes.

Reservations for women in urban and rural bodies eventually led to nearly 9,000 posts being created for women across the state. Perceptive civil servants who worked with these bodies, and thus became enthusiasts for decentralisation, have consistently argued that women members have raised the tone of politics. They insist that the information supplied to them by women councillors is far more reliable than that provided by their male counterparts.[15] But this was not the main gain. Officials in the Health Ministry argue forcefully that women members of local councils are far better able than health professionals to explain the need for attendance at ante- and post-natal clinics to ordinary women in a language the latter understand. And since, where healthcare is concerned, women are the main gate-keepers between households and the wider world, this has increased the uptake on such services, and saved the lives of large numbers of children.[16]

Early Action on Other Fronts

To dramatise the magnitude of the change which had occurred when the new government took over, initiatives were swiftly introduced in several other sectors as well. Some addressed matters of great substance, while others were more cosmetic, although even some of the latter made the administration more accessible and responsive.

---

[15] James Manor's interviews with 27 such civil servants between 1993 and 1995.

[16] James Manor's interviews with health department officials in five districts of Karnataka, in 1993 and 1994.

A conscious effort was made to bridge the gap which had opened up between the government and the people during Gundu Rao's regime. Hegde himself set an example by setting apart time to meet ordinary citizens, who took their concerns to him. Gundu Rao, in sharp contrast, had gone to the extent of erecting a fence around the Vidhana Souda (the building housing both the legislature and senior ministers' offices) to prevent citizens from entering. Hegde had it removed and, together with other ministers, threw open the corridors of power.

Many of the issues that had to be tackled were highly sensitive and needed subtle handling. A fine example of this can be seen in the government's handling of a set of demands from farmers. In the assembly election, various farmers' associations, which had battled Gundu Rao's government, had supported the Janata–Kranti Ranga combine that had made several commitments to them in its manifesto. Several of these were soon fulfilled, but ministers subsequently found themselves drawn into a turf war among various farmers' associations. When they called a meeting of the various organisations, the Raitha Sangha[17] which probably had the widest support and was certainly the most vocal and strident, demanded that the government recognise it as the farmers' sole representative. Ministers rightly saw that this would be politically suicidal, so Hegde and Bommai adroitly set about isolating this association. Embittered, Raitha Sangha leaders called for state-wide strikes and became Hegde's harshest critics. But their attempted agitation went nowhere, since popular sentiment remained with the new regime.

Under Gundu Rao, a '*chaku-churi*' (knife and dagger) culture had enveloped Bangalore city for the first time in its history. Gangsters and underworld dons who had strong contacts in the Congress had made life difficult for ordinary citizens. On several occasions, street fights had occurred between the various factions of these goons, and they had also taken over campus politics. Hegde ordered the police to deal ruthlessly with the problem. Once it was known that political patronage and friendly interventions by important politicians were no longer available, the gangsters either abandoned their activities or finished each other off.

Hegde also dealt with extremely sensitive issues such as those of language with dexterity. Pro-Kannada lobbies demanded that the knowledge of Kannada be made a mandatory requirement for all government servants

---

[17] The term means 'farmers' association'.

at the time they took up their posts. These activists were right in insisting that government servants, who dealt with ordinary people, must know the local language. The new government accepted this, but faced difficulties in implementing such a demand since they also had to take into account linguistic minorities. Hegde took his cue from an order passed by the Urs government and made the knowledge of Kannada essential for government servants, but not at the point of entry. He proposed that members of linguistic minorities entering government service should be required to pass a test in Kannada within two years. This proposal was initially rejected by the pro-Kannada activists who, like the Raitha Sangha, were demanding their pound of flesh for their support during the election, but Hegde skilfully persuaded them to accept his formula.

His style, evident in many of the issues in which the middle class and the intelligentsia had an interest, contrasted sharply with that of Gundu Rao. The latter believed in initiating things on his own and reconsidering decisions later in the teeth of popular pressure. He never attempted prior consultation. Hegde preferred the politics of consensus to the greatest extent possible, and certainly consultation, even when no consensus was possible. An example of this, which had long-term implications, was the creation of an economic and planning council. It included a number of academics, policy planners and experts from diverse fields, brought for the first time from outside the government to interact with planners and administrators, in order to formulate long-term strategies for development.

On all issues, major and minor, Hegde also consulted leaders of parties supporting him. This was a decidedly ticklish job, since the BJP and the two Communist parties which kept his minority government in power occupied opposite ends of the Left–Right spectrum and regarded one another with hostility. (The only thing that they agreed upon was the need to keep the Congress out of power.) So Hegde always met these parties separately, and often shuttled between them, reconciling differences. He nearly always had things his way, but he often had to do a lot of manoeuvring, not just between these other parties, but within his own too.

In 1983, Hegde organised a conference of south Indian Chief Ministers to discuss centre–state relations. One of the aims of this conference was to serve notice on Mrs Gandhi's Congress government at the national level that pressure was building in the south over neglect by New Delhi. Three of the four southern states had non-Congress governments; the Congress ruled only in Kerala. The non-Congress ruling parties — the Janata Party in Karnataka, the Telugu Desam Party (TDP) in Andhra Pradesh, and the All India Anna Dravida Munnetra Kazhagam (AIADMK) in Tamil Nadu — did not shrink from criticising the central government. The TDP's leader, N. T. Rama Rao, had swept to power in 1983 by insisting that the people of Andhra would no longer tolerate remote rule from New Delhi through pliable Chief Ministers. The AIADMK, which had ruled for over a decade on an anti-centre, anti-Hindi platform, was no different.

It was, therefore, quite easy for Hegde to make common cause with them. But to dispel fears of regional chauvinism, he tried to present the conference as an effort on part of the southern states to find their voice. To this end, he also invited the Congress Chief Minister of Kerala, K. Karunakaran. Karunakaran declined, alleging with characteristically calculated inaccuracy that the conference smacked of secessionism when, in fact, no one had been thinking on those lines.[18]

This was followed by a major seminar on centre–state relations to which eminent persons from all over India were invited. It highlighted key issues on which states deserved greater functional freedom. The end result was that Mrs Gandhi, who preferred to avoid conflict on this score, announced the creation of a commission, headed by Justice Sarkaria, a Supreme Court judge, to consider the question and make recommendations.

Electing Hegde to the Legislature

When Hegde was sworn in as Chief Minister, he was not a member of either House of the state legislature, and was legally required to find a seat within six months of assuming office. He had several choices. He could contest from his home district, Uttara Kannada on the coast in the west, or from northern Karnataka where several legislators were ready

---

[18] It is often erroneously claimed that the Dravidian parties of Tamil Nadu (including the AIADMK) continued to pursue separatism well into the 1970s and 1980s. The claim is refuted in detail in Manor (2001). No Chief Minister in the other three southern states has ever flirted with this idea for a moment, and Mr Karunakaran understood this quite well.

to vacate seats for him. However, since the Janata Party and its allies had won 24 of 25 seats in Bangalore district, many by wide margins, it appeared to offer the safest options. Since Bangalore city had afforded the Janata–Kranti Ranga combine spectacular victories in the past, most people expected him to contest from here.

Hegde, however, surprised everyone by settling on rural Kanakapura in Bangalore district. Many thought this decision was downright stupid, and Congress leaders gleefully began devising a strategy to defeat him. In reality, Kanakapura had been chosen very carefully. Although it was near Bangalore, it was underdeveloped in every sense. It was mostly dry and unirrigated. It lacked basic necessities such as drinking water (which Nazirsab's tubewells had begun to provide), roads and transport, and had a large number of poor people. Yet because it stood in Bangalore's shadow, the electorate in Kanakapura shared many characteristics with urban voters who were determinedly anti-Congress in 1983. The constituency was predominantly Vokkaliga and had a sprinkling of Scheduled Castes, Kurubas,[19] Muslims, and a microscopic number of Brahmins and Lingayats.

The choice of Kanakapura was prompted by Deve Gowda and his protégé, P. G. R. Sindhia, who had just won from the same constituency. Deve Gowda, who was trying to rally Vokkaliga leaders around him, had visited Kanakapura to see if local leaders there would enthusiastically back Hegde. The Chief Minister finally chose it for two reasons. First, he wanted to contest from a rural constituency in this predominantly rural state, but one that was close enough to Bangalore to enable him to campaign extensively and, later, to attend to its needs without travelling too far from his duties in the capital. Second, he was keen to demonstrate his acceptance among communities other than his own, and for this reason wanted to contest from a constituency in which fellow Brahmins were not a significant factor. With Deve Gowda heading the campaign, a Vokkaliga-dominated constituency seemed an attractive proposition.

A prominent Congress leader, N. Chikke Gowda, told journalists that Hegde had blundered, that Kanakapura would prove to be his Waterloo, adding, 'I thought Hegde was intelligent.' Many other Congressmen saw this as a way back to power. If Hegde lost, it would only be a matter of days before the government fell. Despite this, they found it difficult

---

[19] Herders — a 'backward' caste.

to field a heavyweight against him. Their stunning defeat was still fresh in the minds of the big guns of the Congress. The party finally chose an ex-police officer, D. J. Linge Gowda, a man who had little political experience. He was chosen because he was a Vokkaliga, and had become president of the Rural Education Society of Kanakapura after the death of its popular founder, who had won multiple elections here.

As always, an auspicious time was chosen for Hegde to file his nomination papers. He interrupted the hour-long drive to worship at the Banashankari temple on way. His wife and children accompanied him, as did many ministers and partymen. He submitted his papers amidst great enthusiasm, made a brief speech and returned to Bangalore. Great care was taken to make this a low-key affair, to convey an air of simplicity.

It was quite evident that the campaign was in the hands of Deve Gowda and his protégé Sindhia, who had vacated his seat in Kanakapura. Deve Gowda had already convened several meetings with important leaders, the most prominent among them being an elderly politician, Thimme Gowda, whose reputation and clout among Vokkaligas was formidable. Hegde formally launched the campaign at a massive public rally in Kanakapura. From then on, he and his wife travelled to practically every village in the constituency. He chose a simple, straightforward approach to appeal to voters. With little fanfare, he, his wife and a small entourage of party workers would set off early in the morning, go from village to village, say a few words to those gathered, and walk down the village street with folded hands, seeking votes. For an electorate used to witnessing the trappings of power, Hegde's style, which clearly stressed modesty and humility, was striking — even touching.

In reality, the Janata Party campaign was more complex than this. Hegde and his entourage were highly visible, but Deve Gowda and Sindhia worked independently, concentrating mainly on Vokkaliga voters. Vokkaliga leaders from other parts of the state were made to criss-cross the constituency. Ministers and other leaders were drawn in to focus on other castes. Under the pretext of dealing with the drought, the government also poured in substantial resources for development work.

The Congress responded by flooding the constituency with money and campaigners from various castes. One standard technique it used to win votes was to organise a mass feeding for a particular caste, at which leaders from that caste appealed for support. Throughout the campaign, there was one such 'meal *mela*'[20] every day, particularly focused on the Vokkaligas and the Scheduled Castes. Enormous sums were spent on these meals and on direct inducements to voters.

At the same time, the Congress's complaints soared. A constant refrain was that the Rural Development Department was 'sinking borewells in Kanakapura left, right and centre' in a bid to win votes. Nazirsab, who was responsible, did not hesitate to acknowledge this, but saw nothing wrong in it.

> I cannot stop drought relief simply because there is an election. It is not as if wells are being sunk only in Kanakapura . . . if providing drinking water is a crime, I would not hesitate to commit more of it.

When the Congress discovered that the borewells were popular, it abandoned this theme.

As the campaign drew to a close, most Congress leaders had largely given up hope, but kept up the pretence of a campaign. On an exceptionally hot afternoon, Raghavan and a colleague had gone round a part of the constituency and, as the sun was setting, stopped near a tea shop. When they saw a senior Congress leader, K. H. Ranganath, standing by his car in a crisp, spotless *kurta*, they asked him, 'Are you arriving now?'. He replied, 'No, I went round some villages this afternoon.' On that sweltering day, there was no way one's kurta could remain clean after an hour or so on the dry, dusty roads. When they looked incredulously at him, Ranganath smiled.

The Janata Party leaders still had their doubts about whether anti-Congress sentiments remained strong enough. They were also anxious because one candidate had secured an election symbol which looked confusingly similar to that of the Janata Party.[21] Moreover, his name, Rajashekara Kasave, listed on ballot papers immediately after Hegde's name, could easily be confused for Ramakrishna Hegde by those not fully literate

The Janata Party, however, needn't have worried. It has been proved time and again that there is no relationship between illiteracy and political awareness. In 1978, for instance, the Congress led by Mrs Gandhi

---

[20] The term 'mela' means a mass gathering.

[21] In India, each party and candidate uses a pictorial symbol to enable illiterate voters to identify the candidate of their choice.

had to adopt a new symbol on the eve of the state election. Voters across the state easily understood the change and returned her party to power. In one constituency, the Congress candidate could not even use the new symbol since his papers reached the returning officer after the deadline. The voters still elected him.

Voting in Kanakapura was peaceful, and the turnout high. Once the counting began, it soon became apparent that Hegde was heading for a massive majority. Even before the totals were out, he along with cabinet colleagues and party workers left for Kanakapura in a bus for a victory rally.

After a splendid start for the new government, Hegde's victory was a heady moment. For most observers, the scale of the victory confirmed that the Janata Party was firmly established as an alternative to the Congress. After 36 years of one-party dominance, multiparty democracy had plainly 'arrived' in Karnataka. It had happened much later than in most Indian states, and the breathtaking ineptitude of the last Congress Chief Minister, Gundu Rao, had contributed considerably to it. But it was still a historic achievement.

Urs had broadened and deepened democracy by breaking the power of the dominant land-owning groups at the state level, and by giving low-status groups what appeared to be — and, in fact, turned out to be — permanent and potent influence at the cabinet table. But Urs had done this in order to maintain single-party dominance. Now Hegde and the Janata Party had pried the political system open still further by introducing party competition, which gave voters genuine choices in state elections.

This change, like the progressive ones Urs had brought about, would also endure. But it did not mean that the Janata government's troubles were over. It soon became clear that Karnataka's discerning voters would remain hard to please. And the Congress was all too willing to exploit this reassuringly democratic reality with a new effort to bring the government down.

7

Struggling for Political Survival

Hegde's victory at Kanakapura in mid-1983 boosted the Janata government's already high morale, but voters elsewhere in the state soon provided sobering reminders of the ground realities. In three subsequent by-elections, the Janata Party made no inroads into Congress support. Convinced of the infallibility of his campaign skills, Deve Gowda took responsibility for a by-election in Maddur, an important constituency in the Vokkaliga heartland of Mandya district, where a Congress incumbent had died. Although all the tricks tried and tested in Kanakapura were employed in Maddur, the Congress retained the seat. The Janata Party met the same fate in two other constituencies. The Congress had been beaten in the state assembly election and in Kanakapura, but it was far from finished.

Most Karnataka by-elections conform to a pattern. First, issues, except for the purely local variety, never come into focus. As a result, candidates' personalities loom large. Second, ruling parties usually lose. All these by-elections, except Kanakapura where Hegde himself was the issue, fit the pattern. One factor, however, could not be ignored. Of these four constituencies, two were dominated by Vokkaligas and two by Lingayats. If Hegde's victory is treated as an exception, this pattern was disturbing for the Janata Party. It meant that the locally dominant castes, a key element in its social base, tended to remain with the Congress. This led the Congress to adopt a fresh strategy to bring down the government, and a succession of altercations ensued. Moreover, a little more than a year later, ghastly events in New Delhi were to thrust the Janata Party in Karnataka into a desperate struggle for political survival.

Congress Efforts to Destroy the Government

Congressmen saw the Janata regime as a minority government with no moral right to remain in power. But since the public perception was entirely different, any overt attempt to scuttle the government was bound to be greeted with widespread derision. This did not, however, deter them from such efforts.

After nearly four decades of dominance, the Congress was not used to working as an opposition party. It missed the trappings of power. The party needed some time before it could find its feet in its new role. In the legislative assembly, it certainly had the required strength — 81 seats — to pillory the government. In the state's Upper House, it enjoyed a majority and could hold up legislative business. Yet the Congress found it difficult to capitalise on this advantage. The Janata government was new; it had had little time to err. Congress criticisms tended to boomerang, since ministers could respond by recalling more serious wrongdoings by Gundu Rao's wretched Congress regime. Hegde, a skilled parliamentarian, mastered the art of selectively using facts and figures to thrust the opposition onto the defensive.

Uncomfortable as they were on the opposition benches, Congressmen realised that the longer they allowed the government to survive, the stronger it would become. After all, they knew only too well that a party in power could use the process of patronage distribution to consolidate political support.

The method Congressmen employed to bring down the Janata government was well-tested. It had been used elsewhere by Mrs Gandhi, particularly in the northern states, against opposition-led alliances. (Indeed, this curious concept of an 'opposition government' was distinctly Indian: the product of decades of one-party dominance by the Congress.[1]) She had often broken such ruling alliances by weaning away a vital component, subsequently declaring that the government was incapable of providing stability, and ultimately recapturing power. This tactic had succeeded even in the Indian Parliament in 1979, when she promised to support Charan Singh as Prime Minister if he would bring down the Janata government by walking out of it. He did so, but less than a month later, Mrs Gandhi withdrew her support, thereby forcing a general election to take place. Having done this, it was easy for her to return to power since she had succeeded in creating the impression that the Congress was the sole source of stability.

To create a similar situation in Karnataka, the government first had to be destabilised. This was not an easy task, since those who had been elected on the Janata ticket were staunch anti-Congressmen who had

---

[1] We are grateful to Rajni Kothari for calling our attention to this odd concept during discussions in Delhi on election night, 1986.

suffered for years at the hands of the Congress. Enticements had little appeal for them. Nor could the parties supporting the Janata government from outside — the BJP, the CPI and the CPI (M) — be seduced since they were even more strident in their anti-Congressism. This left the Independents.

Table 7.1: Composition of the Karnataka State Assembly (party-wise), 1983

Pro-government		Anti-government	
Janata Party	88	Congress	81
BJP	18	Kranti Ranga (Bangarappa)	6
CPI	3	Maharashtra Ekikaran Samiti[2]	5
CPI (M)	3	Independents	4
AIADMK	1		
Independents	14		
Total	**127**	**Total**	**96**

Source: Survey by the authors
Note: The Speaker of the assembly has been omitted from this table.

Among the Independents supporting the government were a few former Congressmen (see Table 7.1) who, when denied party tickets in January 1983, defied the party, contested as Independents and won. Some of them were now considered easy prey by the Congress.

The first attempt at engineering defections began a month or two after the new government had been formed.[3] Such operations are often 'mentioned' in the literature on Indian politics, but seldom *analysed* because evidence is hard to obtain. We have a considerably detailed account of the Congress Party's attempts at engineering defections from the Janata government. The Congress prepared a list of about 35 members (Independents and Janata members) who could be tapped. There were three categories of potential defectors. The first included people without strong party loyalties who might, therefore, succumb to monetary inducements and switch sides. The second consisted of those who thought they had potential for promotion, but had not achieved positions of

---

[2] A sub-regional party in the far north of Karnataka.

[3] All of this occurred before an anti-defection law was passed at the behest of Rajiv Gandhi, Prime Minister from late 1984 to 1989. This act made such tactics difficult, though not impossible.

power. The third included big guns who had been denied office, given unimportant portfolios, or those who resented other bigwigs.

The first attempt, made on two Scheduled Caste legislators, badly misfired. It is probable that some money had been promised, if not paid. However, Janata Party leaders swiftly learnt of this. Their political intelligence worked reasonably well, and Hegde and his confidants quickly repulsed this initial effort.

This and every subsequent attempt was aggressively publicised by the government. Prospective defectors were exhibited before journalists to nail rumours of their impending departures and to expose Congress inducements. Hegde also offered them counter-inducements to stay on board. One prospective defector, for instance, was made chairman of the Warehousing Corporation and another chairman of the Food and Civil Supplies Corporation.

Hegde and his colleagues stressed the squalid nature of these Congress machinations to the full. The people of the state, he argued, had ousted the Congress, and the popular will should not be reversed by such immoral devices. The Congress, however, continued to use these tactics. It soon became obvious that the Congress high command itself fully backed all these moves. C. M. Stephen, a minister in Mrs Gandhi's government in New Delhi, defended the campaign in Karnataka by declaring that 'causing defection is a birth right'. Mrs Gandhi, however, maintained a studied silence and, when asked, stoutly denied any such manoeuvres on the part of her party. Nevertheless, her active interest in the 'operation' was evident from the repeated visits to the state, both official and secretive, by trouble shooters like Buta Singh.

National Congress leaders had grown deeply anxious about south India slipping away. North India had long been more influential over the Congress Party's politics, but the southern states had always stood as a bulwark for it. Even at its worst moment — the post-Emergency election of 1977 — when the party had lost every seat in the Hindi heartland, it had found overwhelming backing from the south. In Karnataka, the Janata Party had won only two of 28 seats, while in Andhra, it managed only one (Manor 1978). But by January 1983, the situation had utterly changed. Both states rejected the Congress for the first time, largely because of the incompetence of the party's Chief Ministers in these states.

These reversals could not be taken lightly. Though Hegde balanced perilously on a tightrope and Andhra Pradesh Chief Minister N.T. Rama

Rao was a maverick given more to theatrics than to substantive pol-itics, the fact was that the non-Congress governments that both led in their respective states were extremely popular. If anti-Congress senti-ments in these states survived much longer, it might prove disastrous for Mrs Gandhi at the next national election, due in January 1985.

Nor was it only Andhra Pradesh and Karnataka. The Congress had reasons to worry about Kerala too, where the CPI (M)-led Left Front, then in the opposition, was quite capable of inflicting a defeat. In Tamil Nadu, the Congress had been a marginal force since 1967, clinging to the apron-strings of the AIADMK or the DMK.[4]

The task before Mrs Gandhi was clear. She could not be sure of the north-central Hindi heartland, so the status quo ante in the once-predictable southern states had to be restored. Hence the priority given to the efforts aimed at destabilising the non-Congress governments in the southern states. It had begun in Karnataka, but was not yet evident in Andhra Pradesh where N.T. Rama Rao, unaware that the carpet was about to be pulled from under him, went about announcing one populist measure after another.

As Stephen was asserting his right to engineer defections, Nanje Gowda, a senior Congress MP from Karnataka, actually called journalists and told them that the Congress was working to a deadline for the toppling of the Janata Party government. He and a Congress legislator in the state claimed that even some Janata Party ministers were in touch with them, awaiting a signal to jump ship.

The brazen manner in which the Congress proceeded in its attempts to entice Independents and Janata legislators to defect signalled a marked degeneration in its political standards in Karnataka and in the self-respect of Congressmen in the state under Indira Gandhi. Before 1972, Congress leaders in Karnataka may have been arrogant at times, responsive mainly to landed castes, and seriously neglectful of the basic needs of lower-status groups (for example, in providing primary education), but to engage so wantonly and openly in attempts at bribery in order to undo a crushing popular verdict would have been unthinkable. Under Urs's Congress

---

[4] These acronyms refer to the All India Anna Dravida Munnetra Kazhagam and the Dravida Munnetra Kazhagam, respectively — two rival parties which emerged from the Dravidian movement in Tamil Nadu, and which have dominated politics in the state since 1967.

government, the state had been spared many of the excesses which Congress leaders in most others states had committed, but now (as the following account will show) all pretensions to political morality had been abandoned.

The names of three prominent Janata Party figures, besides those of a few others, were mentioned as potential defectors. It was a clever ploy, passing off gossip as privileged, unattributable information. If journalists published even speculative stories, the resulting confusion suited the Congress. It was indeed true that the Congress was trying to open communications with three prominent Janata leaders: Chandraprabha Urs, Azeez Sait and V. L. Patil. Of the three, Urs was manifestly unhappy in the government. She felt that she did not get the respect and responsibility she deserved as the daughter of Devaraj Urs. She was also unhappy that the Excise portfolio, given temporarily to her at first, had been taken away. Sait and Patil had no real grouses. But Congressmen thought that they were misfits in the Janata Party government, steeped as they were in the Congress's culture.

Heavy pressure was also applied on various Independents. For instance, a former Congress minister literally locked an Independent legislator in his house and secured his signature on a letter which stated that he withdrew support from the government. Several others signed such letters. When the Janata leaders got wind of this exercise, they hurriedly convened a meeting of the legislature party and passed a resolution denouncing the Congress's tactics. All members, including those considered potential defectors, were made to sign it. It was then presented to the new Governor, A. N. Banerjee.

This was done with a view to preventing the Governor from blindly accepting the Congress's claims. The Janata Party's argument was that since Hegde had a verifiable majority in the assembly, the Governor should not contemplate encouraging the Congress to topple governments led by other parties, as some of his counterparts elsewhere had done. All this was deemed necessary because the Governor did not appear to be above partisan politics. Unlike his predecessor, Govind Narain, Banerjee appeared to be soft towards the Congress. He had received numerous Congress delegations in his first few months, and at one stage, some Janata ministers indirectly accused him of turning Raj Bhavan into an annexe of the Congress.

These allegations, and the public revulsion towards the Congress for its devious game, did not stop it from further attempts at destabilising the Janata government. N. Hutchamasti Gowda, a veteran who had won as an Independent, initially supported the Janata Party in the hope of getting a ministry, but later switched sides when no post was provided. The Congress sent him to work on a Janata Party legislator. When Janata activists got a tip-off about a secret meeting between the two, they *gheraoed*[5] Hutchamasti Gowda and presented him with bangles (a symbolic act which signified that what he was attempting was not manly). Such exposures of the Congress tactics made compelling copy for newspapers, and eventually caused the party a serious setback.

Of all the attempts by the Congress to undermine the government, three stand out for the drama that ensued. The first was the celebrated 'Moily tape'; the second, a raid on the hotel room which Shalinitai Patel, wife of the former Congress Chief Minister of Maharashtra, had checked herself into, and where she had been found with several suitcases, apparently containing money she had carried with her from Bombay; and the third was the 'kidnapping' of a Janata Party legislator.

Moily, leader of the Congress legislature party, was as deeply involved in this game as anyone else. He stood to gain if the government collapsed since, as leader of the opposition, he had a claim to the chief ministership. It was, therefore, not surprising that he should try to woo defectors. He cast his net wide.

Among the several Independents he tried to bait was C. Byre Gowda from Kolar district. The first time Raghavan learnt of this was when Ramesh Kumar, a former legislator from the same district, rang to ask how he could go about surreptitiously taping a conversation. Kumar said that his objective was to catch Moily redhanded in the act of discussing the possibility of Byre Gowda's defection. Moily responded positively when an intermediary from Byre Gowda raised the issue with him. A sum of Rs 3 lakh[6] was agreed upon as the price for defection. A time and place were set for the transaction. Byre Gowda carried a mini tape recorder with him, but could not get the machine to work. The deal was not completed that evening.

---

[5] Crowded round him to temporarily prevent him from leaving the premises.

[6] Rs 300,000 — a substantial amount at the time.

Ramesh Kumar kept Raghavan and a reporter from *Lankesh Patrike* magazine posted. This magazine carried a small report about the meeting between Moily and Byre Gowda. Had Moily noticed it, he would have been more careful. But a second encounter was arranged a few days later. On this occasion, Byre Gowda carried *two* mini tape recorders, and Moily walked into the trap. The following day, a press conference was called at which Byre Gowda played the tape which had recorded his conversation with Moily, and graphically described the sequence of events.

Moily, it appears, had picked him up at Cubbon Park and they had driven to a posh locality. Moily had subsequently gone into the residence of B. V. Desai, returned with a suitcase full of bank notes, and handed it to Byre Gowda after obtaining his signature on a resignation letter. Byre Gowda then dramatically produced the money before journalists, and said he was turning it over to the state government for investigation. In the taped conversation, Moily claimed that Sait, Chandraprabha Urs and V. L. Patil were also on the list of prospective defectors. All three ministers were on hand at the press conference to deny that they were changing sides.

This was a bombshell. Many journalists who heard the tape recognised the voice to be Moily's, with its typical Dakshina Kannada accent. By that evening the full transcript of the tape had been released, and Byre Gowda had become something of a hero. Nothing like this had ever been revealed in Karnataka before.

The Congress camp was crestfallen. Moily met journalists the same afternoon, and stoutly denied having met Byre Gowda. However, it was evident from the expression on his face that he was not being truthful. Much later, Hegde ordered a judicial inquiry into the episode. It ruled that it could not be proved that the voice in the tape was that of Moily. Many technical institutions declined to analyse the voice because of political repercussions. It is also true that the tape contained no explicit reference to any payment. So, even if it could be proved that the voice was Moily's, there was nothing illegal about his having approached Byre Gowda. That it was immoral, nevertheless, was another matter, and the expose served its purpose for the Janata Party. The resulting excitement compounded the Congress's difficulties in scuttling the government.

What transpired in room number 724 of Hotel Ashok, Bangalore in December 1983 was even more bizarre. Two days after Christmas, journalists received a tip-off about something fishy having taken place in this room the previous evening. Inquiries with sources in the intelligence wing of the police indicated that Shalinitai Patel, wife of the former Congress Chief Minister of Maharashtra, had checked in using the surname Kapoor, and had also booked another room. On 26 December, K. H. Patil, president of the state unit of the Congress, had called on her four times. K. H. Srinivas and B. V. Desai, two other Congress leaders, had accompanied him. But few other Congressmen appeared to know that Shalinitai was in town. She had brought with her five suitcases, which the state's intelligence suspected contained money to be handed over to the local leaders to use in pulling down the government.

This information was apparently passed on to the government, which could do nothing since Shalinitai was free to visit Bangalore and do as she pleased. What transpired next is not clear. Apparently someone, possibly from the intelligence wing, informed the income tax authorities about there being suitcase loads of cash in the room booked in the name of one 'Kapoor'. An income tax raiding party promptly went to Shalinitai's room to seize the suitcases. A flustered Shalinitai did not know what to do. She feared that the investigators would not recognise her. She phoned K. H. Patil who rushed to the hotel, berated the officials, and even invoked Mrs Gandhi's name to caution them against further action. The raiding party then beat a hasty retreat, apologising profusely. The entire drama in the hotel corridor was witnessed by a reporter of a news agency owned by the central (Congress) government, which meant that he could not file a report. When Raghavan and his colleagues heard of this the next day, they teamed up with a reporter from the *Telegraph* and confirmed all details. The day after that, when the *Indian Express* and the *Telegraph* broke the story, there was a furore.

The evening of the day this story was reported in these two newspapers, K. H. Patil and others issued a statement to the effect that Shalinitai was in the city for treatment for asthma, and that there had been no raid at the hotel. This was contrary to Shalinitai's version. She told the *Indian Express* that the income tax men had certainly arrived, but left without raiding at the instance of Patil. This left Patil looking rather foolish. So he and Shalinitai issued a joint statement seeking to deny the raid. Finally, the income tax commissioner himself confirmed that his men had sought to raid the hotel room, but that they had called it off after realising who was involved. The secret nature of Shalinitai's mission was blown and, whatever its objective was, it failed. Whether her suitcases contained currency notes remains a mystery. But in the fervid situation, no one believed her claim that they contained woollen blankets, which were in plentiful supply in Bangalore. This incident was extremely embarrassing for the Congress, and temporarily halted their 'operation destabilisation'.

The episode that finally ended it altogether involved Congressman Nanje Gowda, who had set a deadline for pulling down the Janata government. He and a few colleagues timed their campaign well. Hegde was away at a nature-cure clinic where he was required to stay for a prolonged period. Congress leaders saw Hegde's absence as an opportunity to strike since, they thought that no other Janata leader was capable of reacting swiftly. Late one night, many journalists received a tip-off that intense activity was afoot at Raj Bhavan (the Governor's official residence). They rushed there, but could not gain entry.

From the gate, journalists could see K. H. Patil and a few others rush out of Raj Bhavan and jump into a car. The journalists' efforts to stop them were in vain. Soon they learnt that the Governor had been asked to be ready to receive a delegation of defectors who would declare that they had withdrawn support from the government. They also got word from Nanje Gowda that a few legislators were at his home, nearby, and would arrive in a group at Raj Bhavan. When reporters went there, they found only one Independent legislator. Nanje Gowda promised to bring him and other Independents to the Raj Bhavan that night.

A large crowd of reporters, plain-clothed policemen and political activists waited at the gates till well past midnight. No one came. Evidently, Congress leaders had just the one legislator in hand, and they had hoped that more would jump ship if enough confusion could be created. Nanje Gowda and Patil were past masters at this game. In 1978, they had managed to confuse enough legislators to persuade them to desert Urs. As a result, his government had been dismissed and President's Rule[7] had been imposed. This latest exercise was an attempt at a re-run.

---

[7] Direct rule from New Delhi, under the leadership of the state's Governor.

The following morning, Nanje Gowda promised reporters that he would soon parade the defectors before the Governor. He appealed for more time, and continued to do so throughout the day. By nightfall, he still had only one man to offer. Reporters, policemen and partymen maintained a continuous vigil at the Raj Bhavan. The Governor was so incensed at the turn of events that he decided to personally see what the ruckus at the gate was about. A comic scene then unfolded, with the Governor moving through the crowd, questioning those waiting and even passers-by. The next morning, Hegde returned from the clinic and reviewed the situation with senior colleagues. By that time, yet another drama had built up. The would-be defector's wife had lodged a police complaint alleging that her husband had been whisked away in a car by Congress activists, and that she feared for his life. She and her small child were brought from their home in Tumkur by the ruling party. She freely met reporters and complained of a kidnapping.

In the early hours of the next morning, the Tumkur police arrived in Bangalore. By then, Hegde had decided to hit back. He instructed the police to trace the legislator and restore him to his wife, unless he claimed that he was with Nanje Gowda of his own free will. The Tumkur police went straight to Nanje Gowda's house where they were told that he was there of his own volition, so they left. Their visit, however, rattled Nanje Gowda to such an extent that he called up every Congress leader he could reach. They rushed to his residence and began calling up journalists and senior police officers to complain about Hegde resorting to police intervention. Raghavan received a call at 5 a.m. and rushed to the house to find Nanje Gowda, Bangarappa and others calling up the director general of police. Each took turns abusing the senior-most police officer who, being well used to politicians, heard them patiently and assured them that he would investigate the matter.

Hegde's decision to send policemen to Nanje Gowda's house sent an appropriate message to Congressmen. They had believed that he was weak and incapable of playing the game at which Congressmen were experts. His decision signalled to them that he was capable of removing the velvet glove, if need be.

This bungled episode was the 'last' major effort to engineer large-scale defections. We call it the last effort on the Congress's part for several reasons. No matter how hard Congressmen tried, it was proving impossible to wean away even Independents. Legislators were too frightened of public opinion, which reacted with hostility to these ploys. Also, would-be defectors saw that if they switched sides, it would not necessarily put the Congress in power. It could lead, instead, to the dissolution of the assembly and, consequently, to fresh elections, where they would have to face the wrath of patently discerning voters. The negative popular reaction was not confined to Karnataka alone. The media ensured that it attracted nation-wide attention. Hegde thus came to be seen as an embattled hero, fighting against great odds to save a democratically elected government. Even the insensitive Congress high command eventually realised that the tactics they had been practicing were not in their interests. They subsequently turned their attention to neighbouring Andhra Pradesh. There they found a Trojan horse in Nadendla Bhaskar Rao, a minister in the Telugu Desam Party's (TDP) government, quite willing to play their game. But more of this later.

The Congress had actually sought such a person in Karnataka. It had contacted the likes of Sait and Chandraprabha Urs, but they had been unable to bring enough legislators with them, and in any case they could not have been persuaded to try. The Congress's problems were compounded by mutual distrust within its state-level unit. On the one hand, leaders who were members of the legislature held those who had lost in the state election in some contempt. On the other, those who had lost took little interest in their party's attempts to destabilise the Janata government, because they would not benefit if the government fell and the Congress took power. Many potent individuals in the party were so suspicious of one another that they would not share their plans with others. All in all, the Congress's anti-Janata effort was poorly coordinated, and this contributed to its failure.

The Defeat of the Congress's Toppling Tactics in Andhra Pradesh — With a Little Help from Karnataka

By July 1984, the Congress high command had begun to focus elsewhere. It engineered the dismissal of a democratically elected government in Kashmir by devious means, and then turned its attentions to Andhra Pradesh. However, no one expected a sudden change there, since despite his extravagant theatrics, N. T. Rama Rao (or 'NTR', as he was popularly called) was still performing quite well compared to the wretched Congress governments of the early 1980s. Among his critics were many from the Left parties, the Janata Party and the BJP. But none of these parties was interested in causing NTR problems, since doing so would help their common adversary, the Congress. NTR went abroad for bypass surgery, and while he was still recovering, Mrs Gandhi struck decisively.

She had opened communications with Bhaskar Rao, an erstwhile Congressman who had helped NTR form his Telugu Desam Party. Bhaskar Rao and several TDP legislators were used to traditional politics, and chafed at NTR's tendency to run the party and the government as if they were his personal property. It was commonly said in Andhra Pradesh at the time that the TDP was 'a party of heroes and zeroes, and the number of heroes was one' – NTR.[8] Mrs Gandhi exploited this discontent. She convinced Bhaskar Rao that his future lay with the Congress. Subsequently, he resigned from the ministry, persuaded some of his colleagues in the government and the TDP legislature party to desert NTR, and submitted a list of his supporters to the Governor. Though it was clear that Bhaskar Rao had the backing of only a handful of legislators, his breakway group was quickly sworn in by the obliging Governor, Ram Lal, a partisan Congressman who was waiting for an excuse to dismiss NTR's government. As if to maintain some constitutional propriety, the Governor asked Bhaskar Rao to prove his majority on the floor of the assembly within a fixed timeframe. The calculation was that, given a few days and a hold on power, Bhaskar Rao would be able to buy enough support to prevail in the assembly.

The tactic had worked elsewhere, but this time, Mrs Gandhi was proved wrong. NTR quickly returned, took stock of the situation and found that he could keep most of his flock with him. He was still a charismatic leader with mass support. And as in Karnataka, fear of the electorate prevented legislators from crossing the floor. There was a national — indeed, even an international[9] — uproar over what was done to NTR. All the opposition parties united, and insisted on the restoration of the democratic principle. No matter how hard Congress leaders tried to distance themselves from these sordid developments, for once the mud stuck.

---

[8] Interview with G. Ram Reddy, by James Manor, Hyderabad, 3 September 1984.

[9] NTR later told James Manor in an interview (Hyderabad, 2 September 1984) that he believed that the coverage of this episode in the international press had been crucial to his survival.

NTR fought back hard. He took all the TDP legislators to Delhi on a roadshow, paraded them in front of the President, Zail Singh, and proved with a head count that Bhaskar Rao did not have enough supporters to stake a claim to form a government. Judging from the reaction of the media, it appeared that the nation was behind NTR. Parties opposed to Bhaskar Rao decided that he should be defeated on the floor of the assembly. As a result of this public pressure, the Andhra legislative assembly was summoned for a trial of strength by Bhaskar Rao, though this meant waiting for at least two weeks.

NTR realised that a safe haven was needed during these two weeks to prevent legislators from being tempted by Congress enticements. So, NTR and all his legislators flew off in a chartered plane to Bangalore, to a hotel provided by Hegde. When Bhaskar Rao dispatched agents to contact them there, they were moved to Mysore, and when even that became risky, they were shifted to Nandi Hills near Bangalore, where access was extremely difficult. Finally, on the eve of the assembly session in Hyderabad, they left in a convoy.

The assembly in Hyderabad met amidst unprecedented security. Bhaskar Rao, unable to muster a majority, resigned. Prior to this the Governor, Ram Lal, had been forced quit because of his undemocratic role in undermining a popular government. By the time the assembly met, Shankar Dayal Sharma, an old Congress warhorse who had not succumbed to his party's newly degenerate practices, had been sent as Governor. NTR subsequently made a triumphant return to the post of Chief Minister.

After this sordid episode, the Congress more or less resigned itself to the changed political environment in south India. Events in the two states had shown that it was possible to overcome Mrs Gandhi's manipulative politics as long as popular opposition to it remained firm. The upheaval in Andhra Pradesh had captured headlines. Similar attempts by the Congress in Karnataka had been less lurid, but they had changed popular perceptions among people in one very important way.

Before these episodes involving the Congress's attempts to destabilise the government in Karnataka had occurred, many people had believed that the ghastly spell of Congress rule between 1980 and 1983 could be attributed not to the party itself or its national leader, but to one wayward leader, namely Gundu Rao. But after the party had sought, so openly and wantonly, to buy its way back to power in defiance of the popular will, it was difficult to avoid the conclusion that the problem lay with the Congress as an institution and with Mrs Gandhi. Gundu Rao had been uninvolved in this tawdry business, but a leading Congress candidate for the post of Chief Minister — Moily — had played a key role.

The Congress had squandered whatever little goodwill it had retained in the state after the Gundu Rao years. The south was setting standards for the rest of the country where the Congress's disreputable tactics had often worked. Mrs Gandhi's machinations were shown to be not just sinister but silly and self-defeating. Multiparty competition was here to stay.

Both Hegde (Karnataka) and NTR (Andhra Pradesh) owed an ironic debt of gratitude to the colossal bungling of the Congress, as it attempted to force them out of power. In Andhra, if the Congress had waited a little longer to tackle NTR, they might have succeeded, since his extremely inaccessible,[10] autocratic style was alienating legislators. Indeed, he had inspired so much resentment among his legislators that the Congress's attempt at a coup actually threw him a lifeline by rekindling sympathy for him. Let us not forget that later, in 1995, his overweening style led to a palace coup in which his son-in-law ousted him as Chief Minister. In Karnataka, Janata Party legislators were far less discontented. But unlike NTR's regime, theirs was a minority government. It is thus possible that if the Congress had been able to restrain its childish impatience for power, and had given the Hegde government more time to become afflicted by the ambiguities and troubles which every government inevitably suffers from, their effort to bring it down might have succeeded.

The Arduous Business of Governing

Having thwarted the Congress's destabilising tactics, Hegde was now able to focus on other issues, including preparations for the next parliamentary election, expected within a few months' time. He faced plenty of pressures. A group of 38 legislators had begun to lobby for a reconstitution of the ministry, in the hope of senior posts. Hegde himself wanted a reshuffle. He hoped to drop Chandraprabha Urs and Sait, since they were reluctant, uncomfortable members of the team. But he needed

---

[10] It was, for example, NTR's habit to insist on visitors calling on him between four and five-thirty in the morning. Manor once interviewed him in 1984 at 5 a.m.

a good political reason to be able to do so. He also wanted to change some ministers' portfolios, and have a more broad-based, balanced team, bearing in mind the government's minority status and the approaching national election.

On 17 July 1984, at Hedge's request, all the ministers, except Chandraprabha Urs and Sait voluntarily handed over their resignations. The duo were absent from the cabinet meeting on the morning this happened. This news was kept a secret for at least two days, but there was intense speculation about it in the media. On the third day, an official confirmation emerged. Behind the scenes, a minor drama brewed. Both Sait and Urs refused to fall in line. It took them almost ten days to make up their minds. They finally resigned, not only from the ministry, but from the party as well. They claimed that the atmosphere in the government had become stifling. They also complained that it was dominated by Vokkaligas and Lingayats. This was an after-thought, intended to show that they were carrying on the legacy of Devaraj Urs, whose power rested on the Backward Classes. Even as they were resigning, they were in touch with the Congress, to which they finally went.

As this episode unfolded, the BJP, whose support for the government was vital, pitched in with its own demands. It insisted that it be consulted prior to any policy decision. Its legislators not only wished to avoid any policy that would be detrimental to them, but also to practice 'me-tooism' in the hope of sharing the credit for popular Janata policies. And yet while the BJP's support to the Janata–Kranti Ranga combine prevented the Congress from coming back to power, it also made BJP leaders uncomfortable. They did not want to be seen to be too close to the Hegde regime, lest they lose their own identity and become less able to cultivate a popular constituency for the future. Fortunately for Hegde, the BJP's national leaders came to his rescue when their state-level colleagues pitched their demands too high. The BJP high command could not afford to allow a non-Congress government to founder. This was only the first of many occasions, over the years, when interventions from the national level undercut the BJP's state-level leaders.

Though this was reassuring, Hegde still considered the possibility of dissolving the assembly and ordering fresh elections, in the hope of a Janata Party majority that would free him from dependence on other parties. He consulted first the cabinet at an emergency meeting, and then the BJP and the two Communist parties. While the Left parties were agreeable to Hegde's suggestion, the BJP was not. It had more seats (18) than ever before, and its leaders knew that Bangarappa, who had helped them do well in Dakshina Kannada district, was now an adversary. They also wanted time to consolidate their position in the constituencies that they held. In the end, Hegde decided against dissolution.

Meanwhile, he reconstituted the ministry, raising its strength from 22 to 35. He inducted 16 new faces. Deve Gowda, J. H. Patel, two heavyweights, were dropped, so that they could devote themselves to preparing the party for the upcoming parliamentary election.

When the new ministers were sworn in the next day, there was an extremely serious gaffe. B. M. Mujahid, a Muslim to be brought into the ministry in place of Sait, was not present to take the oath of office. Hegde explained that Mujahid was a last-minute inclusion, and that since he could not reach Bangalore from Hubli in time for the ceremony, he would be sworn in the next day. As it turned out, Mujahid refused the offer because he was still a committed Congressman. This was extremely embarrassing for Hegde, especially since a Chief Minister is expected to pick his ministers with great care.

In this instance, Hegde had gone by what Bommai told him. Bommai had suggested Mujahid's name on the grounds that it would be good for the party to have Muslim representatives in the cabinet coming from different regions. Since Nazirsab came from Mysore in southern Karnataka, it was logical that the second Muslim should come from the north. The choice of Mujahid, however, was a huge mistake. It was well-known that he belonged to the Congress. Since Bommai knew him well personally, he mistakenly thought that Mujahid could easily be persuaded to join the ministry.

This episode was a source of glee to Congressmen, who were quick to point out that it was not they but Hegde who was now trying to engineer defections. Even if Mujahid had been prepared to accept a post, it would have been extremely unwise to include him; the Congress's efforts to inspire defections had made it seem morally tawdry alongside a Janata Party government that appeared to be above such squalid tactics.

Seen in this light, the episode involving Mujahid was a major blunder from the Hegde government, since it struck at its claim to moral superiority. Morality looms larger in Indian politics than in some other parliamentary systems. When the British Prime Minister Harold Macmillan was asked in the 1950s why his government did not provide more moral leadership, his reply was dismissive. He knew that all governments must make compromises, and that they are thus assailed by inescapable ambiguities, including what will be seen as moral ambiguities. So he suggested that people should look to archbishops, rather than politicians, for moral guidance.[11] Indian leaders on the other hand, in part because of the legacy of Mahatma Gandhi, have always been more inclined to strike moralistic postures. The Janata Party stood squarely in this tradition. It sought to offer people an uplifting alternative to the morally degenerate Congress, which had committed excesses during the Emergency and was abusing power again, now that Mrs Gandhi had been swept back into office. The Congress attempt to entice defectors from the Janata Party in Karnataka was a vivid example of such degeneracy. The attempt to play the same dirty game with Mujahid squandered the Janata Party's moral advantage on these issues.

After the reconstitution, the ministry became extremely large. Not many objected, however, since the expansion forced Hegde to distribute patronage widely in order to keep the government intact. He continued to maintain a balance, not only between the two factions within his own party (the original Janata Party and the Kranti Ranga), but also (as in Urs's day) between the dominant castes on the one hand, and the Backward Classes, Scheduled Castes and Tribes, and Muslims on the other. Major portfolios went to leaders from less privileged groups. For the first time, the Home portfolio, which had traditionally remained with the Chief Minister or a dominant-caste leader, went to Rachaiah, a Scheduled Caste. Many junior ministers with the potential to excel were given independent charge. Some political heavyweights with less talent got minor portfolios.

Trouble, however, was just round the corner. Hegde had made up his mind even before the expansion of the ministry that the presidency of the party would go to Deve Gowda. Other top party posts would be assigned in ways to maintain a balance between factions and social groups. But Hegde had not consulted all senior party colleagues on this matter. J. H. Patel suggested that the president be chosen by consensus, and later threw his hat in the ring to thwart Deve Gowda. With a parliamentary

---

[11] This was in the days before Margaret Thatcher and Tony Blair adopted moralistic postures, but the troubles that ensued for both of them as a result suggest that Macmillan was right.

election looming, the party president would have a great influence over the award of tickets. Hence the interest of both Deve Gowda and Patel in the post.

This problem was compounded when a group of Lingayats and members of the erstwhile Kranti Ranga indicated that they opposed Deve Gowda. After strenuous negotiations involving Janata's national-level president, Chandra Shekhar, Deve Gowda was finally chosen as president, but Patel was made secretary-general, a new post which was said to be equal to that of party president. After this, things went smoothly.

On 18 October 1984, Hegde, who had long suffered from a throat problem, went to the US for treatment. Two weeks later, while he was still in the US, Indira Gandhi was assassinated. She was succeeded by her son Rajiv, and an early parliamentary election was called in late December. Hegde's government had come through a grim struggle for survival, but in the wake of this stunning event, it was to face a far graver challenge.

8

Nine Weeks, Two Key Elections

The brutal murder of Mrs Gandhi altered the course of the country's history, but its impact on Karnataka was, surprisingly, minimal. There were no acts of retaliatory violence against Sikhs[1] in Bangalore or elsewhere in Karnataka, as there were in several other states. People reacted with sorrow, and Congressmen in particular behaved as if they had been orphaned. With the appointment of Rajiv Gandhi as Prime Minister and later his 'election' as party chief, Congressmen heaved a sigh of relief. Rajiv's appointment meant that despite his inexperience, the dynasty would continue.

The Parliamentary Election of December 1984

Rajiv Gandhi advanced the Lok Sabha elections by a couple of months to capitalise on the sympathy wave sweeping the country. After the trauma of the assassination, the Congress's call for stability would have a wide appeal. And though she had been controversial, Mrs Gandhi had endeared herself to the masses. The election was set for the earliest possible date, so non-Congress parties had little time to prepare. Hegde, who was still away in the US, was persuaded by senior colleagues to rush back. He arrived on 16 November, fully fit. In an uncharacteristic fit of bravado, he declared that the electorate would reject Rajiv Gandhi because he was a greenhorn. When asked whether, as a matter of courtesy, he would call on the new Prime Minister, Hegde said he wouldn't since, in his view, Rajiv Gandhi was only a caretaker Prime Minister.

Two days earlier, the Congress had set up a state-level election committee. Typical of the party, it had left out Krishna, a minister in the central government, and included his name only as an afterthought. By that time it was known that the state would have a one-day poll on Christmas eve. Within a few days, 432 Congress aspirants had applied

---

[1] In the days following Indira Gandhi's assassination by her two Sikh bodyguards, mobs across much of India killed thousands of Sikhs in retaliation, including over 3,000 in Delhi alone.

for the 28 Lok Sabha seats from Karnataka. There was such turbulent lobbying for tickets that the committee could not deliberate properly. The entire committee shifted to Delhi, where calm deliberation was easier, to finalise the list of names.

A week later the Congress Parliamentary Board announced its nominees for Karnataka, and this list contained many surprises. Eight sitting MPs had been denied tickets. Many ardent followers of Gundu Rao had been excluded because they were considered too crude for the new ethos in Rajiv's party. Gundu Rao's alter ego, Khan, had been expelled from the Congress a few weeks earlier because he had undertaken a fast in front of the party's headquarters in Delhi, demanding a greater influence for old loyalists.

The changes in the candidates' list for Karnataka were replicated across India. Rajiv Gandhi was determined to infuse new blood into the party. He and his so-called Computer Boys had clearly spent time identifying constituencies that required changes. After some initial bickering, most Congressmen reconciled themselves to the list and began work in earnest for a campaign that was centrally planned and controlled.

Meanwhile, even before Hegde could open talks with allied parties, the BJP announced that it would contest four of the 28 seats. After negotiations, it got them, partly because one of them, Shimoga, was unpromising for the Janata Party. The Raitha Sangha (farmers' association), which had its headquarters in Shimoga, refused to renew its support because the government had rejected its demand that it be recognised as the sole representative of farmers, on the grounds that it was unreasonable. The CPI was given Chikmagalur. Negotiations with the CPI (M) broke down because it insisted on the Bangalore North seat where the Janata Party wanted to field George Fernandes, a leading light of the national party.

The Janata Party asked more than one aspirant to file nomination papers for each seat that it would contest, and then decided between them on the day of the withdrawal of papers. This naturally led to unnecessary bitterness, so that the campaign was damaged by animosity between aspirants and, in almost all cases, factions. Hegde decided to field some of his cabinet colleagues who had gained influence in their respective districts. By doing so, he was inadvertently acknowledging that the Janata Party lacked strong leaders at the local level.

He did this because this election was crucial to the party at both the state and national levels. Winning a respectable number of seats in Karnataka was vital. If the party failed badly, defections could soon scuttle his government. Rajiv Gandhi was unproven, and the Janata Party actually hoped to improve its position nationally through this election. Among those fielded were Nazirsab, by then well-known for his tremendous work in rural development, R. L. Jalappa, M. P. Prakash and P. G. R. Sindhia. All had earned popular reputations for themselves.

The Congress faced straight fights (contests in which they faced only one opponent) in 25 of the 28 constituencies. The Janata Party campaign was opened by its national-level president, Chandra Shekhar, in Basavanagudi, a party stronghold, in Bangalore. Rajiv Gandhi inaugurated the Congress campaign in Kolar by declaring that Karnataka was in a mess and had to be rescued by the Congress. This was a theme he stuck to throughout the campaign in the state. 'Hegde', he told reporters, 'will be irrelevant after the election.' This came across as being a haughty statement to make. Even Congress leaders were stunned by it.

But barring such minor diversions, the campaign ran on expected lines. The Congress, as expected, proceeded as though it was still observing obsequies for Mrs Gandhi. Video tapes of her funeral were played repeatedly in most villages. Congressmen unashamedly used the imagery of her death to their advantage everywhere, in order to impress upon people the fact that an end to the Congress rule would lead to anarchy.

The results were out on 28 December. Congress won 24 of the 28 seats. Considering the circumstances and the Congress Party's performances in previous elections, the Janata Party can also be said to have performed quite well. It won four seats, and narrowly lost two others. In one, it gave a central government minister the fright of his life: he almost lost to a greenhorn, at a time when the Congress was nearly wiping out the opposition in the Hindi belt.

Despite winning four seats (the best a non-Congress party had done since the Congress split in 1969), Hegde faced immediate demands from the Congress that he resign, on the grounds that having lost at the national level he had no moral right to continue at the state level. Publicly, Hegde ruled this out but, privately, he had begun to consider this option since it might yield considerable political mileage. But any hint of it would have triggered mass defections overnight. This had happened twice before, in 1971 and 1980, when rumours of the resignations of the then Chief Ministers had caused apparently strong state governments to unravel.

On 29 December, Hegde summoned an emergency cabinet meeting and convinced his colleagues that the only option available to them was to face the electorate again. Before he resigned, he had them formally adopt a resolution advising the Governor to dissolve the assembly and proceed with fresh elections. He immediately called on the Governor to present the resolution. Later, he told newsmen that the Governor was bound by the Constitution to accept the advice (which was not strictly true),[2] and that he hoped the Governor would not play politics and induct a Congress government through the back door.

Whether the Governor consulted the newly elected leaders in New Delhi is not known. But it did not take him long to recommend the imposition of President's Rule in the state. This obviously took the Congress leaders in Bangalore by surprise. They called on the Governor and offered to form a government, and many also rushed to Delhi, hoping to persuade Rajiv Gandhi to urge the Governor to let them do so. All they needed was the support of 25 non-Congress legislators, something that looked an easy target in the circumstances. The central authorities dithered, but despite tantalising prospects, neither Janata Party nor Independent legislators switched sides. Hegde then announced that rule by defectors would not be allowed in the state this time, and threatened to start a *satyagraha*[3] if the Congress was invited to form a government. Soon thereafter, a spokesman in New Delhi quoted the new Prime Minister as saying that there would be no Congress government in the state. The state assembly was then formally dissolved, and preparations began for a state election.

The Remarkable State Election of March 1985

Soon after this announcement, on New Year's Eve, several of India's leading political scientists met in Delhi to discuss the outlook for the Karnataka state election. The unanimous view was that things were grim for the Janata Party. The Congress had won a thumping victory in the Lok Sabha election here, the emotions triggered by the murder of

---

[2] Unwritten political conventions, both within India and in other Westminster-style systems, dictate that such requests should be accepted. But India's Constitution does not explicitly require this of a Governor or, at the national level, of the President. See Manor (2005).

[3] A campaign of non-violent civil disobedience — a form of protest developed by Mahatma Gandhi.

Mrs Gandhi were still strong and Karnataka's voters would return to the polls in just a few short weeks. It seemed inconceivable that the Janata Party could win.[4] Most pundits in the Indian press drew the same conclusion, and stuck to it until the votes were counted.

The analyses within Hegde's circle were better informed and less pessimistic. He called a meeting to discuss what had gone wrong in the Lok Sabha election. From these discussions, it turned out that nothing about the Janata Party's campaign had gone terribly wrong since, despite a sympathy wave, the performance of the Congress had actually been a good deal worse than in previous elections. This discussion led to the question of how, then, the state election campaign ought to be run. Hegde was advised to be aggressive, to match what was expected from Rajiv Gandhi. The new Prime Minister had been projected in the Lok Sabha election as the unquestioned leader of the Congress as well as the nation, who was opposed by squabbling opposition parties which, in turn, were depicted in newspaper advertisements as snakes and scorpions. His party's advertisements had also appealed to the popular fears of Sikhs, who had been slaughtered in large numbers by Congress thugs after Mrs Gandhi's assassination — something that would have been outrageous to his grandfather, Jawaharlal Nehru. In Karnataka, the Janata Party was in for a rough ride.

It was suggested that Hegde be projected as the next Chief Minister so that he could ask the pointed question raised by Rajiv Gandhi in the earlier election: 'Who is the leader of the opposition camp?' In Karnataka, the Congress had at least four possible leaders. Hegde liked the idea, but wondered if it was proper to declare that he would remain at the helm.

The next day, Janata Party members of the dissolved legislature met at the party office to consider the situation. Raghupathy, a former minister, moved a resolution naming Hegde as the party's nominee for Chief Minister. This was not to the liking of Deve Gowda and at least a few other leaders. Hegde again said that it would be improper, but that if asked, he would accept the designation as head of the election campaign. This formulation was then adopted. At a meeting with reporters, one Janata Party leader said, 'Hegde is our undisputed leader. I would like to know who is the undisputed leader in the Congress.' This theme served the Janata Party well, since Congress leaders were in disarray. But

---

[4] James Manor took part in this discussion.

it was also disheartening to Janata Party leaders like Deve Gowda and Bommai: they realised that this resolution impicitly foreclosed the issue of post-electoral leadership. They would both have to wait another five years before even aspiring to the top post.

The Janata Party set up an election committee which carefully maintained a balance (both in terms of representing the two factions of the party as well as the different social groups) by including a balance of the original Janata Party and Kranti Ranga members, two Lingayats, two Vokkaligas, two from the Backward Classes, a Brahmin, a Muslim and a Scheduled Caste leader — a veritable rainbow coalition. The Election Commission fixed polling in all constituencies for 2 March, giving precious little time for parties to finalise their lists. Only nine weeks would elapse between the national election (held in December 1984) and the state elections due in early March.

Hegde promptly began talks with the parties that had supported his government. Several Janata Party leaders lobbied against having ties with the BJP for two reasons. The first was the issue of ideological incompatibility, with many Janata Party leaders being from Socialist backgrounds. The second was even more compelling. Over the past two years, the BJP had aggressively increased the price of its support to the extent that it had threatened the Janata Party's self-respect.

For example, when legislators were in the process of electing members to the Rajya Sabha in April 1983, several BJP members refused to honour an agreement with the Janata Party to support one of the latter's candidates. A BJP leader had thrown a tantrum because the Janata Party candidate had not personally requested his backing. The situation was only retrieved when Janata Party members dragged their candidate from a restaurant to personally plead for the votes. This sort of unreasonable behaviour by BJP leaders was common. As Hegde said privately, 'I have had to stomach many insults, and compromise to an uncomfortable degree, because of the BJP.'

Janata Party leaders were not the only ones who wanted to break with the BJP. The two Communist parties, which had vast ideological differences with Hindu nationalism, also favoured a split. So repugnant was the BJP to them that they always insisted that the Janata Party government deal entirely separately with them and with it. This, and the now deep distrust between many Janata Party leaders and the BJP, meant that the link had to be broken. But to do so unilaterally, in the teeth of a potent Congress challenge in the emotionally charged atmosphere after Indira Gandhi's assassination, would have been unwise. So the Janata Party kept the association going for the sake of appearances, while party managers devised ways of terminating it soon thereafter.

To avoid blame for the break, Hegde intentionally approached the BJP before the Left parties for negotiations on seat sharing. He offered the BJP 24 out of the 224 assembly seats. The BJP demanded 40. Hegde refused to budge, but asked the BJP to reconsider. It seems that both parties' leaders suspected that their tenuous ties were about to snap. Each side was positioning itself to blame the other, which explains the BJP's modest goal of 40. (In the 1983 state election it had initially demanded 120.) Despite pressure from the BJP's national leaders for compromise, none was found. The BJP announced the breakdown and ultimately contested 97 seats on its own. One BJP leader admitted that his party had behaved like a 'grumbling wife', adding further, 'we have now decided to divorce'.

As it turned out, the decision to project Hegde as the principal campaigner made an enormous difference. He told voters in very simple terms that 'no matter who won the election, Rajiv Gandhi would not become Chief Minister of the Karnataka'.[5] If the Janata Party won, Hegde would remain in office, but if the Congress won, voters would have to take their chances with one of several state-level leaders, all of whom were linked to the baleful Gundu Rao. To press home the message, he reminded them of how much more than the Gundu Rao regime his government had achieved in its brief spell in power: providing drinking water in rural areas, bridging the gap between the people and the government, achieving progress on the law and order front by tackling youth gangs in urban areas. He said, 'If you elect us, these programmes will continue, but if you elect the Congress, it will mean a return to the old ways.'

Hegde decided to assume close control over most of the key aspects of the campaign. He had seen that the party organisation had not stretched itself to its limit during the 1984 Lok Sabha election. He could never be sure if the money given to the various committees within the organisation had actually been used properly. He also felt the need to maximise efficiency in the drafting of the manifesto, the drawing up of tour programmes for leaders, and in the preparation and distribution

---

[5] Hegde, interview by James Manor, Bangalore, 17 August 1985.

of election material to the constituencies. The committees to perform these tasks, which had been created by party president Deve Gowda, were left in place, but they answered to Hegde on a daily basis. This did not cause any open conflict with Deve Gowda who, as chairman of the election committee, still enjoyed tremendous clout. He appeared to be unhappy about the control which Hegde exercised over these committees, but because a lot was at stake, he said nothing.

Deve Gowda's experience in this campaign is worth noting in detail, not just because he later became India's Prime Minister, but also because it provides key insights into the events that occurred in the years following this election. He chose to contest from two places: his home constituency, Holenarsipur, and Sathanur in Bangalore Rural district. His explanation for doing this was that party workers in the latter district thought that his candidature would help to win several neighbouring Vokkaliga-dominated constituencies. This sounded unconvincing, since in 1983 the Bangalore Rural district had returned Janata candidates in 12 of its 13 seats, in spite of the fact that Deve Gowda had neither contested from the district nor campaigned very hard there.

However, the real reason for Deve Gowda's decision to contest from two places was that Holenarsipur was no longer completely safe for him. By early 1985, he had made a number of enemies in this constituency. Indeed, right from 1967 the constituency had been sharply divided between his supporters and detractors, and at every election since then, the conflict between them had only deepened. After he became a minister, Deve Gowda's capacity to distribute patronage increased enormously, and he began to build a much wider constituency for himself in the districts where Vokkaligas could decide elections. At the same time, however, some of his traditional supporters (including some Vokkaligas), who had either been denied patronage or thought that their share was not in proportion to the service that they had rendered, distanced themselves from him.

One such politician was G. Puttaswamy Gowda. He had long been Deve Gowda's alter ego, and it was through him that Deve Gowda had nursed Holenarsipur and built up a sizeable following among Vokkaligas. He felt so obliged to Puttaswamy Gowda that in 1978, when the Janata Party was in a position to win a couple of seats in the state's Upper House, he saw to it that his alter ego became a member. But after Deve Gowda became a minister, Puttaswamy Gowda complained that his erstwhile patron had begun to depend on him far less, preferring to operate through his sons instead.

The two leaders began to fall out and finally, when Puttaswamy Gowda retired from the Upper House, he was not renominated because by then Deve Gowda had turned against him. Puttaswamy Gowda walked straight into the Congress, which readily admitted him but did not put him to good use. Although he was the strongest candidate to fight Deve Gowda in the state assembly election, the Congress did not select him, disregarding also the truckloads of voters that he brought along with him from Holenarsipur to Bangalore to plead his case with the party leaders. Instead, the party chose a nonentity to oppose Deve Gowda, forcing Puttaswamy Gowda to contest as a Congress rebel. For this act, the president of the Congress, K. H. Patil, expelled him from the party.

This action strengthened speculation that top leaders in all parties had entered into a secret deal to help one another in the election. It was not a merecoincidence that leaders like Deve Gowda and Bommai in the Janata Party, and Patil and Moily in the Congress, faced relatively lightweight opponents. In the case of Hegde too, his Congress rival was a virtual nonentity, but he could at least claim that he made no deal with the Congress leaders, as the others appear to have done.

For Bommai, Patil and Moily, winning their seats was an extremely easy proposition, but not so for Deve Gowda. Puttaswamy Gowda, contesting as an Independent, troubled him no end. There were clashes between their supporters almost every night. When the result of the 1985 state election was declared, Deve Gowda's apprehensions were proved right. He won by a very narrow margin in a constituency (Holenarsipur) where he had swept every election since 1962. Had the Congress had the sense to nominate Puttaswamy Gowda, Deve Gowda would probably have lost. It was this apprehension that had forced Deve Gowda to contest from a second constituency, Sathanur, where he won with relative ease.

The election preparations by the Congress were far less orderly than those of its Janata Party opponents. No Congress campaign in those days was complete without a chaotic scramble for party nominations, but on this occasion, the party surpassed itself. Rajiv Gandhi's emergence as leader suggested that new kinds of candidates might be chosen, and the party's nationwide sweep at the recent parliamentary election (1984) made nominations appear tantamount to victory. So, no less than 10,000 aspirants sought tickets for just 224 seats.

The state Congress election committee could not cope so, as in the past, it decamped to Delhi. A large number of aspirants followed it. Bangarappa, who had become a key player in the party after leaving the Janata Party, was characteristically unhappy that his group was under-represented in the election committee. But for all practical purposes, this committee now had little influence. Rajiv's Computer Boys[6] had taken over and some of them, notably Arun Nehru, were so abrasive that party veterans found it difficult to adjust. They busied themselves cultivating ties with key figures in the party's new corporate culture, but were able to achieve little.

Arun Nehru apparently had his own list of candidates based on constituency-wise profiles fed into computers long before the elections. Whether reliable data had been entered is open to serious doubt. Congress observers had quietly been sent to each constituency, to report to Rajiv Gandhi and his closest advisors on the party's prospects. National intelligence agencies had done the same. This formed the basis for the distribution of tickets.

By 1 February, the party bosses had finalised the Karnataka list, but even though time was short, they waited almost a week before formally announcing it. They decided not to project a single state-level leader, in order to strengthen Rajiv's personal impact (and, later, his influence in choosing the next Chief Minister). When the list was announced, Gundu Rao (the antithesis of the suave Doon School[7] brigade that surrounded Rajiv), along with his followers, found himself excluded. So was the formidable Vokkaliga leader Srikantaiah, along with 26 sitting legislators. The list included 43 Lingayats, 42 Vokkaligas, 66 from the Backward Classes, 19 Muslims, 35 from the Scheduled Castes and Scheduled Tribes, eight Brahmins, and 13 others. The Congress had offered representation to every important social group in the state. Moreover, 14 of those who got tickets were women, and just over half were under 45.

The high command then asked Gundu Rao to keep out of the campaign. The Congress was clearly seeking to stress Rajiv's reputation for being 'Mr Clean', and to check elements like Gundu Rao, whose

---

[6] The mostly young, westernised men who formed Rajiv Gandhi's inner circle, many of whom were skilled in the use of computers.

[7] The elite public school which Rajiv Gandhi had attended.

brutish regime was still fresh in the citizens' memory. After years of being known for taking institutionalised corruption to unimaginable heights, the Congress was now seeking to restore some credibility.

The Janata Party leaders had earlier claimed that more seats would be given to the Backward Classes and minorities than to the dominant castes. As it turned out, this was untrue. The final list revealed that 63 Lingayats and 45 Vokkaligas had been given tickets. Others included 37 from the Backward Classes, 35 from the Scheduled Castes, 10 Brahmins, nine Muslims, two Jains, and two Christians. Twenty four sitting members had been dropped, including two junior ministers. It fielded 206 candidates and left eight seats to the CPI and seven to the CPI (M). Lingayats and Vokkaligas were given disproportionate shares, so that the Janata Party appeared to be somewhat less broadly based than the Congress. As we shall see later, over the long term, the ensuing tensions eventually came close to destroying the party.

Considering that in 1983 the Janata Party had used the Backward Classes platform, assiduously built by Urs in the 1970s, it was surprising that it allowed the dominant castes to assert themselves this time. For those who knew the mindset of the Janata Party leaders, this came as no surprise. It must be remembered that the Janata Party, excluding the members of the erstwhile Kranti Ranga group, was of old Congress (O)[8] stock. And the Congress (O) had always represented the interests of the dominant land-owning castes, forcing Urs, in 1972, to turn to the excluded groups. Both his land reforms and his reservation policy for the Backward Classes had impelled the Lingayats and Vokkaligas towards the Congress (O), which later became the 'original' (that is, before its merger with the Kranti Ranga) Janata Party. All its important leaders — Hegde, Deve Gowda and Bommai — came from the Congress (O), and the Congress (O) culture lived on, to a degree, even after its merger with Urs's Kranti Ranga. Former Congress (O) leaders adapted themselves to the change towards rainbow coalitions that this implied, but where possible, they activated their old networks. Deve Gowda (a Vokkaliga) and Bommai (a Lingayat) sought to carve out bases within

---

[8] The designation described that section of the Congress that had opposed Indira Gandhi between 1969 and the early 1970s. 'O' stood for 'organisation'. In Karnataka, the Congress (O) had been dominated by the Lingayats and Vokkaligas.

the new Janata Party. Hegde (a Brahmin) and others resisted this, but they were also constrained since they needed these two leaders.

In 1985, Bommai and Deve Gowda sought to get all other leaders of consequence tied down to a particular issue or constituency, to prevent them from interfering in the selection of candidates. Deve Gowda refused to issue Nazirsab and Chandre Gowda the all-important 'B' form, an official certificate that they required to secure the party symbol for their followers in their home districts. Angered by this high-handedness, these two threatened to resign. Deve Gowda relented in the case of Nazirsab, but Chandre Gowda had to suffer the mortification of seeing one supporter in Chikmagalur contest as an Independent. On the last day of filing, Deve Gowda and Bommai made a few changes in the list of candidates without consulting Hegde or the election committee, as required.

Hegde was naturally furious, but could do precious little to assert himself. Fortunately for him, the damage inflicted on the party by Deve Gowda's tactics was limited. It could have been worse had Hegde left the subsequent campaign entirely to the organisation, as in the past. This time Hegde and a small circle of leaders took all the vital decisions, thereby preventing Deve Gowda from starving some candidates of resources or delivering them late, as had happened previously. And ironically, Deve Gowda and Bommai, who had sought to tie others down to their constituencies, found themselves tied down to their regions, while Hegde toured the entire state, spending little time in his new constituency (Basavanagudi in Bangalore) which looked reasonably safe.

Hegde introduced an innovation by creating a watchdog committee unconnected to any party, consisting of eminent men from outside politics. This committee was meant to field complaints from citizens about the misuse of office during the campaign. Though it had little work to do, it enhanced Hegde's credibility. One politician who could have gone to the committee, but refused, was Bangarappa (with the Congress at the time). He accused the Janata government of raking in a crore[9] of rupees in a liquor deal with a company in Kerala, in the hope that some mud would stick. The government promptly denied it and, after the election, a judicial inquiry found the charge baseless.

---

[9] Ten million.

The campaign gathered momentum when both Rajiv Gandhi and Hegde hit the road. Rajiv Gandhi characteristically opened his campaign by accusing the Janata Party of wrecking Karnataka's economy. Few, however, took him seriously. Instead, most voters apparently believed the Janata Party's promises to provide drinking water to every village (a pledge that had already been substantially fulfilled) and jobs to the unemployed. Hegde turned the election into a referendum on the performance of his government. 'If you are satisfied with the work we did, elect us again. If not, it is up to you', he repeated in every election meeting.

As the campaign reached its peak, political pundits wrote off Hegde and the Janata Party on the basis of what had happened nine weeks earlier in the Lok Sabha election. Rajiv Gandhi ran a high-profile campaign in the state, putting in abundant money and resources. For once, because it was in power (which helped with 'fund-raising'), the Janata Party was nearly able to match the Congress in this respect. Apart from plastering the urban and rural landscape with posters and banners, Hegde drafted a short, personal appeal to voters and had it distributed state-wide in several languages, including Kannada, English and Urdu. He also addressed election meetings touching nearly every assembly constituency.

It soon became clear to those who made forays deep into the districts that the Janata Party was winning. But in urban centres, this was neither the popular nor the pundits' perception. Although Hegde and many colleagues sensed the voters' mood as being largely positive towards their party, they were still extremely anxious after their all-too-recent defeat in the parliamentary election — and with good reason. The Janata Party had drawn extremely large, enthusiastic crowds then too, and yet fared badly.

To get an accurate picture, Hegde privately commissioned Prannoy Roy, a psephologist with an excellent track record, to conduct a survey two weeks before polling. Roy's report indicated that a further substantial swing towards the Janata Party was needed to win a comfortable majority. Unnerved by this, Hegde quickly consulted colleagues and asked Bommai to announce what became known as a supplementary manifesto. In order to trigger the required swing, Bommai promised economically weaker groups rice at Rs 2 per kilo and subsidised clothes. However, since the announcement was made three days before voting, it is extremely doubtful whether it made any difference. In this election, as in 1983, at least half of the voters had probably made up their minds long before any party drew up its strategy.

Even 48 hours before polling, Janata Party leaders felt very uncertain. Varied reports from pollsters, several of whom used unreliable methods, added to the confusion. In both camps, frenetic calls were streaming in from cash-starved candidates desperately seeking assistance. Neither party was short of resources, but both deployed them very judiciously, pouring more into constituencies where there was a reasonable chance of victory and offering only token amounts to others.

Hegde spent the last morning of the campaign making a whistle-stop tour of rural constituencies abutting Bangalore. That evening and the following morning, he went door-to-door in the city, since public campaigning was forbidden. By that time, several things had become clear to journalists. Despite massive Congress spending, Hegde would comfortably win in his constituency. Urban pockets in almost all districts still favoured the Janata Party. The Congress was not doing as well as usual in its traditional strongholds. Still, it was difficult to get an overall picture. National intelligence agencies, which were hyper-active because of Rajiv Gandhi's close interest in polling trends, were unable to develop a realistic assessment.

Hegde rang Raghavan to find out how things looked to journalists, who had toured extensively. After discussing each district, the two arrived at a figure of 120–25 for the Janata Party. Hegde was pleasantly surprised. However, he had two reasons for apprehension. He did not have the benefit of an independent assessment of trends. Those who briefed him naturally exaggerated the Janata's chances. National intelligence agencies surprisingly came up with a similar figure. Some political pundits gave the Janata Party only 60 to 80, and the Congress over 120.

On election day, roughly 60 per cent of the electorate exercised its franchise. This was a high turnout, another indication of a possible Janata victory. It implied that the middle classes who, in a reversal of patterns in industrialised democracies, are less likely than the poorer groups to vote in India (Linz, Stepan and Yadav 2007), had come out in strength. They were known to favour the Janata Party. In Karnataka, low turnouts had always been to the advantage of the Congress.

When counting began next morning, it soon became obvious that the people had swept the Janata Party back to power. It was a massive turnaround from the Lok Sabha election held only nine weeks before. Hegde himself quietly stayed at the state guest house, trying to get a picture of the results. By noon it was clear that the Janata Party would, at the very least, secure an absolute majority. In Basavanagudi, Hegde was on the way to winning by a record margin (42,780 votes). He found the totals sobering. 'Such a mandate places enormous responsibility on the party, and me in particular', he said in private. 'The mandate is so overwhelming that we cannot afford to commit any mistakes.'

This was indeed a momentous occasion for Hegde. No one before him, not even a Devaraj Urs, had managed a runaway victory against the Congress. Late that night the final figures became available. From being a minority government, the Janata Party had returned with 139 seats out of 224. The Congress ended up with 66. The BJP suffered worst, dropping from 18 to two, and one of their partymen, Vasant Bangera, had already begun thinking of migrating to the Janata Party. The two Communist allies won six seats (CPI four and CPI (M) two). The Maharashtra Ekikaran Samiti won four, and Independents, eight.

By any reckoning, the Janata Party's performance was splendid. This victory was a vote for the Janata government for performance, for clean government, for less ostentation and, above all, an acknowledgement of the tremendous work it had done to provide drinking water in rural areas amidst a drought. Every minister could claim some credit, but Hegde and Nazirsab deserved the lion's share.

This was also a vote against the political manipulations of the Congress and the curious conduct of BJP legislators. In many constituencies, people who had elected BJP candidates only two years back, had become alienated by the behaviour of these representatives once in office. In Dakshina Kannada district, for instance, they found that BJP leaders refused to help those who had not voted for them. This had never been true of Congress or Janata Party leaders. They had always assisted everyone in the hope that the next time, voters might turn to them. The BJP's narrowly partisan approach was forcefully rejected in this election.

Voters also recoiled from the idea of Congress rule by remote control. During the campaign, Hegde had had the state plastered with posters saying that Karnataka should be ruled by its own state government and not New Delhi. The implausible Congress response to this was that Hegde was promoting separatism. People, however, understood that any state-level Congress leader would just not be a free agent. Hegde, on the other hand, had demonstrated that the initiative in running the government lay with him, and that it was not necessary for him to consult the party high command at every turn, as Congressmen had had to do owing to Mrs Gandhi radical centralisation of power in the early 1970s. Karnataka's voters had seen how in Andhra Pradesh Congress Chief Ministers had been changed four times between 1980 and 1983, and that the blundering Gundu Rao had avoided this only by abject pledges of obeisance to Mrs Gandhi.

If in the 1983 state election, the Janata Party had won as a result of a negative vote against Gundu Rao's vile Congress regime, the 1985 result was an overwhelmingly positive vote for the former party. It left Congressmen looking for excuses and scapegoats. The national leader was above criticism, so others had to be found. The president of the Congress's state unit K. H. Patil, resigned and, in public, ludicrously blamed vote-rigging for his party's defeat. Privately, he attributed it to dissension and sabotage in the ranks. Gundu Rao roundly abused the Congress leader from Kerala, Karunakaran, claiming that he had 'tampered' with the candidates' list in order to promote Moily.

The Janata Party's victory in 1985 was, in our view, the most extraordinary to occur both at the state and national levels in India between the repudiation of the Emergency in the general election of 1977 and the present day. We invite other analysts to nominate alternatives, but we have considered all of them and we see nothing to match the verdict of the 1985 state election in Karnataka.

It had not become fully apparent as early as 1985, but India had entered an era in which the re-election of any state or national government was an extreme rarity. At the nine national elections between 1977 and 2004, ruling parties or alliances have been thrown out seven times. And at state elections across the country since 1980, they have been ousted about 70 per cent of the time. If we exclude West Bengal (where, uniquely, re-election has been the norm for a quarter-century) from the latter calculation, the figure for ruling parties or alliances being ousted in state elections approaches 90 per cent. This is a spectacularly high figure in any democracy.

We see, then, that despite the pro-Congress emotional surge after the assassination of Indira Gandhi, it was rejected in Karnataka in early 1985. In a mere nine weeks between the Congress sweep in the parliamentary election of 1984 and this state election, 105 of 224 assembly constituencies swung from the Congress to the Janata Party.[10] This was, and remains, astonishing. Only a sophisticated, discerning electorate could produce such a colossal swing. In the years since then, we have seen abundant evidence of Indian voters' sophistication, for example, from how they split tickets when state and national elections occur simultaneously, or when they single out offensive ministers for special humiliation. But this first became vividly apparent in Karnataka in 1985.

The 1985 state election was important for one other reason. It entrenched, and made permanent, multiparty competition in Karnataka. There would, henceforth, be no going back to one-party dominance, ensuring that voters would have a genuine choice in every subsequent election.

---

[10] E. Raghavan developed these calculations at the time.

9

A Government Like Any Other?

During their first two years in power between 1983 and 1985, the Janata Party's minority government and its Chief Minister had constantly faced the possibility of sudden political extinction. The election victory of 1985 eased this pressure and caused Hegde to relax somewhat. It also made him a potential national leader. This was a potent distraction from the management of state-level affairs and, together with his more relaxed approach as the head of a now secure majority in the state legislature, it made him prone to lapses of judgement, leading his government into avoidable embarrassments. It had suffered them earlier too. The bungled attempt to engineer the defection of a Congress legislator with an offer of a cabinet post, noted in Chapter 7, had been an egregious example. But as missteps and troubles now mounted, people increasingly came to see this supposedly 'values-based government' as something altogether more ordinary and less inspiring than what they had earlier thought it to be — a government like any other.

Hegde Asserts Himself — Briefly

Hegde's election as leader of the Janata legislature party on 8 March was a mere formality. No one, not even Deve Gowda or Bommai, contemplated a contest. His senior colleagues concentrated instead on lobbying for the second, third or fourth position in the government. The legislature party meeting was therefore a subdued affair, and the central party observer, Madhu Dandavate, had little role to play except to formally declare that Hegde had been unanimously elected. As president of the state unit of the party, Deve Gowda made a speech, acknowledging that Hegde's leadership had made the victory possible. But if this was a decidedly tame beginning, there was plenty of drama waiting to unfold, although no one except Hegde had an inkling of it.

As soon as he had been elected, it was announced that the swearing-in ceremony would be conducted not at Raj Bhavan, but on the steps of the Vidhana Souda (the state assembly building) — a departure from tradition. Hegde took his cue from NTR of Andhra Pradesh who, in 1983, had had the swearing-in held at a stadium to enable a large crowd to take part.

Hegde summoned senior leaders for consultation in his chambers. All of them assumed that they would automatically find cabinet berths, but he told them that he needed time to think this through. For this reason, he had decided that only two others, Rachaiah and Nazirsab, would be inducted the next day along with him. In doing this, he was sending a message, especially to Deve Gowda and Bommai, who had altered the list of candidates without consulting him, that he was now his own master. He was also signalling that he would prefer to depend less on the Lingayats and Vokkaligas, and to cultivate a much broader constituency. He did so by picking Nazirsab, a Muslim, but more to the point, a leader whose credentials were stronger that those of others, and Rachaiah, a Scheduled Caste leader. He knew very well that caste would inevitably need to be taken into account, and that a balance had to be struck between the land-owning castes who dominated village life and the others. But this was his day, and if he could settle one or two scores while creating an impression of refreshing change, why not?

Hegde's suggestion was not to anyone's liking, but J. H. Patel immediately accepted it.[1] He felt slighted, but was pleased to see Deve Gowda and Bommai visibly angered after their recent indiscipline. Both of them pointedly said that it was improper of Hegde to keep leaders as senior as they were out of the ministry even for a day. But Hegde did not budge.

Among those affected, Bommai suffered the most. He had been number two in the previous government, and his exclusion implied that he no longer retained the second most important position in the government. This sweetened the pill for Deve Gowda. As long as Bommai was denied that position, it did not matter greatly if he himself had to suffer a bit.

When the swearing-in began on the massive steps of the Vidhana Souda at around 4 p.m., a huge crowd had gathered for their first glimpse of such a ceremony. The Governor first administered the oath to Hegde, and then Rachaiah and Nazirsab were summoned to take their oaths together. Nearly everyone was shocked that senior leaders such as

---

[1] He was a Lingayat but, like Nazirsab (a Muslim), he was less closely associated in the public mind with his social group than with a political orientation. Both were socialists, and Nazirsab was also associated with the provision of basic services at the village level and with democratic decentralisation.

Bommai and Deve Gowda had not been called to take oaths. The two of them sat on the steps along with a few journalists and, while they said nothing, the expressions on their faces were easily read.

Hegde had seldom asserted himself as he did now, but whatever gains he made were short-lived. He did not clip Deve Gowda's and Bommai's wings further. Had Urs found himself in Hegde's shoes, he would have made both cool their heels for a spell, and even after taking them into the ministry, he would have given them portfolios that offered little clout. It would not have been impossible to deal more forcefully with them, particularly when the election results (for which Hegde could claim most of the credit) were fresh in everyone's mind. Deve Gowda's influence among the Vokkaligas, and Bommai's among the Lingayats had not been especially evident in this election. Both had struggled to win their seats, and the former would probably have lost in Holenarsipur had the Congress given a ticket to his old protégé, Puttaswamy Gowda. Both men were patently senior, but neither had developed a firm support base across the state. (Deve Gowda achieved this only later through much hard work and the assiduous cultivation of key interests.)

But Hegde lacked Urs's killer instinct, and this small episode turned out, in retrospect, to be his first political mistake in the new term. He then compounded his error by failing to remain acutely wary of Deve Gowda and Bommai after having publicly snubbed them. For ignoring this fundamental principle of statecraft, he eventually paid a price. For this and other reasons, the Janata Party government was to face rough seas until it eventually collapsed under the weight of internal contradictions in 1989.

Sowing the Seeds of Future Troubles

In the week following his swearing-in, Hegde expanded the ministry, adding 26 ministers, of which 14 held the junior rank of Ministers of State. He thus reduced his cabinet's strength from 34 (in his first term) to 29. Now that he was not running a minority government and was no longer at the mercy of individual legislators, he could afford to be tough. His team included seven Vokkaligas, six Lingayats, seven from the Backward Classes, six from the Scheduled Castes, two Brahmins, one Reddy (who should actually be included among the Vokkaligas), and one Muslim.

Hegde got the social composition of the cabinet more or less right, but he had not summoned the courage to drop some who had performed poorly in the previous government. On the other hand, junior ministers like M. P. Prakash and Sindhia, who had performed impressively, remained at the same level. To maintain a balance between the dominant castes and others, he gave some junior ministers independent charge of departments. Some not-so-efficient seniors, kept on account of caste or regional compulsions, were given such light responsibilities that they were disappointed, as were the juniors who had not been promoted. Hegde had pleased almost no one. At this early stage, none of them expressed public displeasure or took precipitate action. Indeed, it would have been politically unwise to tackle a leader fresh from an electoral victory, but resentments had begun simmering.

Within a few months, however, Hegde's luck began to run out. Between 1985 and the time he left office, he was beset by troubles, including both alleged and actual scandals. His administration, which had earned quite a good name during its first two years, began to run downhill. The unusual cohesion which the fear of collapse had enforced within his former minority government now vanished since the Janata Party's clear majority had removed anxieties about a sudden toppling.

From mid-1985 onwards, it appeared as if nearly everyone was only interested in self-preservation, and that they failed to see that this was impossible if the collective good was disregarded. The Chief Minister unwittingly helped to create the conditions for the prevalence of such an attitude within the government. Hegde was many things at the same time: intelligent, sophisticated, articulate, and scheming. His urbane ways naturally won him many admirers. But two traits of his created major problems. First, although he felt genuine personal warmth towards almost everyone he dealt with, there were many who thought it was a ruse. This impression gained credence from his habit (in his official capacity) of keeping a certain distance even from those who were completely trusting, so that many wondered whether he could be depended on in a crisis. Second, he was often too indulgent with colleagues.

Apart from all this, Hegde was also a media star. Magazines like *India Today*, *Sunday* and other glossies portrayed him in soft-focus and attributed to him virtues and values which he probably did not possess. Like any other politician, he enjoyed this attention. And like many leaders from the south, he also had a complex about being a state-level leader whose potential role beyond his state was going un-recognised. Hegde was not the first leader from Karnataka to suffer from this. Before him Urs too had nursed hopes of becoming a national-level leader, and Gundu Rao certainly thought that he was on his way to becoming one, until people back home ended his career. Hegde's ambitions were partially fuelled by the national media which claimed that he was prime ministerial material and, in a typically flippant and unhelpful fashion, began to ask whether he was a bigger and better leader than the Janata president at the national level, Chandra Shekhar. As we shall see in the chapters which follow, these speculations eventually led to trouble.

Moreover, because Hegde assiduously cultivated the national press, he antagonised many local journalists, who concluded that half of what he did was a sham or a gimmick. This would also become a major prob-lem, but their distrust took time to crystallise. For the present, Hegde's honeymoon with the people continued apace.

A 'Values-Based Government' Encounters Ambiguity

A change within the Congress created acute strains between the ruling party and the main opposition. Bangarappa was made leader of the Congress legislature party, and thus became the official leader of the opposition. He was imposed by the party's national leaders, against the wishes of most Congress legislators, because the former knew of Bangarappa's pathological hatred for Hegde, and expected him to go hammer and tongs at the Chief Minister. He did not disappoint. Every time he opened his mouth in the assembly, he poured scorn on the Chief Minister, so much so that after a while, Hegde dropped all attempts at civility and reciprocated the sentiment. At the very first opportunity in the legislature, Bangarappa once again charged Hegde with having made Rs one crore[2] in a liquor deal with a party in Kerala on the eve of the election. The debate that followed was, to put it mildly, extremely acrimonious. Hegde denied the charge but, to establish the credentials of the government, ordered a judicial inquiry into the so-called deal. A couple of years later, the inquiry cleared him of this charge.

As this was happening, A. K. Subbaiah (a maverick who had been bitterly critical of the Congress for the best part of his life, but later

---

[2] Ten million rupees.

became sympathetic to it after he too developed a deep loathing of Hegde) alleged that just before the elections, the Janata government had collected money from housing co-operatives with a promise to clear their proposals for the acquisition and distribution of sites. Hegde sought to deny this too, but he did not agree to subject it to an inquiry. Instead, he asked Subbaiah to place it before the Lokayukta, a statutory body to look into corruption and the misuse of office. Subbaiah did so, found fault with the Lokayukta's procedures and, out of frustration, stopped pursuing the case. The allegation, however, resurfaced from time to time throughout Hegde's tenure, and an official committee finally found that the government had allowed many co-operative societies to violate the law.

The problem for Hegde was not that all these allegations were true, but that they undermined the image that he sought to project. In one of his first encounters with the press after the election, he promised to provide a 'values-based government'. This promise tended to magnify the impact of even minor cases of malfeasance, or mere allegations, which in any other circumstance would have been largely ignored.

There was certainly a contradiction between what Hegde preached and what he and others in his government practiced. Corruption had not, and probably could not, come to a grinding halt. It is difficult to quantify the level of corruption with any precision, but it is almost certain that the Janata government, both before the 1985 election and in the first two years or so of its new term, was much less corrupt than the Gundu Rao regime.

Both Gundu Rao's and Urs's governments had been corrupt, but no one made much of it because they had offered no promises of probity. But under Hegde, the issue became acutely sensitive because he wanted everyone to believe that he was lily white. For many, both in and out of politics, disenchantment with him began at this stage.

These allegations of corruption — some of which had substance — remind us of a glaring irony in the story that we stress in this book. Urs and Hegde were responsible for a largely constructive transformation in the politics of Karnataka, but they also presided over high levels of corruption, which surged during the Urs years. This merits condemnation, but we also need to examine, when assessing corruption among these and nearly all other Indian politicians, the *uses* that the illicitly raised funds were put to. Chief Ministers of Indian states manipulate systems of corruption for six main purposes:

(a) self-enrichment,
(b) funding election campaigns,
(c) payments to their parties at the national level,
(d) payments to important political actors within their states,
(e) payments to important social groups within their states, and
(f) as a distraction, to keep important political actors from interfering in policymaking.

When we consider each of these in turn, we encounter some surprising complexities. The first two motivations in this list should be seen, for different reasons, in an entirely negative light.

(a) There can be no doubt the fact that the use of illicit funds for self-enrichment is utterly reprehensible, and we do not think that this requires explaining.

(b) Corrupt acts to raise resources for election campaigns are not just morally objectionable but, to make matters worse, they are almost entirely *pointless*, because money does not win elections in India. This point is not difficult to prove. Parties in power always have far greater opportunities to raise money illegally than do parties in opposition, because they have far more influence to sell. Therefore, parties in power almost always go into election campaigns with more money than their opponents. *And yet*, at five of the six national elections in India before 2009, and at over 70 per cent of state elections since 1980, the parties in power have been thrown out by voters. If money decided elections, this would not have happened. India's voters are far too sophisticated to be swayed by lavish campaign spending. They cheerfully accept the gifts and payments that parties hand out, but decide how to vote based on the merits of the competing parties.

The use of illicit funds for the other four purposes are usually thoroughly objectionable, but not always. Consider the following:

(c) Nearly all ruling parties at the state level in India which have ties to national parties face pressure from their national leaders to provide payments to fund national-level activities. This is always an unsavoury business, but such payments can sometimes serve constructive purposes. Urs regularly sent massive contributions to Indira Gandhi, in part to prevent her and her hare-brained son Sanjay from interfering destructively in state-level affairs. These payments were crucial in ensuring that the Gandhis never inquired very closely into Urs's implementation of Emergency measures. This enabled him to send false reports of large numbers of sterilisations, so that the people of Karnataka were spared this outrage.[3] Hegde's payments to the Janata Party's national leaders, while the Congress held power in New Delhi during the 1980s, helped to ensure that multiparty competition would be sustained in India.

(d) Payments made by Chief Ministers to important political actors within their states is again an objectionable practice. But Urs made use of them to enable penniless politicians from disadvantaged groups to establish themselves and, thus, to prevent moneyed Lingayats and Vokkaligas from using their resources to re-establish dominant-caste rule at the state level. Hegde used such payments to prevent legislators from his minority government, between 1983 and 1985, from being bribed to defect by Congress opponents. In this way he kept his minority government afloat and ensured that multiparty competition survived in Karnataka.

(e) The provision of illicit funds to social groups is also morally repugnant, but Urs made use of these to bankroll caste associations for low-status groups in order to strengthen their collective capacity to withstand efforts by the Lingayats and Vokkaligas to take back control of state-level politics.

(f) It is also objectionable to see Chief Ministers permitting their subordinates to enrich themselves. But both Urs and Hegde did so in order to distract these people and prevent them from scuttling constructive policies that both were implementing. Urs had numerous Lingayat and Vokkaliga ministers and legislators in his camp who were unhappy with his policies meant to benefit and empower disadvantaged groups. By enabling them to engage in private profiteering, he prevented them from thwarting his constructive initiatives. Hegde used the same technique, between

---

[3] Urs made this point in some detail in interviews with James Manor between 1978 and 1980.

1983 and 1985, to prevent subordinates from defecting to the Congress, and from opposing the empowerment of panchayats — which most legislators and ministers wanted to do.[4]

The comments above are not intended to justify corruption, but they indicate that this issue is complex and ambiguous and that it requires subtle analysis.

Hegde's government soon, and quite inevitably, faced further embarrassments. Less than a week after Subbaiah's allegation about housing co-operatives, the newly appointed chief whip of the Janata Party, C. Rajavardhan, was accused of practicing bigamy (which is illegal). A young woman claimed that he had married her and she had borne him a child, but that he had subsequently abandoned them both. Charges of bigamy were not new in Karnataka's politics. Many leaders had allegedly practiced it before and when it came to public attention, they had stepped down. Although the chief whip denied the charge, several magazines wrote colourful copy about him, and the issue finally figured in the assembly itself. Many thought that he should resign. Two ministers in Urs's government had been forced out of office when allegations linking them with women had been made. Women's organisations took up the cause of the 'second wife', and demonstrations against Rajavardhan were organised.

The response of the political establishment to this episode is worth noting, since it indicates the double standards politicians often applied to their own conduct. Within the Congress, which could have made much of the controversy, there were many who thought that unnecessary noise was being made because Rajavardhan belonged to the Scheduled Castes. Many Scheduled Caste leaders, notably the influential Congressman Basavalingappa, thought Rajavardhan should be rescued. Basavalingappa's argument was that there were at least three senior politicians in the assembly who unabashedly practiced bigamy. There were probably several other legislators who practiced it but went scot-free because they were less prominent and their private lives were largely

---

[4] These are not isolated cases. For example, Digvijay Singh, Chief Minister of Madhya Pradesh between 1993 and 2003, permitted ministers and legislators to enrich themselves in order to distract them from opposing progressive policies which he sought to implement. This is examined in detail in Melo, Ng'ethe and Manor (forthcoming).

unknown. He asked why, when members of the dominant castes could openly indulge in bigamy and get away with it, Rajavardhan should be made a scapegoat. For this reason, and because the Congress did not wish to see some of its own leaders accused, the matter was allowed to die down. But despite that, this episode caused some damage to the ruling party — again, because it stood in stark contrast to Hegde's promise of a 'values-based government'.

In the short period between 1983 and the Janata Party's extraordinary victory in the state election in early 1985, Hegde had become one of the most formidable Chief Ministers seen anywhere in India since independence. This was especially remarkable because, unlike most other potent Chief Ministers, he had no personal base in a numerically powerful social group or in an important region of his state. His rise was based instead on two other things. First, he had demonstrated an unrivalled mastery of the art of political *presentation*, that is, of finding just the right words and postures at any given moment, to turn events to his and his party's advantage. Of several hundred politicians at the national level and in over 20 Indian states, interviewed by one of us over the last 35 years, Hegde was one of the two most articulate.[5] Second, he had been consistently brilliant in his political *judgement*. It is difficult to identify a single instance in that initial phase in office when Hegde put a foot wrong.

However, when he promised a 'values-based government' in his second term, his skills on both fronts — political presentation and political judgement — deserted him. It was as if, after dazzling people with his presentational gifts on so many occasions, he felt driven to offer people yet another incandescent moment. This was entirely unnecessary. The Janata Party's triumph in the state election so soon after the Congress had obtained a brute majority in the Lok Sabha was seen by most observers across India, and by many within Karnataka, as something of a miracle.

Many of his previous public statements had been brilliant precisely because they were low-key and because he avoided overblown rhetoric. This style had marked him out as a different kind of Indian politician. In the immediate aftermath of this election, it would have sufficed to offer a modest assurance that he and his team would do the best they

---

[5] This is based on James Manor's interviews with leaders since 1971.

could. But by promising something spectacular, like a 'values-based government', he had set himself an impossible standard. Even if his government continued to perform as impressively as it had in its first two years (and it did not), it would be seen to have fallen short. This 'tall promise' of moral purity had the effect of undermining the accurate perception that his government was morally superior to the Gundu Rao regime, which was, in fact, one of the main pillars of its popularity and legitimacy.

Hegde thus violated a fundamental rule that all adroit politicians understand: it is unwise, indeed dangerous, to create unrealistic expectations. When ambiguities and untoward events afflict a government, as they always do, such expectations inevitably lead to popular disillusionment, posing grave threats to those in power.

Hegde, who was well read in the literature on statecraft, might have recalled former British Prime Minister Harold Macmillan's views on the subject: when asked why his government did not provide more moral leadership, Macmillan replied that people should look to archbishops rather than political leaders for moral inspiration. Politicians and governments could not hope to provide it because they inevitably became entangled in ambiguities. They had to make tough choices between competing interests and competing moral imperatives. This led, inescapably, to the perception among many observers that they had compromised on issues of right and wrong. It was a lesson that should have been heeded by his moralistic successors, Margaret Thatcher and Tony Blair, by American presidents, and by Hegde. On this occasion, Hegde's much-vaunted political judgement deserted him. He had fashioned a rod for his own back.

'Populism' — Or Rather, Programmes for Disadvantaged Groups

None of these issues seriously dented the image of the government at this early stage. If proof were needed, it came in two by-elections. Deve Gowda, who had won from two constituencies, resigned at Sathanur. Another seat fell vacant when its Janata Party legislator died. The Janata Party managed to retain boths seats in the by-elections held in late April.

In May, a few days before Hegde went for rest and voice therapy to Kodaikanal, his Education Minister, Raghupathy, announced a massive scheme to distribute free textbooks to nearly half a million children at a cost of about Rs 4 crore.[6] A similar scheme for distribution of free uniforms to children followed. Both schemes were based on recommendations of a think tank — the Economic Planning Council — established by the government. It met frequently and addressed specific issues in the social sectors. These schemes were based on the premise that such inducements would bring down school dropout rates. Subsequent studies indicated that some success had been achieved both in improving attendance and reducing dropout rates.

Two later schemes provided a pair of sarees and dhotis at subsidised rates to families with annual incomes below Rs 3,600, and subsidised foodgrains to those below the poverty line. The subsidy components in both cases were quite high. All these initiatives, and others such as maternity allowances for daily wage earners in the unorganised sector, were scoffed at for being populist.

Hegde disagreed. He argued that while wage earners in the organised sector[7] were partially insulated from inflation, since their wages included an index-linked dearness allowance, the unorganised sector got little. As he put it:

> First of all, the statutory minimum wages for the unorganised sector cannot be strictly enforced, even though they are prescribed under law. Second, since even the statutory minimum wage does not take into account the inflation rate, the daily wage earners end up paying more and more for their daily necessities. Our schemes are meant to protect them to some extent from the vagaries of price increases of essential articles.

His preference for such schemes was based on his own experience, particularly as Finance and Planning Minister in the Congress-led state governments during the 1960s. Hegde had begun as an advocate of massive developmental projects, which had consumed a substantial portion of the state government's meagre resources. Irrigation and power projects were special priorities in that era. It took him many years to understand that such investments mainly benefited the land-owning elite. He had also seen during the Urs years that programmes costing far less than major development projects, but aimed specifically at poorer

---

[6] 40 million rupees.

[7] The minority of workers who belonged to unions and who, therefore, enjoyed strong legal protection.

groups, made a far greater impact on their lives. On the advice of the government's think tank, he decided to direct substantial resources to the social sectors.

Such schemes may be 'populist', but as analysts have demonstrated in more recent times, if carefully designed, they ease poverty. They also yielded quick results, which helped the Janata Party to make headway in its efforts to win the support of the disadvantaged groups which Urs had drawn into politics a decade earlier. Also, since Hegde associated himself closely with these programmes, they also added to his own already immense popularity.

This caused acute concern within the Congress. Thanks to Indira Gandhi's early promises to abolish poverty, followed by Urs's impressive efforts in that vein, the Congress had come to think of the poor and unorganised as its vote bank. Now it faced a shrewd rival who was out to hijack this constituency. Congressmen could not criticise Hegde's programmes too severely because doing so would give him and his colleagues the opportunity to claim that the Congress was anti-poor. So Congressmen picked holes in the schemes without opposing them outright.

They found a useful ally in Deve Gowda, even though he never made common cause with them. He was very concerned about the implications of these programmes for his core constituency — the Vokkaligas of southern Karnataka.[8] Since most Vokkaligas own and cultivate land,[9] their interest lay in maximising agricultural production. For this, irrigation was crucial, and Deve Gowda's knowledge of the topic was immense. When he had led the opposition during the tenures of Urs and Gundu Rao, he had displayed a deeper understanding of irrigation than the ministers in charge of this portfolio. As Minister for Irrigation in Hegde's cabinet, he brought his vast expertise to bear and ran the department very efficiently.

He realised that allocations for the social sector, even if they were moderate in size, would divert resources from irrigation and, thereby, from his constituency. Hegde publicly pledged that social programmes

---

[8] Almost all Vokkaligas reside in southern Karnataka. Lingayats are found mainly in the north, although sizeable pockets can also be found in certain southern districts.

[9] The term 'Vokkaliga' literally means 'those who thresh'.

would not erode funding for irrigation, but failed to convince Deve Gowda. In August 1985, the latter openly criticised the social programmes, even though, as a minister in Hegde's government, he had been party to the decision to implement them. This breach of the principle of collective responsibility forced Hegde and his loyalists to defend their policy, not just in the teeth of criticism from the opposition but from within as well.

Deve Gowda continued to run down these programmes as long as he was a minister. This suited him, since among land-owning Vokkaligas, and even landed Lingayats, he emerged as a champion. In private, he used every occasion to poke fun at Hegde and his pet programmes. When legislators pleaded for funds for irrigation or for interventions to expedite sanctioned work delayed for want of funds, he pleaded helplessness and, in bitterly sarcastic terms, told them to take their cases to 'the Brahmin'. He consciously adopted the posture of being a 'son of the soil', to stress the contrast with the 'Brahmin intellectual' whose ambitions to be a national-level politician were damaging the interests of the state.

For all his pretensions of being a simple village politician, Deve Gowda was an extremely shrewd operator, capable of anticipating events and preparing meticulously to face them. He rightly sensed that the massive mandate their party had won would heighten expectations and, since no government or leader could satisfy every interest, disenchantment was bound to grow. He bided his time, allowing legislators' frustrations to build. When they did, he first indirectly and then directly encouraged them to snipe at Hegde. For the time being, this could achieve little since Hegde's popular image and his control over the party and the government remained strong. However, Deve Gowda was a patient man, and not one to concede defeat easily.

Allegations of Scandal

Now that Hegde's government had begun to encounter inevitable ambiguities, his adversaries in the opposition could attack him with far less restraint. Bangarappa's caustic comments in the assembly were a painful nuisance, but the Chief Minister soon encountered much more troubling attacks from the maverick Subbaiah, who had developed a deep personal animus for him. Subbaiah had a formidable reputation for his sharp mind and ferocious unwillingness to strike deals with those in power. Urs had once remarked that he was one of only two politicians who never sought a personal favour from him during his spell in power. Subbaiah delved meticulously and relentlessly into every action of Hegde's, seeking to sow doubts about his lily-white image.

Several exposes ensued. Apart from the aforementioned housing co-operative scandal, Subbaiah also alleged the misuse of office by Revenue Minister V. L. Patil who had reportedly twisted the arms of applicants in a land reforms case to which he was a party. In October 1985, he dropped a much bigger bombshell. He accused Hegde's only son, Bharat, and his cousin of collecting Rs 2.5 lakh[10] from the daughter of a coffee planter, with a promise to secure her a postgraduate medical seat in a private college.

This allegation assumed serious proportions, as unlike the earlier charges against him, this touched Hegde's family. The deal, if there was one, would have remained a secret if the lady had secured the seat. But her father approached Subbaiah when she did not and the money was allegedly not returned. The father had tried to file a police complaint, but he found that officers were reluctant to pursue the case. He then approached Subbaiah who, after he was convinced that there was truth in the unsubstantiated allegation, went public. The charges sent shock waves through political circles. Not many believed them, but since such cases were not uncommon in the prevailing political culture, few were prepared to dismiss them.

Hegde stoutly denied the allegation. 'The law will take its course and if my son is guilty, he will be punished', he said. He did not stop at this. Within two days, he persuaded the cabinet to agree to set up a judicial inquiry in order to prove that he was setting high standards of probity, and to establish that his promise of a 'values-based government' was not a hollow slogan. This decision enhanced his image considerably, since it was not often that politicians willingly exposed themselves or close relatives to such scrutiny. People also assumed that Hegde would not have dared to set up the inquiry if the charges were genuine.

Before long, however, the Congress leader Moily fired another salvo. He alleged that the Andhra Pradesh government was constructing a massive irrigation system in the Krishna river basin in violation of the award given by an inter-state river waters tribunal which allocated

---

[10] 250,000 rupees.

specific quantities of Krishna waters to Andhra Pradesh, Karnataka and Maharashtra. His main target was not, however, the Andhra Pradesh government. Moily sought to establish that the Andhra Chief Minister, NTR, would not have taken this action without tacit approval from his ally Hegde.

Both Hegde and Deve Gowda (who held the Irrigation portfolio) promptly denied the charge. The Karnataka government had, in fact, lodged a strong protest against the Andhra Pradesh project. But when the issue figured in the legislature and in debates outside, Hegde appeared to be less strident than expected in his criticism of Andhra. This was exploited to the hilt by Moily and other Congressmen who cleverly sought to draw a distinction between Deve Gowda's commitment to the state and Hegde's ambitions to figure in national politics, which would be served by cordial ties to the Andhra Pradesh Chief Minister. Such devices to drive a wedge between him and Hegde suited Deve Gowda, since they showed Hegde in a poor light.

For reasons that are not totally clear, Hegde consistently refused to be extremely critical of NTR. It was well known that he was capable of exceedingly sharp reactions when they were called for. NTR had always treated Hegde with great respect, and it is likely that Hegde did not want to cross swords with another non-Congress leader in the south. He may also have calculated that he would require NTR's support at a future date. These things probably explain his mild approach during this controversy.

Conflict with Deve Gowda

What Hegde probably did not anticipate was that Deve Gowda's stock was rising. It was around this time that Deve Gowda began to press for the commitment of much larger sums of money to complete on-going irrigation schemes to utilise Karnataka's share of waters from the Krishna and in the Cauvery basin, where another dispute between Karnataka and Tamil Nadu remained unresolved.

It was also in this context that Deve Gowda began criticising the government's populist programmes, both inside and outside the legislature. As far as he was concerned, irrigation required top priority. A commitment to the poor and workers in the unorganised sectors could wait. He often cited the example of Andhra Pradesh which had diverted massive funds to construct the Nagarjunasagar Dam, and emphasised the need for similar action by Karnataka.

There were other reasons for Deve Gowda's discontent. During the first two years of Janata Party rule, Hegde had never failed to consult him and to be guided by his advice. But now the Chief Minister had begun to rely heavily on the government's think tank. And the list of those consulted on all major issues included not just Deve Gowda and Bommai, but Nazirsab, J. H. Patel and sometimes Rachaiah. Hegde had also come to depend on several junior ministers who, inspired by his confidence in them, began announcing policy decisions before the issues had been discussed in the cabinet or with the Chief Minister. This reached a point where Hegde had to upbraid them and ask them to desist. All of this naturally left Deve Gowda feeling aggrieved.

He correctly concluded that there was a deliberate attempt to sideline Vokkaliga ministers and ignore Vokkaliga interests — interests that should have been a key concern of the government. Since almost all Vokkaliga ministers had been appointed at his behest, he was in a position to influence, even control, them. Resentments eventually surfaced at a couple of meetings of the Vokkaliga lobby to discuss perceived injuries meted out by Hegde or his trusted lieutenants. These meetings remained a secret for a while, until it was decided to invite all Vokkaliga legislators for detailed discussions. By the time this larger group met for the second time, resentments over perceived neglect and raw treatment had sharpened sufficiently for a sharp, precipitate reaction to be considered.

The entire Vokkaliga membership in the Janata legislature party was invited for a dinner at a junior minister's residence. According to a source who attended, Deve Gowda and others were quite critical of Hegde for encouraging non-Vokkaliga ministers and not treating Vokkaliga ministers in the same fashion. Some of them vented their spleen on Rachaiah, Raghupathy and Laxmisagar in particular. These targets were not chosen at random. There were Lingayat ministers who were guilty of whatever Rachaiah, Raghupathy and Laxmisagar were guilty of. But these three were chosen because they represented non-dominant castes and therefore could not rely on a strong caste lobby to retaliate on their behalf. Had the Vokkaliga lobby taken on, for example, Lingayats like J. H. Patel or Bommai, the consequences would have been very serious, since the Lingayat lobby would certainly have reacted sharply.

There was also a widespread feeling that all Vokkaliga ministers should offer to resign as a mark of protest. But the idea was dropped since it was recognised that it would do more harm than good. An important objective had in any case been achieved in the creation of solidarity among Vokkaliga legislators, which could be used to press Hegde for a greater share of the spoils.

The plan came unstuck when details of what transpired at the dinner meeting were discussed in the legislature lobbies and reported in the newspapers. The next day the issue was promptly raised in the state's Upper House by a Congress member, K. N. Nage Gowda. It was widely rumoured that he had raised the issue, which was of no consequence to the legislature, at the instance of the Vokkaliga lobby in the Janata Party, in order to provide an opportunity to Deve Gowda and others to set the record straight. Hegde responded by asserting that there was absolutely no danger to the ministry. But Deve Gowda did some plain speaking:

> If Hegde sits and discusses issues with Khadri Shamanna [a senior journalist and member of the Upper House who was quite close to Hegde] and B. K. Chandrashekhar [another confidant of Hegde in that House, and like Shamanna and Hegde, a Brahmin], no one describes it as a Brahmin conclave, but when some of us sit and discuss issues that we think are important, it is described as a Vokkaliga conclave.

He implied that there was a conspiracy among the so-called Brahmin intellectuals to portray him as a leader who could not rise above Vokkaliga interests. Ultimately, the dinner meeting had little impact because of the exposure it received. Some Vokkaliga legislators were at pains to explain that it had not been organised to challenge Hegde, but as an attempt at pressure tactics.

The unexpected beneficiary of this entire episode was the Lingayat lobby. In order to capitalise on the discomfiture of the Vokkaligas, Lingayat legislators, led primarily by J. H. Patel, held an informal but well-publicised meeting at the residence of a junior minister considered close to Hegde and Patel. Bommai, who was consulted beforehand, blessed the idea, since it gave Lingayat legislators an opportunity to demonstrate their strength without damaging the government's image. It was billed from the outset, in constrast to the Vokkaliga conclave, as a meeting in support of Hegde. Bommai, Patel and others went out of their way to deny that the Lingayat gathering was intended to act as a pressure group. Nothing much transpired at the dinner, but in the long run, it served an extremely important objective. The message broadcast was that Janata's Lingayat legislators would stand by Hegde at all costs. Some members even expressed anxiety about the occasional comments that Hegde made about wanting to move to politics at the national level before his full term elapsed.

These comments had naturally persuaded Deve Gowda and Bommai to position themselves as Hegde's successors, should he depart. But they adopted sharply contrasting strategies. Deve Gowda appeared to be in greater hurry than Bommai. He sought to build a strong lobby, first among the Vokkaligas and later among legislators who had become disenchanted with Hegde. Bommai stayed close to Hegde and culti-vated the pro-Hegde lobby, while simultaneously nurturing Lingayat legislators without ever giving the impression of indulging in group pol-itics. Both leaders made considerable headway. As months passed and more and more legislators grew wary of Hegde, they looked to Deve Gowda, who readily offered sympathy and long-term protection. Those who remained loyal to Hegde naturally relied upon Bommai.

Hegde did surprisingly little to tackle problems that had the potential to snowball and overwhelm him. In private conversations, he told Raghavan more than once that he no longer found his office attractive or challenging. He had tired of the routines of administration and of grappling with the petty politics that had become the order of the day. Legislators were now freed of the anxieties that they had felt between 1983 and 1985, when the government was a minority one, leading to fears that it might be toppled at any moment. Moreover, the new government's hold on power was bolstered further by a new anti-defection law passed by Rajiv Gandhi's government in New Delhi which required any break-away faction to muster one-third of a party's legislators[11] — a daunting task during Hegde's post-1985 government since the Janata Party held such a large number of seats. Now that the government's survival was scarcely in doubt, the discipline and unity of purpose seen in the Janata Party's first term diminished markedly.

Legislators now threw off much of their old restraint about seeking favours from the Chief Minister. And yet, since he now felt less compelled to keep legislators happy lest they defect, Hegde did less than in his first

---

[11] Defectors who mustered less than one-third would be stripped of their seats, so they would have to recontest in by-elections.

term to respond to them. This inspired rising levels of frustration among the legislators, opening the way for increasingly troublesome factional conflict.

The Arrack Bottling Controversy

There was only one occasion between 1985 and 1989 when Janata Party leaders and legislators achieved unanimity. This was in February 1986, when the Karnataka High Court cancelled the award of arrack[12] bottling contracts to people who allegedly had close ties to Janata Party leaders. This triggered a major controversy.

Until the mid-1980s, arrack vending rights had been auctioned district-by-district, and contractors who bid successfully secured the rights to sell arrack in retail outlets. After the infamous hooch tragedy in 1981, in which over 300 people had died after consuming illicit liquor (not arrack, which was far safer) bought from bootleggers (see Manor 1993b), a judicial inquiry had recommended that arrack be sold in tamper-proof bottles to prevent adulteration.

Hegde decided to deny bottling contracts to those who were already engaged in the liquor trade. Ministers claimed that they wanted to encourage new entrepreneurs, but their real motive was to deprive major liquor barons, most of whom strongly supported Bangarappa, of opportunities. However, the government failed to follow proper pro-cedures set out in the Excise Act, when it selected eight bidders out of 131 applicants. An additional factor was that none of the eight chosen had the resources to set up bottling plants on their own.

The award of the contracts was promptly challenged through public interest litigation, in which specific charges were levelled against Hegde, but were later withdrawn. When the High Court struck down the award, Hegde found that even some old allies were unwilling to support him. The CPI, for example, termed it a black mark against the ruling party. The Congress and the BJP called for the resignation of the government. An added inconvenience was that the verdict came while the legislature was in session.

This issue arose in the assembly the next morning, but the government asked for time since, it claimed, it did not have a copy of the judgement. Late that evening, Hegde called in his senior colleagues for

---

[12] A strong, distilled alcoholic drink.

a strategy session. They concluded that the Congress challenge could be squarely resisted, since the verdict said nothing about the personal involvement of either Hegde or other ministers in the award of contracts. Many decisions of the government are challenged and set aside by the High Court, and it was argued that every such instance did not represent moral failure.

Deve Gowda, to the surprise of some, offered to defend the government on the floor of the House when the issue arose again the following day. Everyone readily agreed for two reasons. First, Hegde was personally on the defensive since he had held the Excise portfolio when the contracts were awarded. Deve Gowda, on the other hand, would not be inhibited by such considerations since he had nothing to do with the contracts. Moreover, everyone acknowledged his debating skills. Though not a great orator, he had trained himself over the years to marshal facts and arguments very tellingly on any issue.

When a Congress adjournment motion was taken up, Deve Gowda led for the government. Hegde refused to comply with the Congress's demand that he quit, asserting that he would have stepped down if the High Court had indicted the government or if there was any suggestion indicating the government for corruption or nepotism or even loss of revenue. After Deve Gowda successfully made the government's case, the adjournment motion was disallowed, forcing Congressmen to stage a *dharna*.[13]

But legal aspects apart, the issue simply refused to die down. The Congress repeatedly harped on Hegde's promise of a 'values-based government', to show that Hegde had feet of clay. There were heated arguments in the state's Upper House, leading to its adjournment, and a walkout in the Lower House by the Congress.

Hegde was clearly rattled since this issue had a potent moral dimension. To atone for the lapse, he wrote a confidential letter to national party president, Chandra Shekhar, offering to step down to uphold the government's moral claims, and asking him to find a replacement. Hegde did not take any senior colleagues or trusted lieutenants into his confidence to discuss this move, and the letter was sent by a special courier to Delhi. Chandra Shekhar was not in Delhi when the letter arrived, so it was delivered by Hegde's trusted personal assistant to Shekhar's

---

[13] A sit-in strike; a protest.

personal secretary. To Hegde's surprise, the letter soon found its way to the *Statesman* (a daily newspaper), which prominently published a report on it. How the letter got leaked remains a mystery, but the personal establishment of the Janata Party president had always been suspect. Hegde's loyal colleagues believed that Chandra Shekhar himself arranged the leak.

The Statesman's report hit the Karnataka state assembly like a tornado. As soon as he learnt about it, Hegde left the assembly and went to the Air Force guest house, which he often used as a hideout and, without consulting any of his colleagues, sent a formal resignation letter to the Governor, A. N. Banerjee.

When Raghavan along with Nazirsab, met him a short while later, he asked Hegde, 'What next?' 'Let us see', he replied. 'It is now for the party to decide'. What he meant was that it was up to the party to decide who should succeed him.

By this time Deve Gowda, Bommai and Patel had arrived at the guest house to check the veracity of the report in the *Statesman*. Hegde informed them of his action which left them nonplussed. Bommai, according to Nazirsab, then asked what the next course of action should be. Apparently, Patel and Nazirsab said there was no question of letting Hegde go. The High Court verdict was a setback for the government, the party, and for all of them. They felt that Hegde should not be left to bear the odium alone. He had proved a point by formally resigning. Now the party must decide his fate and, in their view, it should ask him to continue. Hegde heard them patiently but refused to budge. The others then insisted that, as a disciplined soldier of the party, he should leave the final decision to the Janata legislators.

All the legislators were in agreement with Patel and Nazirsab. They made this amply clear the following morning even before a formal meeting of the party was held. All of them, without exception, gathered at the Chief Minister's office, 'Krishna', where Hegde and a few senior leaders had gathered. They virtually *gheraoed*[14] Hegde, insisting that they would not let him step down. In their view, he was not in the wrong in the bottling case. One of them even prostrated himself before Hegde and pleaded with him. The entire drama at 'Krishna', though spontaneous, bordered on sycophancy. Legislators, however, were not ashamed

---

[14] Surrounded him to take prisoner temporarily.

of their behaviour. As one of them put it, 'All of us would feel politically safe only with Hegde at the helm. It is not only that we admire him for what he is; to us, his leadership is a compelling necessity. He simply cannot run away from us.'

It was this instinctive need for self-preservation, coupled with sympathy for the leader's moral dilemma, that propelled them unanimously to argue that offering resignation as an atonement was fine, but that it was the right of the party to direct Hegde on his next step. Even Deve Gowda agreed: 'As captain, he cannot run away. He has resigned on a moral issue. It is all right. But as a disciplined soldier of the party, he has no choice but to abide by its decision when it re-elects him.'

The following day the cabinet met without Hegde, and passed a resolution expressing faith in him and asking him to continue. The Janata legislature party formally followed suit. Hegde, meanwhile, had left for Delhi in the hope that after passions had cooled, the legislators would look beyond him. He remained adamant on the question of resignation. 'It was not an emotional decision at all. It was dictated by conscience and reason', he said. Although a full 48 hours had elapsed since he submitted his resignation, the Governor had not acted on it. He waited another 24 hours before accepting it. This was naturally resented by the Congress which formally registered its protest by submitting a memorandum to him.

Meanwhile, Bommai followed Hegde to Delhi where other Janata Party leaders were pressing Hegde to continue. Chandra Shekhar held informal consultations with Hegde and Bommai, and suggested a formula according to which Bommai and Deve Gowda would be chosen Chief Minister and Deputy Chief Minister respectively. It appears that the three leaders from Karnataka were agreeable to this arrangement. Another option that Hegde tentatively canvassed was to select Nazirsab. This naturally failed to win approval from Deve Gowda and Bommai.

Chandra Shekhar next decided to convince other senior leaders to accept his formula. He summoned Deve Gowda, J. H. Patel and Nazirsab to Delhi. Nazirsab refused to go, on the plea that his views on the matter were too well known and because he was unlikely to be convinced of any alternative to Hegde. Patel went to Delhi to argue the same line. When asked to accept the formula, he bluntly told all the leaders present that he could not accept any formula that was unacceptable to the legislators.

I told them to come to Bangalore and first convince the legislature party. Chandra Shekhar knew that was not possible. He thought that if we endorsed his formula, it would be up to us to convince the legislature party. That, however, did not work.

Following these developments,the Janata Party's national parliamentary board asked Hegde to simply accept the decision of the legislators. They met the next day and re-elected him as Chief Minister, and Hegde accepted the 'collective decision of the party, notwithstanding my own feelings'. He was sworn in that afternoon along with all the ministers in the previous cabinet.

While a full-scale crisis had blown over, Hegde felt quite uncomfortable for a while because many in the media felt that he had deliberately contrived a situation to take complete hold of the party apparatus, and especially because an influential section in the party had begun to feel disenchanted with him. He, as always, was sensitive to media criticism which, in turn, was magnified by his uncharacteristic blunder of promising a 'values-based government'. This rash promise ensured that the various allegations of malfeasance, most notably (but not only) the arrack bottling controversy, struck at popular confidence in him and his party. They had begun to appear to be a government like any other. He soon recovered from his embarrassment and inhibitions following this controversy, and for some time, things went smoothly. But before long, signs of dissidence in his party resurfaced.

10

Rampant Factionalism — and the Deepening of Democracy

Democracies sometimes present us with strange juxtapositions. Humane achievements which, very occasionally, are quite remarkable co-exist with tawdry, selfish narrow-mindedness. And the same political actors are responsible for both. Karnataka and the leaders of its Janata Party government after 1985 provide us with just such a spectacle. Tedious, small-minded factional in-fighting reached embarrassing proportions. Yet, the very leaders who engaged in factional squabbles introduced one of the most adventurous and successful experiments with democratic decentralisation in the recent history of Asia, Africa and Latin America — an experiment which carried forward the agenda of deepening democracy that Urs had done so much for a decade earlier.

Factions Clash, Hegde Blunders

Hegde knew better than anyone that his image had taken a considerable pounding because of the High Court verdict in the arrack bottling case. Regardless of all the brave talk among party colleagues, and the faith that they had unhesitatingly reposed in him, his government's actions were now as suspect as those of any of its predecessors.

Both the Janata Party and the Congress soon elected new state party presidents, and since both were mature and modest men who were not given to theatrics, it was expected that the affairs of both parties would remain low-key for a while. Within the Janata Party, however, this was not to be. Several legislators thought, some justifiably and some not, that they deserved to be ministers. They began mounting pressure on the Chief Minister for a reshuffle. In doing so, they were acting on a precedent. Only a year earlier, when 40 or so legislators had pressed Hegde, he had given some of them ministerial posts.

Taking a cue from the Vokkaliga conclave which had strongly criticised several non-Vokkaliga ministers, these legislators — they called themselves 'memorialists', because they were petitioning Hegde — wanted 12 ministers, whom they regarded as either inefficient or arrogant, to be dropped. Significantly, many of their targets were from the Backward Classes.

Equally significantly, the leadership of the 'memorialists' was provided by the dominant caste groups, notably the Lingayats.

These groups had long sought to increase their influence within the government. As they saw it, Urs's destruction of their dominance at the state level had been partially reversed, and it was only natural that they should try to consolidate their position. The Lingayats and Vokkaligas in the party had come to believe that the Backward Classes, the minorities and the Scheduled Castes had not supported the Janata Party in the last election, and they attempted to persuade others of the same. This, however, was not true. The Janata Party could not have come to power merely on the strength of Lingayat and Vokkaliga votes. If these two groups had been capable of electing governments, then Urs's Congress would not have won in 1972 and 1978. The Backward Classes, minorities and Scheduled Castes had traditionally supported the Congress, but they partially transferred their votes to the Janata Party in 1985. Without them, the party could not have won such a sizeable majority.

These were hard facts, but the dominant-caste legislators refused to recognise them. As far as they were concerned, the Janata Party was their property. Nevertheless, the leaders of the 'memorialists' proceeded cleverly. To avoid giving the impression that the dominant castes alone were putting pressure on Hegde, they forged a nexus with several legislators from other castes, including the Backward Classes, to project a wider support base for their cause. They were receiving guidance and moral support from Deve Gowda, although he remained in the background throughout their campaign.

Meanwhile, the Chief Minister suffered a back injury in April 1986, and was hospitalised for a considerable time. The 'memorialists' became extremely active during this period. They worked hard to persuade everyone that they were acting within the bounds of party discipline, and were primarily interested in protecting the image of the party and the government. This ensured there was no severe backlash from the party establishment. Hegde himself appeared indirectly to encourage them when he remarked that he was in favour of a ginger group within the party, as long as it did not undermine unity. Emboldened by this and by the covert patronage they were receiving from Deve Gowda, the 'memorialists' became increasingly aggressive and clear sighted. They scaled down the list of 'inefficient and arrogant' ministers from 12 to seven, and insisted that these seven be dropped.

As if to oblige them, Hegde summoned a meeting of legislators to discuss, among other things, toning up the administration. It was quite stormy. Deve Gowda berated Jeevaraj Alva (who was close to Hegde, so that it effectively meant that he was berating Hegde) for reproducing in a government publication a piece that had appeared in a local magazine. This article contained critical references to him. Deve Gowda is a sensitive politician who finds it extremely difficult to take fair criticism in his stride. But he was not the kind to object to what appeared in a magazine. Indeed, the magazine in question had earlier published articles which were even more critical of him, and he had ignored them. He objected this time because it suited him politically to do so. He put Hegde and his followers on the defensive to such an extent that Alva offered to step down, owning responsibility for the publication.

At a meeting, a junior member attempted to speak out against the 'memorialists', he was physically manhandled and prevented from opening his mouth. Hegde sat through the meeting, silently observing such shocking behaviour. As if this was not enough, a junior minister loyal to Deve Gowda made a deliberately offensive remark about members of the Kranti Ranga. 'People who put us in jail during the Emergency have become ministers with us' — a reference to those who had originally been in the Congress with Urs. The man making this charge had not actually gone to jail during the Emergency, and some of those who had, including Hegde, Deve Gowda and J. H. Patel, had no qualms about aligning with those who had then been Congressmen. In fact, both Alva and Patel, who had been in the Janata Party in 1977, had left to join Urs because they had become disgruntled with Deve Gowda who (Alva once told Raghavan) ran the party like a fiefdom. Strangely, Hegde did not defend his colleagues from the erstwhile Kranti Ranga. Only Bommai did.

This meeting was a crucial turning point. Hegde was known to be indecisive, but this episode showed for the first time that he could remain a passive spectator even when an issue affected his own vital interests. Thereafter, many legislators and leaders who had had complete faith in him began to wonder whether he could be relied upon. Former Kranti Ranga members were especially aggrieved.

When Raghavan asked him about this, Hegde angrily retorted, 'Why should I do anything at all? It is for them to sort out the issue.' This was surely a sign of weakness from a leader who had, only a few months before, been regarded as the uncrowned king of the state and a figure larger than even Urs, who had never won an election largely by himself.

Hegde took the 'memorialists' so seriously that over the next couple of weeks he met Janata Party legislators in groups. To avoid giving the impression of a weak-kneed response, he saw them in district-wise delegations. This made it appear that he was involved in a genuine review of the situation in each district. As a result of this exercise, however, at the next meeting of the council of ministers, Hegde sought and secured the resignations of all his colleagues in order to reconstitute the ministry. The 'memorialists' had plainly secured part of what they sought.

In an attempt to pretend that the 'memorialists' had not gained ground, Hegde jettisoned not one or two but 17 ministers at the end of June 1986, for reasons no one except he understood. Most of them were junior ministers, all of whom had held independent charges. Almost all of them had done reasonably well, and some, like M. P. Prakash, exceptionally well. So the reshuffle lacked logic. Instead of improving matters, it generated discontent in all camps. Hegde loyalists were the worst hit and felt betrayed. The 'memorialists', now openly described as 'dissidents' in the media, were equally unhappy. The ministers whom they had targeted remained in office, and Hedge had brought only one from their faction into the ministry. The Chief Minister sought to explain away this bungled exercise by insisting that the junior ministers were needed to prepare the party for elections to the district and local councils which were round the corner. This was hardly convincing, as these elections were still many months away.

The dissidents were now both angry as well as aware that Hegde was rattled, vulnerable and capable of ineptitude. This and their surprising success at the legislators' meeting whetted their appetite for power. From this point onwards, they increased the pressure and eventually gained such substantial influence over Hegde that he had virtually no room for manoeuvre. Outwardly, however, he pretended that he was still in charge. In the long run, both Hegde and the Janata Party suffered severe, irreparable damage.

Panchayat Elections and State-Level Politics

The last great achievement of the Hegde government was the generous empowerment of Panchayati Raj institutions. It deepened democracy in Karnataka and, along with a similar experiment in West Bengal, opened the way for democratic decentralisation across India. But before we consider its constructive implications, it is necessary to examine a less uplifting theme: the implications of the first elections to these panchayats for state-level politics.

Getting to the point where elections could be held was a slow, complex business, since an exceedingly thorny problem had to be addressed first. A vast number of constituency boundaries — 54,000 in the 2,400 local councils or Mandal Panchayats — had to be demarcated; 30 per cent of the seats had to be reserved for women, Scheduled Castes and Scheduled Tribes; and since the voting age had been lowered, voters' lists for those over 18 had to be prepared. Eventually, however, these tasks were completed, and elections were scheduled for 3 January 1987 (to district councils or Zilla Parishads) and 21 January (to Mandal Panchayats).

The official policy was that elections would be fought on party lines at the higher Zilla Parishad level, but not lower down for the Mandal Panchayats. In practice, however, here as in every other system on earth that had sought to exclude parties from local elections, party loyalties mattered at both levels. When parties finalised their candidates' lists, it became clear that the dominant caste groups had been given a disproportionately large share of nominations.

This was discouraging for the Backward Classes and other disadvantaged groups who, since 1972, had shared power with the Lingayats and Vokkaligas at the state level. But it was expected that this would be a passing phenomenon as the non-dominant groups became more assertive over time. To a considerable degree, that is how it eventually turned out. This was crucial to the historic contribution which the Hegde government's panchayats have made. If the dominant landed castes had used the system to strengthen their grip on local communities, then the panchayats would have done much less to *deepen* democracy. But partly because the Backward Classes and other low-status groups have been able to assert themselves, partly because some Lingayat and Vokkaliga leaders at lower levels have become exasperated by the challenges from these lower-status groups and exited the panchayat system, and *crucially* because the old caste hierarchies have lost much of their old potency,[1] democracy has indeed been deepened by this change.

---

[1] See, for example, Karanth, Ramaswamy and Hogger (2004).

All parties campaigned intensively during the Zilla Parishad elections, since the new district councils had substantial powers. Polling was attended by some tension and a little violence. The results came as a shock to Hegde's Janata Party. Many had expected these elections to be a mere extension of the assembly elections, with the Janata Party winning an overwhelming number of seats. But they had overlooked the ground realities. Even in the worst of times, the Congress had attracted about 40 per cent of the votes, give or take a few percentage points.

Its support held up at the Zilla Parishad elections and it won 394 seats, as against 450 for the Janata Party. Others fared badly. Independents took 24 seats; the Maharashtra Ekikaran Samiti, eight; the BJP, a mere six; and the CPI, two. The results startled even Congress leaders. They were mightily enthused since, for the first time since 1985, they began to realise that they were not completely down and out. For the Janata Party, the categorical message to be got out of the verdict was that people treated elections to various levels quite differently. Hegde himself realised that to enlarge its support base at the grassroots, the government had to do much more than it had. 'It is a lesson to all political parties that people should not be taken for granted', he said. He saw that voters might bring the Congress back to power if the Janata Party did not deliver.

The Congress ended up controlling a smaller percentage of Zilla Parishads than its percentage of seats. In 12 of the 19 districts, the Janata Party took control. When Parishad presidents were being selected, Hegde and Nazirsab sought to strike a balance between the dominant groups and others, but the new councillors preferred their presidents to be from among the Lingayats and Vokkaligas.

The Janata Party did better in the elections to the Mandal Panchayats. It won 27,333 seats, accounting for 50.3 per cent of the seats as against 38 per cent (20,679 seats) for the Congress. (The BJP again found itself in an embarrassing position, winning only 1.1 per cent of the seats.) The Janata Party gained control of 49.9 per cent of these bodies; the Congress, 26.3 per cent; and in the rest, no party had overall control.

The Janata Party performed better at the Mandal level partly because the Zilla Parishad results had punctured its over-confidence, so that this time it chose its candidates more carefully, playing extremely safe. It also campaigned well and avoided the mistakes it had committed in the Zilla Parishad elections. And the Congress, buoyed by the verdict in the Zilla Parishad elections, committed all the errors that the Janata Party had made in the earlier round, and paid a price for it. Having shocked the Janata Party three weeks earlier, the voters appear to have shrewdly decided to reiterate their confidence in the ruling party.

This further sign of the discernment of the electorate should have reminded Janata Party leaders that they needed to tread carefully. But they refused to learn this lesson. They promptly decided that control of the levers of power was more important than credibility, and used their power to appoint two extra members where no Backward Classes candidates had been elected, to insert people loyal to them into the Mandals. And they did so before these councils had chosen their *pradhans* (leaders), in order to maximise the number of Janata Party *pradhans* eventually elected.

Nazirsab, the Minister for Panchayati Raj, had initially directed that this not be done, since it was anti-democratic. But Janata legislators trooped into Hegde's office and demanded that they be allowed to appoint these two Janata Party candidates to the Mandals. Hegde picked up the phone and asked Nazirsab to withdraw his order, and going further, pointedly asked the minister in front of the assembled legislators whether he had taken leave of his senses. This hurt Nazirsab so deeply that he seriously considered stepping down. He told Raghavan at the time:

> My work has been completed. Whatever I had set out to do, I have finished. Now that the Chief Minister himself finds me inconvenient, there is no point in continuing. After all, if people voted Congress in a particular Mandal or Zilla Parishad, we should accept that gracefully. Defeat is part of the democratic process. That does not mean we give up a cause altogether.

He believed that an alert opposition was healthy for any democratic set-up, and that, therefore, a significant presence of the opposition in these councils would enable the system to work better. 'What can be better than that in democracy', he used to say publicly. Nazirsab's problem was that he was so idealistic that he was considered foolish, although those who knew him understood that that was not the case. Indeed, had his idealism prevailed in this instance, it would have yielded concrete political gains for the ruling party which, in turn, would have emerged with its reputation for fairness enhanced. But this was not to be.

The Constructive Implications of Karnataka's Panchayats

Evidence from a large number of experiments with democratic decentralisation across the developing world plainly indicates that such systems work well only when substantial powers and resources are transferred to elected councils at lower levels. Karnataka's panchayats were given such powers and funds, so that they were among the six or seven strongest out of more than 60 such systems in Asia, Africa and Latin America (see Manor 1999). They gained a considerable influence over almost every sphere of the government that matters to rural development and village life. The only exception was the co-operative sector. It was originally included in the list of subjects that they would control, but was, readers will recall, later withdrawn through an unsavoury manoeuvre within the state cabinet, after Nazirsab (who would, no doubt, have protested against such a move) had left the meeting.[2] But despite this, Karnataka's panchayats remained very powerful by both Indian and international standards.

As a comparative study of Karnataka, Bangladesh, Ghana, and Cote d'Ivoire has clearly demonstrated, the elected councils at the lower levels worked extremely well (Crook and Manor 1998). The preferences of local residents influenced decisions about development projects far more effectively than ever before, since the elected members of these councils felt immediately accountable to their constituents, who could observe their actions at close quarters. Where legislators and ministers had concentrated on grand, expensive projects — major roads, large dams and hospitals — the panchayats instead emphasised small-scale local projects such as minor roads, small irrigation works and primary healthcare centres, which had been starved of funds because so much money had been spent on grand undertakings. Because elected members of these new councils had greater local knowledge than ministers or even legislators, development projects were tailored to distinctive local conditions and needs and, in the process, less money was wasted. Villagers thus acquired a strong sense of 'ownership' vis-à-vis these projects, and therefore maintained them more energetically, with the result that development works became more sustainable.

The greater accountability which the panchayats entailed helped reduce absenteeism by local teachers and healthcare workers. Elected councils had the power to discipline those who failed to turn up for work. As a result, the delivery of education and health services in rural areas improved at no extra cost to the state exchequer.

---

[2] Interview with S.S. Meenakshisundaram (a long-time close aide to Nazirsab), Bangalore, 25 January 2007.

Panchayat members knew that not just accountability but transparency had also increased over what had existed earlier. Before decentralisation, when development funds from the state government reached the taluk (sub-district) level, a group of four or five bureaucrats and elected officials would meet behind closed doors, pocket a sizeable proportion of the funds (sometimes as much as 40 to 50 per cent), and then claim to local residents that the remaining 60 to 50 per cent of the funds was actually the full amount of the development budget. They could get away with this because the old system was opaque. Under the new system, hundreds of people in every taluk knew exactly what amount had been allocated to a particular development project, so that larceny on a grand scale became impossible. The head of one Mandal Panchayat, who had been party to such thefts at the taluk level before decentralisation, complained that he could make far less money under the new system.[3] Many more people were involved in corrupt acts than before, because so many more now had a little influence to peddle, but they also consistently estimated that the transparency of the new system, by virtue of which villagers could easily see who was profiteering, prevented them from diverting more than around 5 per cent of the state funds. Thus, the *overall amount* of corruption decreased.

Information flows between the higher reaches of the government and the villagers increased greatly as a result of decentralisation, and this happened in both directions. Civil servants at the district level consistently reported around a ten-fold increase in the amount of information passing *upwards* to them from the local level, through elected panchayat members. They also received early warnings from remote localities about problems that might mushroom into disasters: incipient floods, droughts, outbreaks of disease, etc. (Manor 1993a). They felt empowered by this information, since it enabled them to respond swiftly enough to prevent disasters from occurring. They felt further empowered by an increase in the *downward* flow of information to villages. One example of this is worth noting. Health department officials realised that elected members of local councils, especially women, were far better able than were health professionals to explain to village women why they should take advantage of ante- and post-natal care services, in a language that

---

[3] Interview with James Manor in a village in Mandya district, 7 April 1993.

these women could understand. As a result, the uptake on such services increased, saving many lives in turn.

Perhaps the most crucial gain from the new system was in terms of government *responsiveness*, which increased in three ways. The *speed* at which the government responded (government actions) increased because the panchayats were empowered to take prompt action without waiting long periods for permission from higher authorities. The *quantity* of responses increased because funds were now spent on numerous small projects rather than on a few large, expensive schemes. And most importantly, the *quality* of responses improved, if we measure quality by the degree to which responses conformed to local preferences. A large-scale survey among villagers clearly indicated widespread satisfaction with the government responses under the new system.[4]

The newly decentralised system also eased the frustrations of politically ambitious people at lower levels — frustrations which might have become destabilising. As we noted earlier, the number of elected posts in the state suddenly increased from just 224 (seats in the legislature) to over 50,000. The new system also provided the main political parties in Karnataka with structures that could be used to strengthen their organisations, and thus their ability to respond to citizens, by creating a framework that reached the grassroots.

We saw in Chapter 1 that as early as 1972, demands from a great diversity of social groups had already begun to overwhelm the state government's capacity to respond adequately. The political awakening which made it possible for Indira Gandhi and Urs to win elections with support from the disadvantaged groups plainly implied an increase in the level of demands. Even though mounting demands pose huge problems for any Chief Minister, Urs had encouraged more demands from these disadvantaged groups, even as he favoured them in his responses. This triggered still more demands from them, and he welcomed them too. It made Karnataka more difficult to govern, but it helped him prevent the land-owning Lingayats and Vokkaligas from re-establishing their grip on the lion's share of the resources flowing from the government.

---

[4] This and all the points discussed in this section are examined in more detail in Crook and Manor (1998: chapter two).

The Hegde government carried this process further. Its social welfare programmes for poorer groups, which Deve Gowda saw as mere 'populism', were intended to reassure the disadvantaged groups that Urs's legacy would live on. And the decision to empower the panchayats was a further step in this direction. The target group here was not just poor people, but ordinary villagers who had long been unable to decide how to use government resources to tackle local problems of great concern to them. Their elected representatives in the district and village councils now had the power to make such decisions, and there is unimpeachable evidence that ordinary people, including those from the disadvantaged groups, welcomed both this empowerment and the decisions that the elected councils made.[5]

By decentralising so generously, Hegde and Nazirsab, like Urs, compounded the state government's problem of a demand overload in two ways. They stimulated more demands from the villagers, although they also provided them with the power and the resources to address many of their felt needs. Further, they reduced the funds available to those at the state level to meet demands from below, since a hefty percentage of the government's funds was now transferred downward to the panchayats. Even state-level bureaucrats who sympathise with Panchayati Raj have often spoken of their chagrin when they see large sums of money, which used to be under their departments' control, passed to elected bodies at lower levels as soon as they are appropriated.[6] But Hegde and Nazirsab were prepared to accept this worsening of the state government's problem in responding to the overload of demands, because they believed — and rightly so — that the empowerment of the panchayats would enhance the legitimacy and popularity of both their government and party.

So just as Urs broadened democracy in Karnataka by providing leaders from disadvantaged groups with a substantial influence at the state level, Hegde and Nazirsab deepened it by generously devolving powers and resources onto panchayats at the district and local levels.

The Congress, the main opposition party in the state, at first looked upon the new panchayats with some suspicion. But over time, their doubts were eased. They were reassured somewhat when they won a substantial

---

[5] Ibid.

[6] This is based on numerous interviews with civil servants, by James Manor in Bangalore since 1987.

number of seats in the new councils, especially at the district level. And when Hegde organised a massive rally of the newly elected panchayat members from every political party, he invited the then Minister for Human Resources in Rajiv Gandhi's cabinet, P. V. Narasimha Rao, to inaugurate the convention. The latter told the throng of (roughly) 50,000 people gathered, 'Mr Hegde may belong to the Janata Party while I belong to the Congress Party, but we both belong to the "Panchayati Raj Party".' And then, as if this was not enough, Rajiv Gandhi himself, late in his term as Prime Minister, took up the cause of panchayats by seeking passage of a constitutional amendment empowering them all across India. This may have been an attempt to steal the thunder of parties opposed to him — the Janata Party in Karnataka and the CPI (M) in West Bengal, both of which had decentralised generously — and he may have intended to bypass and thus undermine the role of state governments in decentralising power by linking New Delhi directly to the grassroots. But this endorsement by the supreme leader quelled most suspicions regarding decentralisation within the Congress in Karnataka.

The Road to Disintegration: Hegde and Deve Gowda

The panchayat elections were the high-water mark of the Hegde regime. Thereafter, gradually, but inexorably, internal conflict within the government led towards disintegration. Many things contributed to this process, but much of it hinged on the growing rift between Hegde and Deve Gowda, and on the latter's vaulting ambition.

It is difficult to separate the two strands. As long as Deve Gowda enjoyed a good relationship with Hegde and saw him as a vehicle to realise his ambition of becoming Chief Minister, things worked wonderfully well. But when he concluded that Hegde was not helping him by hastening this process, disenchantment set in. To understand first the nexus and later the struggle between the two men, one needs to look into their character traits and the ups and downs in their career paths.

Having cultivating support from the Lingayats, Hegde now drew much of his strength from northern Karnataka, where he had, in the past, sometimes had difficult encounters (as a Brahmin) with the Lingayat leadership which is strong in this region. This appears to have persuaded him that Vokkaliga leaders (of whom Deve Gowda was one) were easier to deal with. But he also appears to have concluded that while the Lingayats tended to remain consistently level-headed, the Vokkaligas were prone to giving in to emotions, in ways that could make or mar a relationship. This trait has been attributed to many Vokkaliga leaders, particularly to those from Mandya and Hassan districts. Deve Gowda, from Hassan, was no exception. He could be warm and trusting at one time and antagonistic at another.

Throughout their years together in the Congress (O), and later in the Janata Party, Hegde and Deve Gowda got on extremely well. When Veerendra Patil had to step down as president of the Karnataka unit of the Janata Party soon after the parliamentary election of 1977, Hegde played an important role in installing Deve Gowda as Patil's successor, and he supported him fully thereafter. After the Janata Party came to power in 1983, Hegde relied heavily on Deve Gowda and Bommai (a Lingayat), in that order, for fashioning strategies to resist the Congress's efforts to destabilise the government. Deve Gowda, who had abandoned his campaign for the chief ministership when he realised that it would fail, then supported Hegde for the post. He genuinely believed that, but for his support, Hegde could not have made it. This is probably not true; the outcome could not have been otherwise because members of the erstwhile Kranti Ranga would accept neither Deve Gowda nor Bommai.

Because he had backed Hegde, Deve Gowda naturally thought that he deserved to be treated respectfully. Hegde was grateful for Deve Gowda's support but did not entirely believe that he owed his job to the latter. However, whatever may have been his estimation of Deve Gowda, he certainly relied on him more than on others in the first two years of the Janata regime. He went out of his way to keep him happy. Hegde felt even more indebted to him for running the successful by-election campaign in Kanakapura in mid-1983, which provided him with an assembly seat. That result convinced Deve Gowda that he had emerged as *the* leader of the Vokkaligas — '*Gowdara Gowda*' (the Gowda of Gowdas), as many of his ardent followers claimed. But there were reasons to doubt this. Shortly thereafter, the Vokkaligas in the neighbouring Mandya district, who thought they were, as a community, superior to all other Vokkaligas from other parts of the state, ignored Deve Gowda altogether when he headed an unsuccessful by-election campaign. There is no denying, however, that he had acquired huge importance in state politics.

Relations between the two leaders began to turn sour soon after the December 1984 parliamentary election (held after Mrs Gandhi's assassin-ation), which the Congress swept. Hegde was unhappy with Deve Gowda's tight control over the Janata Party's organisation, as a difficult state election was to be held shortly thereafter. Deve Gowda and Bommai distributed tickets to their clients and impeded surefire winners who stood outside their personal networks. Consequently, Hegde took personal charge of the campaign by hastily constructing a parallel party apparatus. He turned to activists loyal to him and had them carry out crucial tasks without any reference to the party's president, Deve Gowda. This parallel structure was so low-key that it was invisible to many, but it proved highly efficient, and naturally irritated Deve Gowda.

Further, after the Janata Party won the state election, Hegde delayed appointing Deve Gowda and Bommai to the cabinet, to suggest that they had dropped down a couple of notches in the new scheme of things. Had Hegde continued in this vein, he would probably have secured greater control. He was in a position to do so, since (as we have discussed earlier) the state election victory was largely attributed to him. Most Chief Ministers would have consolidated their control but, inexplicably, Hegde chose not to. Instead, he blundered in three ways. He encouraged speculation that he might move to the national level, which persuaded Deve Gowda and Bommai to bolster their personal networks in preparation for a struggle for succession. He eased the pressure on these two leaders, which allowed them to resume their faction-building. And he unwisely promised a 'values-based government', thereby inspiring dangerously unrealistic expectations of the state government.

Many in the Janata Party believed that there was a tacit understanding between Hegde and Deve Gowda to the effect that the former would clear the way for Deve Gowda to succeed him. In 1983, some had thought that Hegde would give way to Deve Gowda soon after the minority government had consolidated its position. However, certain events foreclosed this possibility. Grave threats to the government's survival made it inevitable that Hegde should lead the party into the 1985 state election. Hegde once claimed that later, on several occasions in 1986 and 1987, Deve Gowda had sought his endorsement as his successor. 'I studiously avoided saying yes or no', he said. In Hegde's view, it was for the party to choose the next leader. He was, however, not averse to advising Deve Gowda on how he should position himself. For instance, he told him to cultivate an image of being the representative of all castes and regions, and to avoid being seen as a Vokkaliga leader from southern Karnataka.

Deve Gowda soon realised that Hegde was unlikely to back him to the hilt, and discord began to develop. For example, Deve Gowda did not wholeheartedly approve of Hegde being projected as party leader in the 1985 state election. He was stung by his initial exclusion from the cabinet after this election had been won. Cleverly, he sought to create the impression that while Hegde was interested in protecting the state's interests, he was not above compromising them in order to enhance his image as a potential national leader who could rise above parochial or regional considerations.

The clearest example of this was the controversy over the sharing of waters from the Cauvery and Krishna rivers with other states. Some observers suspected Deve Gowda of leaking documents which indicated that Karnataka's farmers were getting less access to water for irrigation than they deserved to the opposition leader, Moily. By doing this, Deve Gowda sought to cultivate the impression that he was the farmers' most committed champion in the government, and that Hegde was too willing to compromise with other states in order to enhance his image at the national level. When Moily's charges were debated in the state assembly, Deve Gowda argued the government's case, but adroitly refrained from defending Hegde, who had become the opposition's principal target.

Deve Gowda focused the blame on Hegde yet again when legislators complained about the related issue of insufficient funding for irrigation. In the not-so-private meetings with legislators who approached him on the issue, he would point out that he was helpless since Hegde was not providing enough resources, and suggest that the legislators approach the Chief Minister himself. When he met those who were supporters of Hegde, he would make what he considered subtle comments against the latter.

Relations between the two leaders became thoroughly embittered when Hegde chose not to defend Deve Gowda against charges of corruption and nepotism made by his one-time protégé, Puttaswamy Gowda. The charges focused on his alleged misuse of office to secure sites for his relatives from the City Improvement Trust Board in Mysore. When the issue figured in the state's Upper House, Deve Gowda responded in a roundabout way, defending his actions and denying the charges. The Governor then referred the matter to the Lokayukta (the state's ombudsman), who indicted Deve Gowda in connection with the allotment of one site, but found insufficient evidence on 48 others. As a result of these findings, the Governor refused permission to prosecute Deve Gowda.

However, the political significance of this episode lies in Deve Gowda's anger over what he saw as a conspiracy to finish him politically. He suspected Hegde's involvement. He knew that he was not the first or the only politician to have done what he was accused of. The issue refused to die down. A BJP legislator raised it again and challenged the Chief Minister to hold an inquiry. Hegde agreed and promptly turned the evidence over to the Corps of Detectives.

This further incensed Deve Gowda who, like anyone else in his position, decided to strike back. His moves were meticulously planned. He first provided support to dissident legislators, who mounted a campaign against half a dozen ministers. Next, he mounted another against a report on the division of river waters. Finally, he decided to provoke open strife over the selection of a new president for the state unit of the Janata Party. Hegde sought consensus on the choice of Nazirsab. Deve Gowda did not oppose it frontally, but hinted that there might be conflict over the issue. He then encouraged and backed a formidable alternative candidate, Gurupadaswamy, a highly respected Lingayat leader and a known Hegde-baiter.

Deve Gowda had two objectives in mind. The first was to offer resistance to Hegde and, if possible, win the presidency and control of the party. But even if he failed, by supporting a prominent Lingayat, he was conveying to this community that he was not unsympthetic to their interests. Hegde and his associates countered this move by proposing another Lingayat, M. P. Prakash, who was not only completely loyal to Hegde, but also an acceptable choice to the younger elements in the party and to the Lingayats.

Hegde and several prominent leaders sought to work out a compromise with Deve Gowda, but when it failed, the Chief Minister finally declared that he was quite prepared for a showdown. At the last minute, Gurupadaswamy withdrew. While officially there had been no contest, it was evident that both sides had informally tested each other's strength. It was, in a sense, a defeat for Deve Gowda. But it was also a defeat for Hegde since a serious division in the party, hitherto concealed, had become apparent.

From then on, the two factions engaged in open battle. Each began issuing statements and making allegations against the other. The schism soon turned into a revolt. The opportunity to show active dissent arose in March 1988, at the time of the election by state legislators of members of the Indian Parliament's Upper House, the Rajya Sabha. A few days before nominations opened, Hegde, as usual, summoned senior colleagues, including Deve Gowda, to finalise the list of candidates. Deve Gowda proposed one of his followers, but the other leaders decided on Ram Jethmalani, a leading and often controversial lawyer, besides two others. Deve Gowda, it appears, did not dissent.

The choice of Jethmalani triggered an immediate controversy. He was from outside Karnataka and it was widely, perhaps rightly, felt that Hegde was doing him a favour for fighting his son's case before an inquiry set up to probe if he had offered to secure a seat in a medical college for a consideration. At this point, Jethmalani was relentlessly pursuing Rajiv Gandhi in the Bofors scandal. The Congress, therefore, bitterly opposed him, lest he use the seat in the Upper House to throw mud at their leader.

There were also technical and moral questions about his candidature. The law stipulates that to be a member of the Rajya Sabha, a candidate had ordinarily to be a resident of the state from which s/he is nominated and a voter there. It was well known that Jethmalani was neither. To circumvent the requirements, he hurriedly enrolled himself as a voter in Bangalore and declared that he was a permanent resident at the Bangalore guest house of the *Indian Express*. The moral dimension of the controversy arose because the Janata Party had on several earlier occasions criticised the Congress for fielding outsiders for elections to the Rajya Sabha. It had famously opposed the registration of Indira Gandhi as a voter in Karnataka in 1978 after her post-Emergency defeat.

When the nominations closed, there were 10 candidates, which naturally caused concern within the Janata Party. Apart from the official candidates, two rebels propped up by dissidents in Deve Gowda's camp were also in the fray. Even at this stage, Deve Gowda was expected to strike a bargain. The national-level president of the party, Chandra Shekhar, was unhappy about the turn of events and spoke to the state unit's president, expressing disapproval. Chandra Shekhar, who had once been extremely close to Hegde, had grown disenchanted with him. Without Chandra Shekhar's sometimes tacit and sometimes open support, it would have been difficult, and probably impossible, for Deve Gowda to challenge Hegde.

Two other issues became additional irritants, impeding efforts to resolve the crisis. Deve Gowda was clearly feeling the pressure from the inquiry into charges of nepotism in the allotment of sites for houses in Mysore. He told the state assembly that he was quite prepared to rebut the charges made against him and his son, but later at a meeting of Janata legislators, he expressed annoyance that officers from the Corps of Detectives were questioning his relatives. He also prepared the ground for a final break with Hegde by voicing displeasure over the fact that the promised allocation of Rs 300 crore[7] for his Irrigation Department had not been made by the Chief Minister, who also held the Finance portfolio. Deve Gowda had told the assembly months before that he would resign if the promised funds were not forthcoming.

The dissidents and loyalists in the ruling party began preparations for a showdown. Hegde's camp, however, had not expected what turned out to be a major rebellion. They had either been complacent, or their intelligence sources, including the police network, had let them down. There was no doubt that Deve Gowda had been preparing for a confrontation. Two days before the Rajya Sabha election, he summoned 50 Janata Party legislators to a meeting. On the morning of the election, they gathered and decided to defy the party whip, and to vote for rebel nominees, to protest against Hegde's 'style of functioning' and his support for a coterie. Sensing trouble, Chandra Shekhar, who probably knew of Deve Gowda's plans, dispatched Dandavate as a central observer to Bangalore. When Dandavate went to Deve Gowda's meeting and sensed the belligerent mood, he tried to placate those gathered by promising to take up later the issues that concerned them.

Meanwhile, Hegde and his loyalists anxiously waited at the Vidhana Souda, where a meeting of the Janata Party legislators was scheduled, after which the party's election managers were to allot votes to the candidates. They waited in vain, since none of Deve Gowda's supporters turned up. Congress legislators were gleeful at this. They took Jethmalani's challenge so seriously that Buta Singh, an adroit political manipulator, was dispatched from Delhi to ensure that no Congress member voted for Jethmalani.

Some Janata Party managers were trying to buy the support of some Congress legislators for Jethmalani. Since the Congress had surplus votes, securing them for a price was considered easy. There was nothing unusual about this practice, as political parties over the years had indulged in it.

---

[7] Three billion rupees, a huge sum.

But these efforts were foiled when Buta Singh got wind of them late at night on the eve of the election. He summoned all the suspect elements to Raj Bhavan, gave them a dressing down and literally held them captive there all night, in order to prevent contact with Janata Party managers. Next morning, as utter confusion reigned in the Janata Party camp, Buta Singh and other Congress leaders decided not to fish in troubled waters. They played safe by simply allotting all votes to their candidate.

Even when this became known to Hegde, he and his supporters could not summon the courage to take on Deve Gowda in a fight to the finish. Once the Congress had ensured that all its votes went to its candidate, Hegde could afford to ignore Deve Gowda's faction. But since nearly 50 Janata Party legislators had backed Deve Gowda, it would have been better for Hegde to provoke a winner-takes-all confrontation. Instead, as had become his habit, he dithered.

It was at this stage that Deve Gowda, having received a call from Chandra Shekhar in Delhi, advising him not to defy the party whip, left his supporters and came to the Vidhana Souda for a private meeting with Hegde and the others. He had come to communicate two things: he was quitting, and that he would persuade the legislators supporting him to vote for the party nominees. He handed his resignation letter to Hegde who, in turn, did not disclose it until it suited him. Just before voting closed, Deve Gowda arrived with his supporters and voted for the official candidates.

He may have yielded in the end, but this episode was, nonetheless, a clear show of strength. Deve Gowda had demonstrated that he commanded the absolute loyalty of nearly a third of the Janata Party legislators, and that his support base was no longer exclusively Vokkaliga. His other emphatic message was that he was not a leader to be ignored. If, at a time when admiration for Hegde remained undiminished in the ruling party, he could muster the support of around 50 legislators, he would be able to do much more should Hegde's image lose its gloss. Through this entire episode, he had delivered a body blow to the party and the government. Thereafter, Deve Gowda preoccupied politicians of all shades. His public posturing and private behaviour became more and more aggressive.

There was an element of ambiguity in the wording of Deve Gowda's resignation letter. In characteristic style, to indicate that he was quitting not because of factional politics, but on policy differences over the allocation of funds (or the lack of it) to the Irrigation Department, he had couched his letter in sarcastic language, and offered his resignation in a roundabout way. This was interpreted, perhaps deliberately, by Hedge to imply that Deve Gowda sought a change of portfolio and that he was not actually offering to resign. So the next day, Deve Gowda sent the Chief Minister a clarification: 'I would like to reiterate that I want to be relieved of my ministerial responsibilities and that I did not seek a change in my portfolio'. When this second letter reached Hegde, he summoned senior colleagues for consultation. While most of them favoured its acceptance forthwith, Bommai suggested that the situation might still be salvaged. Hegde considered this, but ultimately sent the resignation letter to the Governor for acceptance.

With this, Hegde and his supporters appeared to have won the first round in the battle. Despite the threat of a revolt, all the official nominees in the Rajya Sabha election had won, there was no defiance of the whip by the dissidents and with Deve Gowda's resignation, it would not be difficult to split them. But both sides had been bruised in this sordid fight. Hegde himself admitted remorsefully that 'there is no charm left in heading the government because of the division in the party'. The reporters who were crowded around him in his small office could see that this statement came from the heart.

For a leader who had begun as a mere compromise candidate, but who had then led the party to a convincing and, for many, an astonishing victory, the thought that almost a third of his legislators no longer favoured him was an acutely painful realisation. From then on, Hegde and Deve Gowda were irreconcilable. To keep the battle going, there was no shortage of excuses or crutches other than the real issue of a struggle for power. Some of these were provided by the Janata Party's national leaders.

National-Level Factors Compound the Problem

Chandra Shekhar, Janata Party's national president, did not admonish the dissidents as expected. In most other parties, such activity would not only be frowned upon, but retribution would have followed. In this case it did not, largely because Chandra Shekhar himself welcomed Hegde's discomfiture. Deve Gowda's followers claimed that their leader was acting at the behest of the national president, with whom Hegde had fallen out some time before. Chandra Shekhar appeared to want Hegde to be tied down by this crisis, so that he would be unable to trouble him at the national level. He had reason to be concerned. Hegde and a few others were making a concerted effort to secure control of the national party apparatus, and this contest was likely to reach a climax at an upcoming meeting of the national executive.

There was another strand to the national-level story. Hegde and some like-minded friends in the party wanted to unify several opposition parties. To this end, at several meetings in Delhi over many months, a consensus had been reached about a merger of the Janata Party, Devi Lal's Lok Dal, the Congress (S), and the small but significant group, the Jan Morcha, led by V. P. Singh, who had resigned from Rajiv Gandhi's government over the Bofors issue. Devi Lal, who had taken an enormous interest in this, even suggested that the leaders had agreed upon a new party name and flag. Chandra Shekhar, who opposed this plan because it would have meant accommodating so many parties, suggested that those who sought unity should instead join the Janata Party. He did not seem very enthusiastic about V. P. Singh either.

In Karnataka at this time, the drama was building up into a slanging match between the two Janata Party factions. The Congress in the state did nothing, at least publicly, to add to the confusion. A senior Congress leader explained their passivity this way: 'We see in Deve Gowda a potential Charan Singh. But we are not interested in helping him.' He was referring not to the rural roots which Deve Gowda and Charan Singh shared, but to the latter's key role in bringing down Morarji Desai's Janata Party government in 1979. Deve Gowda, many expected, would do the same in Karnataka. He was rumoured to have met Rajiv Gandhi more than once, although he stoutly denied this.

The Congress did not want to be seen helping Deve Gowda because it might be misunderstood as yet another dubious effort to destabilise a non-Congress government. On the other hand, if internal contradictions were seen to destroy the state government, it would enhance the image of the Congress which would, in contrast to the Janata Party, be seen as a party that remained united despite internal tensions. The Congress could then go to the people and appeal for support with a promise of stability.

The Congress had plenty of opportunities to create problems for Hegde. It could have offered a no-confidence motion in the state assembly in the hope of a split in the ruling party, or it could have encouraged the dissidents to corner the government on the floor of the House. But it did neither; it simply watched and waited, while the Janata Party factions slashed away at each other. In the end, as the Congress had rightly anticipated, both factions became sufficiently sullied to inspire public revulsion.

When the issue of Deve Gowda's resignation figured in the assembly, he sought to dispel the impression that he had quit because of the inquiry against him by the Corps of Detectives. He insisted that he had stepped down because he had made a commitment to the assembly, months before, that he would not remain a minister if the promised funds for irrigation were not forthcoming. Hegde scoffed at this:

> More than Rs 47 crore[8] was provided for irrigation, and I had indicated in the budget that additional allocations for irrigation depended entirely on the mobilisation of additional resources. I had also clearly stated that if the resource position did not improve, there would be a proportional cut in the plan outlay.

He pointed out that on at least three occasions, the availability of resources and the need for proportionate cuts were discussed in the cabinet and that 'Deve Gowda did not protest at any time'. Hegde argued that Deve Gowda claimed to have resigned on a matter of principle with two objectives. He wanted to show that he was not afraid of facing an inquiry. And more importantly, he sought to cultivate a broad constituency that was not exclusively based on caste.

There was some substance in this line of argument. From the time Deve Gowda decided to confront Hegde, he had meticulously projected himself as a 'son of the soil' who was interested in the welfare not just of the Vokkaligas but of the entire farming community, which could prosper only if extensive irrigation facilities were made available. His criticism of the government's welfare measures was also made in this context.

Meanwhile, the dissidents' attacks on Hegde continued unabated. They seized every opportunity to prove that they had numerous Janata Party legislators on their side. For instance, they claimed to have collected signatures for a memorandum to Chandra Shekhar, opposing any change in the name, symbol or flag of the party. Their objective was two-fold. They sought, first, to establish a principled opposition to Hegde and second, to show that more than half of the legislators opposed him. Both factions mounted such signature campaigns, but ultimately these

---

[8] 470 million rupees.

amounted to little since, while some legislators were quite willing to sign almost any paper, when it came to the crunch, they behaved altogether differently.

Amidst all this, Hegde and his men continued to mount pressure on Deve Gowda's camp. When the Zilla Parishad of Hassan district, which was controlled by Deve Gowda's followers, passed a resolution asking Hegde to quit (though it had no locus standi to make such demands), Hegde promptly hit back. He asked K. B. Mallappa, a junior minister and ardent follower of Deve Gowda, to resign within 24 hours for taking part in the meeting which had passed the resolution. Mallappa promptly distanced himself from that decision and reiterated his faith in Hegde, causing a setback for the dissidents.

The drama temporarily shifted back to Delhi when the main players went to the capital city for a meeting of the national executive on 5 April. Chandra Shekhar privately put enormous pressure on Hegde to take Deve Gowda back into the cabinet. There was also, Hegde claimed in private, a hint that the Corps of Detectives inquiry should be quietly dropped. Hegde stood his ground, and on returning to Bangalore, summoned the council of ministers, which reaffirmed full faith in him. A few days later, Chandra Shekhar arrived to meet both factions. He spent a considerable time with Hegde, and eventually met a delegation of dissidents at his hotel. It was then that their strength became publicly known for the first time. Deve Gowda had long claimed to have the support of more than 60 legislators, but only 32 called on Chandra Shekhar. Hegde clearly had a solid majority with him. More importantly, the dissidents were far short of the magical one-third of the total number of Janata Party legislators needed, under the new anti-defection law, to cause a split. So if they defected, they would be disqualified from membership in the House. This greatly reduced their bargaining power.

Bargaining Swallowed Up by Mutual Recrimination

Although Hegde and Deve Gowda appeared to be waging a fight to the finish, they were actually privately engaged in hard bargaining through intermediaries. The desire for an amicable solution stemmed from the fear that a showdown would leave both sides so politically bruised that any victory would amount to a defeat. Each faction contained large contingents of both 'hawks' and 'doves'. The doves felt somewhat helpless at the turn of events, but thought that the status quo ante might somehow be restored if only the two leaders would make up. Frequent appeals for a truce were sent from each side to the other, with the hawks being kept in the dark. But just as often, when severe verbal attacks needed to be mounted, the hawks were called into service.

Such contradictory efforts proceeded constantly, almost on a daily basis. At any given time, mediatory efforts between Deve Gowda and Bommai (serving as mediator), or Bommai and Hegde, could be taking place even as the hawks were busy abusing one another. In other parties, secret meetings would remain secret, so that problems like this did not get out of hand. But the Janata Party was an open book: nothing ever remained concealed for more than a couple of hours. And these troubles were compounded by a number of busybodies who constantly carried tales from one group to the other, adding to the confusion.

Public posturing apart, Deve Gowda was still interested in re-establishing his position within the party. This became evident when dissidents called on Chandra Shekhar a second time. For the public record, they urged him, one, to attend the legislature party meeting a few days later, and two, to accept their demand that Hegde should step down. Deve Gowda then met Chandra Shekhar privately, and the latter summoned Hegde and Bommai for a meeting next. He told them that an amicable solution was possible if Deve Gowda were offered presidency of the state unit of the party. Hegde refused, pointing out that only recently, M. P. Prakash had been elected president after Deve Gowda's faction lost the battle for control of the party machinery. So there was no question of a change now. Soon a delegation of ministers called on Chandra Shekhar and stoutly opposed accommodating Deve Gowda. They argued that it would only enable him to open another front against Hegde from within the organisation which, mercifully, was then under loyalist control. Later the same evening, Hegde told Raghavan, 'We [he and Deve Gowda] are not really far from each other. It is just that a thick wall that cannot be broken separates us.'

Chandra Shekhar's suggestion that Deve Gowda be made president more or less confirmed whose side he was on. As national party president, he ought to have upbraided the dissidents for causing trouble, and even taken action against some of them. But his personal animus towards Hegde persuaded him to ignore such rank indiscipline to the extent that he was willing to risk the overthrow of the only state government in India controlled by his party.

Neither Hegde nor Chandra Shekhar ever admitted it, but the latter's antipathy developed after 1985, when Hegde became the focus of attention in the media, and some magazines began to project him as a potential Prime Minister. In a private conversation with Raghavan, Chandra Shekhar blamed the national press (meaning the Delhi press) for promoting personality cults, and he specifically mentioned Hegde in this context.

Chandra Shekhar made an attempt to break the ice between the factions during his stay in Bangalore, but failed since positions had hardened on both sides. It appeared as though the die was cast for a split in the party.

Hegde began a tour of the state to try to explain what had happened. He also wanted to feel the pulse of the people and to gauge how they were reacting. He set 3 May 1986 for a legislature party meeting where he proposed to seek a vote of confidence from Janata Party legislators. To strengthen his position and project an image of toughness, he asked seven ministers aligned with the dissidents to choose between remaining in the ministry or supporting the rebels.

A few days before this meeting, Chandra Shekhar summoned Hegde and Deve Gowda a second time to make a last-ditch effort at compromise, but failed again. By then, the loyalist camp had done its homework and could claim confidently that there was no threat to the ministry from the dissidents. According to one calculation, loyalists had the support of 110 of the 139 Janata Party legislators, which contradicted the dissidents' claims of 70 favouring Hegde's ouster. By this time, the seven ministers from the dissident camp had resigned.

When the legislators met, anxiety was writ large on the faces of nearly everyone. The meeting, which lasted nine hours, had all the ingredients of a tense political drama. Hegde began by declaring that he was seeking a vote of confidence since the dissidents disputed his majority. There was a prolonged dispute over whether members of the state's Upper House, the legislative council, could vote. The dissidents opposed it on the premise that a Chief Minister's power rested on his support in the Lower House, the legislative assembly — and in this they had a point. The issue was finally settled when Dandavate, who had arrived as a central observer, declared that legislative council members could vote too. This was followed by another long dispute over whether ballots should be open or secret. The dissidents preferred the latter, to give greater freedom to members to express their views on Hegde. A voice vote on this point was clearly won by the loyalists. This itself made it vividly apparent that they constituted a large majority.

Hegde, emboldened by this, sprang another surprise. He accepted that the vote should be taken through a secret ballot after all. This unnerved and infuriated the dissidents, some of whom let off steam. Deve Gowda, an otherwise cool and calculating politician, lost his temper and shouted at Dandavate for allowing legislative council members to vote in violation of a directive that Chandra Shekhar had issued, and produced a letter from the national Janata president as evidence. This further exposed the nexus between him and Chandra Shekhar.

The dissidents were not prepared for Hegde's acceptance of a secret ballot. They had insisted on it in the hope that, if it was rejected, they could walk out of the meeting. When Hegde pre-empted them by agreeing to a secret ballot, they needed another excuse, and none was evident. Finally, even as the loyalists were casting their votes, two Janata Party members of India's Upper House from Karnataka, who were entitled to attend but not vote, objected to the wording of the resolution. This provided a convenient reason for Deve Gowda and his followers to troop out. Efforts were made to bring them back, but they refused. At 4.30 p.m., the results were announced. Hegde had won the intra-party vote of confidence with support from 109 legislators, including 15 members of the state's Upper House.

The dissidents had clearly suffered a setback and were now forced to state, at least publicly, that they supported Hegde. Hegde clearly had a majority in the legislature party, but with many Janata Party legislators in the dissident camp, it was at least theoretically possible that he could be defeated on the floor of the assembly. Instead of his initial, comfortable majority of 139 Janata Party members in a House of 224, he could now bank on only 103. With the support of the BJP and the Communist parties, he was still one short of an absolute majority.

Even then, his government would probably not be overturned because the dissidents were a few short of the required one-third of Janata Party legislators, which they needed under the anti-defection law to split the party. But if their strength increased, this would change. Though the dissidents publicly promised to support the government, privately they frantically sought to wean away loyalists to achieve the requisite one-third. This would have enabled them to convincingly threaten to split the party if their demand for Hegde's replacement was not conceded. Peace had clearly not broken out.

11

Endgame

The generous empowerment of the panchayats was a remarkable achievement, but it was the Hegde government's last. Even as over 50,000 elected members of councils at the district and sub-district levels began learning to make local democracy work and matter in the lives of ordinary people, the wretched squabbling among the ruling Janata Party's legislators proceeded apace. It was as dismal a spectacle as the new panchayats were encouraging.

A Downward Spiral

The next skirmish between Hegde's faction and Deve Gowda's camp occurred over the election of members of the legislative council, Karnataka's Upper House. On 26 May 1987, the Janata Party prepared a list of 12 candidates and sent it to the high command for clearance. The rebels submitted a separate list. It was at this stage that Deve Gowda put forward his terms for a truce. He suggested that Siddaramaiah, a Backward Classes leader[1] in the dissident camp, should be made president of the state unit of the party. He also set 30 May as the deadline for the Janata Party to agree to his suggestion.

He thus made it clear that he was still prepared for a compromise, but on his terms. By setting a deadline, he was conveying that he was quite prepared to cause further problems if his terms were rejected. And by suggesting Siddaramaiah, he was trying to disprove claims that he was pro-Vokkaliga. This, however, did not wash with the loyalists. M. P. Prakash, the sitting state president, who was in the uncomfortable position of having to answer questions about Deve Gowda's demands, made what he considered was a fair gesture from the loyalist camp: he proposed a discussion of the party presidency after the election to the state's Upper House. This occurred after the party high command had given the state unit a free hand to finalise the list of candidates.

---

[1] He belongs to the Kuruba (herding) caste which has considerable numerical strength.

Since the loyalists did not meet his demands, Deve Gowda fielded three rebel candidates of his own. He also went on the offensive by declaring at a public meeting in Hassan that any attempt to 'crush him would ruin Hegde and the Janata Party'. Hegde reacted promptly by saying, 'I am not here to be bullied by anybody.' He had invited Deve Gowda and another prominent dissident leader for consultations on candidate selection. Both had attended an initial meeting, but did not participate thereafter. Instead, Deve Gowda responded by fielding those candidates of his own.

Deve Gowda regarded his demands as an olive branch. By accepting them, Hegde could have bought peace, at least in theory, for some time. But by doing so, he would have exposed himself to the criticism that he was buckling under pressure yet again. Hegde knew from experience that once he gave in, he would be pushed around both by loyalists as well as dissidents. So instead, he steeled himself to losing a couple of seats to the rebels. Although politics in Karnataka had not witnessed such a rebellion in the past, upsets in elections for the ruling faction were nothing new. But at this particular juncture, it suggested a threat to the very survival of the government, so there was enormous interest in the unfolding drama.

A few days before the election, Deve Gowda met Prakash and offered to withdraw the rebels, provided the party agreed to field candidates of his choice in five constituencies. This was turned down, and when legislators cast their votes in the election on 6 June, two of the three rebels won, defeating the official candidates. More importantly, the rebel candidates secured 50 votes which meant that the strength of the dissidents in the legislature had gone up from 32. A few days later, Hegde suffered a further setback when all the seats in the election to the legislative council from the graduates' and teachers' constituencies were lost on account of in-fighting in the party in every district. This revealed that the schism had occurred not only within the legislature but at every level of the party organisation. Subsequent elections from the local authorities' constituency reinforced this message. Dissidents fielded by Deve Gowda won from two districts.

The party was plainly facing a full-blown crisis from which there was little chance of recovery. The dissidents may not have formally broken away from Hegde's camp, but the separation had acquired a certain finality. Deve Gowda told Raghavan in the lobbies of the legislature that as far as he was concerned, it was only a question of time before the government fell. In fact, he had already begun looking beyond this possibility:

Right now I am in a position to ensure that the Janata Party is defeated in the next general election. Unfortunately, I am still not in a position to turn that into a victory for myself. They are finished. I need some time to turn a negative factor — my ability to halt them from returning to power — into a positive factor — winning support of the people for myself.

This was an accurate assessment. It had taken him about a year to turn public admiration for Hegde and the Janata Party into revulsion. Destroying Hegde was not an end in itself, but a means of thwarting what he considered to be a concerted effort by Hegde and the people around him to finish him politically. Despite all the confusion and the conflicting claims of rival factions, it was becoming clear that only two possibilities existed. Hegde and Deve Gowda had to resolve their differences, or the people would render a verdict which, given their proven sophistication, was likely to be damning. Since the first outcome was unlikely, a mid-term election following the collapse of the government was on the cards.

Deve Gowda could have toppled the government quickly if he had acted in concert with the Congress. There was no need to parade legislators before the Governor to prove that Hegde had lost his majority. The dissidents had only to vote against the government on the budget. If a finance bill had been defeated, the government would have automatically collapsed. But Deve Gowda resisted such a temptation. He did not want to bear the odium of being seen as a wrecker. He preferred instead to create the perception that Hegde's misdeeds caused the collapse. The Congress welcomed this. It wanted to avoid the impression of unseemly haste. Why should it assist in destroying the government (which would have made it unpopular) when the Janata Party leaders were doing such a splendid job of it on their own? This, however, would take time.

At this point, Ajit Singh, the Janata Party's new national president, arrived in Bangalore and went through the motions of trying to mediate between the warring factions. He got nowhere and in exasperation, declared, 'The party in Karnataka is a brakeless vehicle hurtling downhill.'

But on returning to Delhi, he took sides in the dispute. Yet another election was looming, this time to the Rajya Sabha, the Upper House at the national level, members of which were elected by state legislators. Deve Gowda telephoned Ajit Singh to confirm that the Janata Party high command had neither given the state unit of the party the authority to select candidates, nor had it approved the list sent by Janata Party's state president. When Singh said nothing to the contrary, Deve Gowda effectively gave dissidents the green light to field their own candidates. So this election would also be an embarrassing free-for-all.

Three of the party's five official candidates lost because of in-fighting. Hegde was furious. He believed that the rebels would not have contested but for the party high command. He threatened to step down if the party's national leaders continued to encourage indiscipline. They promptly announced that the Janata Party's parliamentary board would discuss the crisis. Hegde went on to suspend six dissident legislators from the party. But this action came too late to frighten others into restraining themselves. From this point on, the crisis moved inexorably to a denouement.

The situation soon grew still more embittered. The loyalists mounted one last campaign against Deve Gowda. For the first time, one of his former followers alleged that Deve Gowda had offered to join the Congress at the height of the Emergency:

> Deve Gowda had not only expressed willingness to join the Congress during the Emergency, he had tried hard along with Veerendra Patil . . . When he was in jail, he once sent for me and urged me to join the Congress and promised to follow. I did join the Congress and persuaded Urs to release him so that he too could join the party. However, within a week the Emergency was lifted and Deve Gowda said it would be politically immature to join the Congress at that stage.

Urs himself had once told Raghavan about this, but no one had gone public with the account. This disclosure only served to inject yet more poison into the conflict.

The Action Shifts to the National Level

Most of the remaining drama took place in Delhi. As loyalists and dissidents rushed to the capital to lobby with various leaders before the parliamentary board met, Chandra Shekhar, who was questioned by reporters about his own role, stoutly denied that he was backing the rebels. 'A section of the press is deliberately spreading falsehood', he asserted. But Hegde loyalists soon had fresh evidence to suspect that the party's national leaders were indeed biased against them.

The *Indian Express* carried a transcript of a telephone conversation between Ajit Singh and Deve Gowda on the eve of the election to Karnataka's Upper House. There was nothing sensational about it, since Deve Gowda had already given journalists the gist of the conversation. But the transcript plainly established that Ajit Singh had lent support to Deve Gowda. It appeared to have been provided to the newspaper by Hegde or one of his supporters. After it appeared, Hegde was accused of tapping telephones, since this was the only way such a conversation could have been taped. Hegde immediately denied the charge and further went on to say that he was morally opposed to any such practice. This comment, as we will see in the next section, was to prove fateful for him.

Two days later, the Janata Party's national parliamentary board affirmed that it 'appreciates the good work done by the Karnataka government under Hegde and feels proud of its several significant achievements'. It also set up a committee to discipline recalcitrant elements in Karnataka. For the Chief Minister, this endorsement appeared to be an important victory.

Meanwhile, other developments at the national level intervened. After much dithering, several opposition parties which had been discussing unification finally decided to act. Leaders of the Janata Party, the Lok Dal (B), the Jan Morcha, and the Congress (S) agreed to name the new party the Samajwadi Janata Dal. Devi Lal, a powerful figure from Haryana and a prime mover in this initiative, even announced that the new party would have V. P. Singh as president, Hegde as vice- president, Ajit Singh as secretary general, Dandavate as its leader in Parliament, and that he himself would chair its parliamentary board.

This was an event of real significance because of the ghastly mess that the Congress government in New Delhi had created for itself. By early-to-mid 1987, Prime Minister Rajiv Gandhi had reversed his initial policies in several very important areas.[2] This revealed deep confusion about

---

[2] Economic liberalisation (rather tenuously tried earlier) had been abandoned, as he had returned to a 'socialist' strategy. The much-trumpeted reform and re-democratisation of the Congress Party (15 years after Indira Gandhi had ended intra-party democracy) was given up. Upcoming elections within the party were announced on 14 occasions, but never happened under Rajiv Gandhi. His initial reliance on many new Congress leaders of his own generation substantially ceased, as he turned again to the circle of sycophants who had surrounded his mother, several of whom were semi-educated and incompetent. He did an about-face in his approach to the crisis in Sri Lanka, with deadly consequences for the Indian Peace Keeping Force. Late in his term, he discovered a sudden enthusiasm for democratic decentralisation, which suspiciously looked like an attempt by a leader who had achieved precious little to steal the best ideas from opposition governments in Karnataka and West Bengal.

fundamentals at the very apex of the government. His alarming inconsistency tended to alienate people on every side of every issue. Moreover, it was a sign of political incompetence, particularly since he had left himself with too little time for his new policies to produce results. Popular disapproval of all this, and of the Bofors controversy[3] in particular, had soared. People had begun to see V. P. Singh, who had resigned as Rajiv Gandhi's Finance Minister to become a crusader against corruption, as an attractive alternative. An opposition victory in the national election due in 1990 seemed a distinct possibility. In this context, a combined force of like-minded parties posed a formidable challenge to the Congress rule at the centre. For Hegde, the offer of the number two position in the new party was a compelling recognition of his position in national affairs.

Significantly, Chandra Shekhar, who had been the Janata leader for more than a decade, did not figure in the new party's pantheon of leaders. He remained a reluctant passenger. The dissidents in Karnataka, who had made much of their sentimental attachment with the name, symbol and flag of the Janata Party, saw in this proposed unification another opportunity to distance themselves from Hegde. They met and declared that they would not join the new party.

Hegde reached Bangalore from Delhi on 8 August to participate in a meeting of the loyalist legislators, convened to endorse the formation of the Samajwadi Janata Dal. They now expected to see less and less of Hegde since, as vice-president of the new party, he would need to be present more often in Delhi. Senior ministers worked out arrangements that would, nevertheless, enable him to continue as Chief Minister. At this point, no one expected or foresaw that he would be out of office in two days' time.

The Telephone-Tapping Controversy and Hegde's Departure

The day after Hegde reached Bangalore, the *Times of India* carried a prominent story, stating that the telephones of several politicians had been tapped in Karnataka at the behest of the state government. Among those targeted were Deve Gowda, Gurupadaswamy, Gundu Rao, Moily, and Raghupathy (a surprise, since he was a strong Hegde loyalist). The

---

[3] It was alleged that massive kickbacks had been received by leading figures in the ruling party when guns from the Bofors company of Sweden had been purchased by the Ministry of Defence.

list gave details of the period covered by the intrusion and the phone numbers tapped.

By itself, the disclosure did not come as a shock to many because successive state governments had long been suspected of resorting to such surveillance. A few years before, when a scandal about mail interception had broken out, Gundu Rao had even defended the government's right to spy. But this latest revelation was acutely embarrassing for Hegde since, after the leak of the transcript of the telephone conversation between Ajit Singh and Deve Gowda, he had pleaded ignorance of this practice and took a moralistic stand against it. Events had taken a serious turn this time.

Hegde believed that the list of phones tapped had been obtained from central government intelligence agencies, and made available by Rajiv Gandhi to Subramaniam Swamy, a Janata Party leader who constantly looked for opportunities to bait Hegde. But it was also clear that the tapping itself had been done not by central government agencies, but by Karnataka's intelligence department. In his public statements, the Chief Minister maintained that he had not personally ordered the taps, and that the state intelligence wing must have done it on its own as a matter of habit.

Even if this were true, it was difficult to believe that Hegde, to whom the head of the state intelligence wing personally reported at least twice a day, was unaware of it. Meanwhile, a new, damaging interpretation was now put on the earlier leak of the Deve Gowda–Ajit Singh transcript. It had been supplied to the *Indian Express* in Delhi, which had a Bangalore edition as well. If the leak had been made possible by Karnataka's intelligence department (acting on its own), it would have occurred in Bangalore. Its release in Delhi strongly suggested that either Hegde himself or someone acting at his behest was responsible. His protestations of innocence were therefore regarded as too clever by half.

On 10 August 1988 Rajiv Gandhi told Parliament that the Karnataka government had flouted accepted norms by indulging in tapping. Hegde, who was back in Delhi by then, continued to plead ignorance and demanded a judicial inquiry to examine tapping all over the country. When this was rejected by the central government, he accepted moral responsibility and told journalists of his intention to step down.

Many in Delhi who had seen his complex manoeuvres before were skeptical. They need not have been, for Hegde returned to Bangalore, met the Governor and formally submitted his resignation, bringing to a close a career as Chief Minister that had begun amidst uncertainty, soared to great heights, and finally turned sour and sordid.

Unexpectedly, Deve Gowda reacted very somberly at this sudden development. He described the event as 'painful' and added, after some reflection, that his relation with Hegde had passed through happy and difficult moments in the last 15 years. 'In the past few months, some people tried to break it . . . I now feel that maybe both of us were partly responsible for indirectly encouraging such forces. I feel it should not have happened.'

He believed that Hegde's image had been enhanced by his decision to resign. There were many others who thought similarly, but a large number also felt that he had paid a price for one ploy too many. This may have been a serious flaw in his character, but, regardless of what his critics might say, he had brought a genuine sensitivity to politics. Even in the phone-tapping episode, he had shown courage by owning up to a mistake and stepping down on moral grounds. Not many politicians in his place would have done it. In this regard, Hegde stood apart.

It is true that Hegde and most of his colleagues suffered from the same weaknesses that run-of-the-mill politicians suffer from. No more than one or two ministers in his government — here Nazirsab comes to mind — were entirely above board, although in most cases the others' weaknesses were kept within tolerable limits. And from 1983 to 1987 (four out of the five years that Hegde was at the helm) the government did not lose sight of its primary objective of working for the welfare of the people. Working within tight financial constraints, it managed a substantial number of achievements, most notably its success at providing some of the basic necessities of life to ordinary people, and its empowerment of democratic institutions at the grassroots.

Hegde's departure was attended by a note of tragedy. By the time he stepped down, the minister who had contributed most to these achievements, Abdul Nazirsab, had fallen terminally ill with lung cancer. Had he been in good health, he might even have emerged as Hegde's successor. His integrity and commitment to constructive work were beyond question, and his unassuming, disarming conduct with legislators had earned him immense goodwill in the party. Hegde himself preferred Nazirsab as a successor. This became known at a legislators' meeting held to elect a new leader. After Hegde's successor had been chosen, he broke down and wept uncontrollably, saying that, but for Nazirsab's illness, he would have preferred him to head the government.

A New Chief Minister

As soon as Hegde had revealed his intention to resign, intense lobbying had begun in both the loyalist and dissident camps. While Bommai and Deve Gowda were expected to contest for the leadership, J. H. Patel and Rachaiah (both from the loyalist camp) also considered entering the fray.

Deve Gowda made an all-out bid. He even called on Hegde, Nazirsab, Rachaiah, and a host of other loyalists, seeking their support. This may appear astonishing to many, because those outside politics do not expect equations to change overnight. But sometimes they do. As one phase of politics closes, yesterday's adversaries might turn into friends, depending on political compulsions.

Both in terms of numbers and of caste considerations, Deve Gowda appeared to be trailing Bommai. In one sense, caste was not a major consideration since factional alignments counted for more. Caste, however, could not be discounted altogether since, for the first time since 1972, there was a clear chance for a member of the once-dominant Lingayats and Vokkaligas to become Chief Minister. In theory, Bommai (a Lingayat) should have been on a stronger wicket than Deve Gowda (a Vokkaliga) on two counts. First, the loyalists outnumbered the dissidents, and there had been no realignment of forces after Hegde's resignation. Second, Lingayats outnumbered Vokkaligas in the legislature party (and in the state), and most Lingayat legislators were loyalists.

But despite this, there was uncertainty in the loyalist camp because Hegde declined to express a preference, and Patel and Rachaiah brought the number of candidates from the loyalist camp aspiring for the chief ministership to three. The disunity among the loyalists was countered by solidarity among the dissidents: Deve Gowda was their unquestioned choice. As such, he could single-mindedly focus on enticing the loyalists.

When the legislators convened, Patel quickly realised that his chances looked dim, so he withdrew in favour of Rachaiah (a Scheduled Caste leader). Apparently, even Deve Gowda, when he had met Rachaiah earlier had, in order to avoid a contest, offered to support him if he emerged as a consensus candidate. When Patel offered to support him, Rachaiah reminded Deve Gowda of his promise. The latter, however, backed out of the so-called promise and a sullen Rachaiah protested that he had been let down. He finally withdrew, which left only Bommai and Deve Gowda in the contest. Bommai won in an informal head count, after which the meeting went through the motions of formally electing him unanimously.

If there was a surprise in these developments, it was that a party which had passed through crisis after crisis was still capable of producing a smooth transition in an orderly and democratic fashion. But this did not mean that its troubles were over. Bommai inherited plenty of them, the most daunting being the factional conflict. And new problems also arose. Two were especially troubling.

First, Bommai had to live in the shadow of Hegde — a hard act to follow. Hegde had projected a certain charisma that enabled him to gain respect without demanding it. Bommai was less colourful, which meant less clout and more compromises. To establish a distinctive persona for himself, he also had to approach things in new ways. But he could not overdo it, since doing so would have cast doubt on what had gone before, in the previous government, when he himself had been an influential, even a guiding, figure.

Second, the issue of caste suddenly became important in a new sense, because Bommai was a Lingayat. Like his three predecessors (Urs, Gundu Rao and Hegde) he had to maintain a certain balance of political representation between the dominant castes and the rest. But he also had to deal with the heightened expectations of the Lingayats, who were overjoyed that one of their leaders had been elected after 15 long years.

These difficulties made it impossible for Bommai to make quick decisions on the composition of his team. So, for the first time in the state's history, a Chief Minister was sworn in all alone. A couple of days later, he expanded the cabinet but did not make Deve Gowda his 'number two'. The dissidents initially thought that Deve Gowda should be made Deputy Chief Minister or, failing that, be given the number two post, that is, the second most important position without the formal title. Bommai could offer neither since both alternatives would have annoyed Hegde and his followers. Instead, he offered Deve Gowda a position as a mere cabinet member with his pet portfolio of Irrigation. Apart form Deve Gowda, Bommai accommodated only two other dissidents in the ministry.

For a short while thereafter, it looked as if the government could carry on till the next election without much hindrance. Since the cabinet was not yet fully constituted, legislators, particularly the loyalists, were hoping that they would soon be rewarded. But this took time because the Janata Party and the other parties which eventually merged into it at a convention in Bangalore were still working out the internal modalities for the newly enlarged party, both at the state and national levels. A national party convention was to be held in Bangalore to coincide with the birthday of Jayaprakash Narayan. Though leaders at the national level had agreed that four parties should merge, unifying them was no easy task. Till the last minute, Chandra Shekhar and Ajit Singh continued to oppose the merger. They finally relented when Hegde and a few others threatened to call a meeting of the national executive to endorse the unification.

The Bangalore convention was finally held on 11 October 1988 at which all the leaders, including Chandra Shekhar, endorsed the creation of the new Janata Dal.[4] They addressed a rally of roughly two lakh[5] people that evening, where Hegde was a huge draw. The dissidents, who had hoped that the merger would somehow flounder, now faced a dilemma. They would have little clout in the new party, and feared that when tickets would be distributed for the state assembly election, due 14 months later, they would be shunned. They therefore preferred to opt out.

Once the Janata Dal was formed, legislators of the newly united party had to complete the legal formality of changing the nomenclature, which meant that every member was required to sign an affidavit. In the first week of 1989, Bommai set 15 January as the deadline for the dissidents to do so. When the deadline passed, many of them had been won over by various, and sometimes dubious, methods. Bommai's managers were extremely active in weaning away dissidents who, having seen the back of Hegde, were no longer interested in a fight. Several leaders who had been close to Deve Gowda, including Siddaramaiah, signed the affidavit.

Deve Gowda, however, declared that he would not join the new party and would step down if asked to do so by Bommai. The new Chief Minister finally made up his mind and on 17 January dispatched a letter to Deve Gowda asking him to join the new party or resign. The next day, the two met in Delhi and Deve Gowda, as expected, handed over his resignation. Bommai hesitated in accepting the resignation at this stage, and it required some pressurising from Hegde loyalists to persuade him to accept it.

---

[4] What had originally been called the Samajwadi Janata Dal was now widely referred to as the Janata Dal.

[5] 200,000.

At the end of this exercise, only 28 Janata Dal legislators had declined to sign affidavits. This meant that Bommai was quite safe for the time being. Deve Gowda and his supporters, now considerably reduced, were out of the way. But Bommai's problems did not end since he now had, yet again, to construct a cabinet. Ministry-making is a thankless job at the best of times, and the high expectations of those to whom he was indebted turned this exercise into an even more nightmarish experience. He ended up making almost everyone unhappy.

The day Bommai inducted 13 ministers, trouble broke out and gathered momentum so swiftly that he could not respond. First, a one-time supporter of Deve Gowda felt aggrieved at not being made a minister and resigned from the assembly. Then Jeevaraj Alva, Hegde's blue-eyed boy, gathered some legislators to express dissatisfaction with the process of cabinet-formation. Since some observers (both inside and outside the Janata Dal) suspected Alva was acting at Hegde's behest, it was felt that the latter might be out to destabilise the government.

Deve Gowda sought to capitalise on this general sense of uncertainty and disillusionment among legislators by encouraging Janata Dal legislators to join him. This generated great confusion. One legislator got 20 colleagues to sign a letter withdrawing support from the government, but then within hours, they relented. A few others decamped to the Congress.

The Governor, P. Venkatasubbaiah, who had been in the Congress before his appointment, promptly reported to New Delhi that instability in Karnataka was rife and recommended the imposition of President's Rule. This was uncalled for since, by then, Bommai had offered to face a vote of confidence. The Janata Dal legislators who voted against the government in the assembly, would have lost their membership in accordance with the anti-defection law. But Rajiv Gandhi's Congress government was impatient and President's Rule was indeed introduced on 21 April 1989.

Thus, de facto, Congress rule was restored in Karnataka, since national Congress leaders would now select the key advisors to be appointed to the patently pro-Congress Governor. It required an act of administrative fiat to end a stretch of over five years in which the Congress had been unable to defeat the Janata Party in two elections to the state assembly and in elections to the municipal councils, the Zilla Parishads and the Mandal Panchayats.

By indulging in an excruciatingly long spell of factional warfare, the erstwhile Janata Party had discredited itself for the time being, causing the newly united Janata Dal to lose the 1989 state election to the Congress. But it had been in power long enough, and performed constructively enough to ensure that it would remain a potent alternative to the Congress. The old Congress dominance could now not be restored. Far from destroying the Janata Dal, the 1989 election ushered in an era in which the major parties alternated in power in successive state elections.

Assessing Hegde

We have provided an unvarnished account of Hegde's many mistakes, especially after 1985. He, like Urs before him, is a study in ambiguity. But the sorry end to his career as Chief Minister, and the undignified period of in-fighting that preceded it, should not obscure the scale of his achievements.

1983 onwards, there were many contradictions within the Janata Party, and conflicting interests worked at cross-purposes throughout the Hegde era. Especially, but not only, between 1983 and 1985, Hegde, by his adroit management and by practicing genuine consensus politics, was able to keep these tensions in check and provide reasonably good administration in most sectors, and historic achievements in some. This was a refreshing change after Gundu Rao's dismal three years in power. It endeared the Janata Party government to the people and earned it a resounding renewal of its mandate in 1985.

In Karnataka's history, Hegde was the only leader, apart from Indira Gandhi, who was able to carry his party largely under his own steam to a convincing election victory. This is something that any politician would envy. Even Urs, an immensely compelling figure between 1972 and 1980, could not achieve what Hegde did in the mid-term election of 1985. After losing 24 of the 28 seats in the parliamentary election in October 1984, very few thought that he could bring his party back to power. But just nine weeks later, he achieved it by directly appealing to the people on the strength of his government's performance during its first two years in power.

In this initial period, his government was constantly haunted by the threat of destabilisation, which the Congress actively pursued in an era before the anti-defection legislation had come in place. Despite its tenuous hold on power — or perhaps because of it, as such a situation enforced restraint among factions within the Janata Party — the government performed exceedingly well in addressing basic issues. It altered the very approach to governance, with Hegde himself setting a personal example by his simplicity and approachability, and by labouring tirelessly to see that his ministers delivered. Crucial problem areas were tackled effectively enough to make a tangible impact. The most striking example was of the provision of drinking water in rural areas. It was such a success that a hostile Congress government at the centre adopted Karnataka's strategy for the rest of the country. In the first two years after its renewed mandate in 1985, the government consolidated its earlier achievements, implemented new programmes to deliver a measure of social justice to disadvantaged groups, and saw the newly empowered panchayats through their first round of elections.

It then began to be overtaken by serious dissidence and drift for several reasons. Instead of heroically struggling against external threats to his government's survival from the Congress Party, as he had before the 1985 election, Hegde had to grapple with tedious squabbling within his own ranks. He found this disheartening, even boring, and his resulting inattention led to damaging misjudgements. He began looking beyond the confines of the state, and unwisely articulated his desire to move out. As he himself put it, this caused 'the suppressed ambitions of some [he meant Deve Gowda] to be rekindled'. The ensuing personality conflict ended in political fratricide. A degree of complacency set in among the legislators once the threat of destabilisation receded, particularly after Rajiv Gandhi brought in the anti-defection law. They threw away the self-restraint that they had exercised between 1983 and 1985 (out of a grim determination to maintain their and their government's survival), and now indulged in the aggressive pursuit of ministerial posts and extravagant factional squabbling.

Hegde, distracted by thoughts of a national role, often failed to respond decisively to this strife. Unlike Urs, who was not afraid of staking everything in a fight, he was often too cautious, too unwilling to strike back hard when he was assailed. Nearly every chief minister of Karnataka — from Kengal Hanumanthaiah in 1955, through Nijalingappa, B. D. Jatti, Veerendra Patil, Urs, and even Gundu Rao — had at one time or another faced groupism in the ruling party, but not one had taken the kind of beating that Hegde did. His inability to join issue with his adversaries and his desire to be seen as a politician who was above petty considerations ultimately cost him dearly.

His was a sad exit for a leader who had emerged as if from nowhere in 1983 as a mere compromise candidate, but who had then, astonishingly, led a minority government to historic achievements, and won a stunning victory in 1985 so soon after a crushing defeat in a parliamentary election.

Hegde had won many admirers in the state, but also inspired bitter resentment among those who thought that his high-minded promises were mere trickery. In particular, his exceedingly unwise promise of a 'values-based government' set a standard which he and his government — or any government — could not reach. Had he acknowledged his faults, as Urs occasionally did, and as Gundu Rao did too often, the people of the state would probably have forgiven him. But despite his resignation on what he argued was a point of principle, much of the good that he had done was overlooked at the time of his going.

With the passage of time, however, there is no doubting the scale of his and his governments' achievements. They sustained Urs's commitment to give leaders from disadvantaged groups substantial influence at the state level and to serve the interests of every section of society, so that this became standard practice in subsequent Karnataka governments. They established multiparty competition as a permanent feature of the state's political system, so that voters have had genuine choices at every subsequent election. And they deepened democracy by creating one of the strongest and most successful experiments with democratic de-centralisation to be found in Asia, Africa and Latin America. These are monumental accomplishments, however tedious the factional strife of the later Hegde years may have been.

Conclusion

This book has focused on three historic changes in Karnataka. First, between 1972 and 1980, Devaraj Urs broke the control which the land-owning castes, the Lingayats and Vokkaligas, had exercised over state politics since independence. In its place, he developed a system, that has endured, in which power was widely shared within very broad, rainbow coalitions of interest groups. The net effect was a broadening of democracy. Then in 1983, after an inept interregnum under Gundu Rao, opposition forces defeated the long-dominant Congress Party. They then united under Ramakrishna Hegde to govern well enough to ensure that multiparty competition became a permanent feature of the state's politics. At every subsequent election, voters have had genuine choices. The Hegde government also tackled the over-centralisation of power at the state level by introducing a strong system of Panchayati Raj, deepening democracy in the process.

These changes transformed Karnataka's politics, by making it more inclusive and more responsive to the vast majority of ordinary people living in villages. Further, the changes occurred here earlier and more smoothly than have similar changes in most other Indian states.

We have explained not only *that* these changes occurred, but (in great detail) *how* they happened. We have concentrated on the actions of Chief Ministers because they played a decisive role in the political transformation of Karnataka. We therefore offer a corrective to most analyses of politics in and beyond India, which have under-emphasised or ignored the role of senior politicians.

In devising their strategies, the two main architects of change in this story, Urs and Hegde, drew heavily upon the political tradition of Karnataka, especially that of former princely Mysore. So, they transformed the system by borrowing key elements from it. Three of these were especially important: political accommodation, enlightened governance, and reforms which anticipated and defused conflicts before they could acquire destructive force.

These two leaders were not saints. If we wait for saints to cleanse politics, in India or anywhere else, we will probably have to wait forever. But fortunately, saints are not required to bring about enlightened change. What *is* needed is political vision and manipulative skill, and both men met these requirements. Urs, Hegde and their colleagues became progressives mainly because political compulsions impelled them to be so.

Urs had to broaden democracy by bringing people from disadvantaged groups into the process, in order to survive inevitable attempts by the Lingayats and Vokkaligas to re-establish their dominance at the state level. But he also had the imagination to recognise that the kinds of programmes which earlier Chief Ministers had undertaken to enhance the state's prosperity — large-scale irrigation projects, agricultural development schemes for land-owning groups, electricity generation projects to supply power to farmers and urban industries, etc. — had disproportionately benefited prosperous groups. They had increased inequality between the landed castes and lower-status groups. Urs saw this both as unjust, and as a political opportunity to be seized because lower-status groups had become more politically aware and assertive. He therefore concentrated on removing social disparities and reinforced this with efforts, notably land reforms which benefited tenants, to ease economic disparities.

Hegde had to deepen democracy through decentralisation in order to persuade voters, in Karnataka and across India, that the Janata Party's rule offered them greater benefit than the Congress, which was then ruling at the national level and in most other states. He had been the Finance Minister in the governments that had preceded those of Urs, and had thus participated in promoting the development programmes that had increased the disparities which Urs then addressed. But Hegde also had the imagination to recognise the injustices which had troubled Urs, and the political utility of easing them as Urs had done. So his government developed new programmes to carry that process further, even as it created new opportunities for ordinary people at the grassroots to influence public affairs. He thus both built upon the broadening of democracy begun by Urs, and deepened democracy by empowering local councils.

Both men stressed the enlightened nature of their policies, and both took pride in their reputations as progressive leaders. But both knew that if they wanted to survive atop the greasy pole of state politics, they had little option other than enlightened reform which they saw both as morally just and as good, advantageous politics.

These two leaders did not solve all of Karnataka's problems. Indeed, in some ways, by broadening and deepening democracy, they made

Karnataka a more difficult state to govern. The state's governments, which had faced excessive demands from prosperous groups before Urs took office, were beset by still more demands after Hegde stepped down, because politics now included disadvantaged groups and penetrated deeper into rural areas. This provides much of the explanation for the failure of every state government since 1985 to get re-elected. Both men knew that this problem would arise. But they were forced by circumstances to embrace the risks that enlightened reform implied, and they regarded it as the right thing to do.

The Broader Context: Karnataka's Politics Since Independence

Readers might well ask how the politicians discussed in this book fit into the broad sweep of Karnataka's post-independence history, and how they appear when they are considered alongside those who came before and after them. In our view, only four Chief Ministers in Karnataka have managed to shape the fundamentals of the state's politics and to transcend regional and caste origins. Two of them — Urs and Hegde — have been discussed here, and our reasons for including them are by now obvious. The other two, who preceded Urs and Hegde, are K. Hanumanthaiah (Chief Minister, 1952–55) and S. Nijalingappa (1956–58 and 1962–71).

Hanumanthaiah, who assumed office after the state's first Chief Minister had made a somewhat hesitant start, brought acute intelligence and immense drive to the job. These qualities enabled him to gear up the machinery of the government to tackle the daunting tasks that confronted it in those early days, and to entrench, for the next generation, both accommodative politics (an admirable achievement for a Vokkaliga) and the dominance of his Congress Party.[1]

Nijalingappa led the campaign for the unification of the Kannada-speaking areas into an enlarged state in 1956. He came from old princely Mysore, but despite some hesitations in that region about unification, he pressed for the change and earned strong and enduring support from northern Karnataka as a result. He then presided very skilfully over the administrative and political adjustments which necessarily followed.

---

[1] For a more detailed account, see Manor (1974).

He is sometimes criticised for partiality towards fellow Lingayats, but his contribution was still substantially constructive.[2]

To name only the above-mentioned four men as the architects of fundamental change may seem unfair to the Chief Ministers who came after 1988, several of whom performed well. But this is less a negative verdict on later leaders than a comment on the circumstances in which they found themselves. These later leaders had fewer opportunities to achieve great things, precisely because the four earlier Chief Ministers had completed most of the basic tasks that modern democracies require. The first two had developed administrative structures that functioned quite well and prepared the ground for economic development. They strengthened mechanisms for accommodative politics and united the state. Later, Urs and Hegde broadened and deepened democracy, making it more inclusive, competitive and responsive. After 1988, much remained to be done, but no task undertaken by later leaders was on quite the monumental scale as of these earlier challenges. It is worth reiterating that while ruling parties led by all the four earlier Chief Ministers were re-elected, no other government since 1985 has accomplished this feat.

This phenomenon is partly explained by the tight fiscal constraints which confronted all governments in this state, and in every place on earth, after 1990. Since then, all Chief Ministers of Karnataka have been less able than the earlier four to respond to the demand overload with well-funded initiatives.[3] And it is to the credit of recent Chief Ministers that they, unlike their counterparts in several other Indian states, have not succumbed to the temptation to spend so lavishly that fiscal destabilisation ensued. As a result, Karnataka has remained one of the most fiscally sound states in the country.[4] But the main explanation for the less monumental achievements of recent Chief Ministers is not economic but political: they had fewer opportunities to scale great heights because, as noted earlier, four of their predecessors had already tackled most of the foundational problems.

---

[2] His early years are examined in Manor (1977b). Both Hanumanthaiah and Nijalingappa are assessed in Manor (1977c).

[3] Since 2003, this problem has eased somewhat as economic growth has yielded more government revenues across India.

[4] This is based on James Manor's interviews with officials from India's Planning Commission, September 2006.

Bommai (a Lingayat) succeeded Hegde in 1988. Though he had sufficient political experience, he was bound to appear less distinguished than his predecessor. To make matters worse for Bommai, he inherited the Janata Party's bitter factional squabbles, which we have discussed in great detail. He compounded them in one significant way. Although the bulk of his support in the legislature party came from Hegde's supporters, he meekly tried to break free from them. This cut short his tenure in office. He thus had only eight months in power — too short a span of time in which to achieve much.

A state election in 1989 brought the Congress Party back to power, but it was as severely wracked with in-fighting as was the Janata Party. Its first Chief Minister, Veerendra Patil (another Lingayat), had held this post before once, between 1968 and 1971. His great problem in his second term was that he governed more or less as he had done earlier, that is, before the immense changes that Urs and Hegde had introduced. He thus seemed unresponsive and old-fashioned, a 'Rip Van Winkle'.[5] This swiftly brought factional strife within the Congress into the open, and after just 11 months, the party's national leaders installed Bangarappa (an Idiga or 'Backward Caste' leader) in his place.

As Chief Minister, Bangarappa overplayed his hand as extravagantly as he had always done earlier in lesser roles: overcentralising power, elevating dubious civil servants to key posts and taking actions that alarmed Congressmen in Karnataka and New Delhi.[6] Corruption soared during his tenure, and he was accused of encouraging tension between Kannadigas and Tamils during a dispute with neighbouring Tamil Nadu over the sharing of river waters. When violence broke out between these two linguistic groups, he faced further charges that he was slow to respond.

These and other troubles persuaded the national-level Congress leaders to change the leadership in Karnataka once again, bringing in Moily (another 'backward caste' leader) after only two years. He found himself in a position similar to Bommai's. When he assumed office, there were only two years left before the next state election in 1994.

---

[5] E. Raghavan, in discussion with James Manor, Bangalore, 18 July 1990.

[6] Alarm in New Delhi was apparent when James Manor spent a week in February 1992 observing the daily routines of the then Congress Prime Minister, P.V. Narasimha Rao.

As such, he had very little time to do anything substantial. He shared none of Bangarappa's unbridled tendencies, but he was less adroit than many previous occupants of this office, so he found it impossible to repair the damage done by his predecessor. As a state election loomed, some expected a third party, the Hindu nationalist BJP, to be the main alternative to the Congress. It had done remarkably well in Karnataka in the parliamentary election of 1991.[7] Forseeing the threat, Hegde, Bommai and Deve Gowda sank their differences and toured the state as a group, both to encourage their various sets of followers to unite, and to demonstrate their new-found unity to voters. In the event, the Janata Dal handily won the 1994 state election and Deve Gowda (a Vokkaliga) became Chief Minister.

He started well, bringing to bear his strong work ethic and the capacity to analyse policy proposals. However, in 1996, after a national election had thrown up a hung Parliament, he was chosen by leaders of a third front ('third' alongside the Congress and the BJP) to serve as Prime Minister of India. The implication of this development for Karnataka's politics was that J. H. Patel succeeded him as Chief Minister.

Patel was an intelligent, cosmopolitan Lingayat with a record for advocating enlightened policies in the socialist tradition. But he was also relaxed to the point of inattention, both in the performance of his official duties and in his relations with the media. He acquired a reputation for being a bon viveur which went down badly with many socially conservative Kannadigas (of whom there is no shortage). This term could also have been applied to some of his predecessors, but most had taken greater care than he had to conceal their recreations. The appearance — and to a degree, the reality — of drift overtook his government, and in the state election of 1999, the voters turned once again to the Congress.[8]

---

[7] On the role of the BJP in Karnataka's politics in the 1990s, see Manor (1998).

[8] It should be noted that reforms in the state's excise sector and professional education admissions under Congress Chief Ministers Veerendra Patil (1989–90) and Veerappa Moily (1992–94) respectively, and those in primary school teachers' recruitment and tax administration under Janata Dal Chief Ministers Deve Gowda (1994–96) and J. H. Patel (1996–99) had significant implications, and were hailed as models at the national level. We are grateful to Narayana Gatty for calling attention to these points.

The new Congress Chief Minister was S. M. Krishna, an intelligent, urbane Vokkaliga who had studied in the US and served in Parliament and as a minister in New Delhi. These long absences from the state made it appear that he was losing touch with Karnataka and with the concerns of rural dwellers. This suspicion was especially strong among fellow Vokkaligas, who dubbed him 'US Gowda' and even 'London Gowda', though he had never lived in England. His development programmes for Bangalore (which by this time had become a global icon), deepened these suspicions, even though his efforts in this regard did not require him to divert funds from the rural development projects. This was exploited by both the BJP and the Janata Dal, so that the 2004 state election produced the state's first hung assembly.

The Congress won the most votes, but the BJP won the largest minority of seats. As a result, an uneasy Congress–Janata Dal coalition government led by a somewhat maladroit Congressman, Dharam Singh (who came from a north Indian caste), took power. After only 19 months, in which he could accomplish little, a revolt by some Janata Dal elements led to a new, similarly uneasy coalition between the Janata Dal and the BJP, with Deve Gowda's son H. D. Kumaraswamy as Chief Minister. He worked hard to provide the media with photo opportunities of his overnight stays in villagers' houses, and his constant efforts to project images of himself interacting with ordinary people won him some personal popularity.[9] But in substance, his government achieved as little as had Dharam Singh's before it. The Janata Dal had agreed that after half of the remaining 40 months (that is, those that were left of the 5-year tenure after the first 19 months of Dharam Singh's government) elapsed, a BJP leader would take over, but when the time came, it refused to keep its side of the bargain. A period of unseemly manoeuvring involving the Janata Dal and the BJP ensued. President's Rule was briefly imposed, after which the BJP's B. S. Yediyurappa[10] (a Lingayat) was named Chief Minister. However, when the Janata Dal again reneged on a supposed 'agreement' to back him, his government collapsed within a week.

---

[9] We are grateful to Sandeep Shastri for sharing polling data for 2007 and 2008 which demonstrate this.

[10] Amid this turmoil in late 2007, Mr Yediyurappa changed the spelling of his name on the advice of a numerologist, so that the correct rendering now is 'Yeddyurappa'. His initials remain unchanged.

After a spell of President's Rule, a state election in May 2008 gave the BJP just under half the seats in the state assembly. With the help of Independents and defectors, it then formed a government under Yediyurappa.

The Broader Context: South Asia's Politics

It is also worth considering the account of Karnataka politics given in this book against the backdrop of politics across India, and indeed, South Asia. In South Asia, most political parties have always been, or have eventually degenerated into, insubstantial institutions dominated by individual leaders or their families. This has always been true of the main parties in Bangladesh and Pakistan and, to some extent, of those in Sri Lanka. It is also true of many regional parties in India, and of the Congress Party at the national level after 1971.

But parties in Karnataka have defied this trend to a remarkable degree. The Janata Party, after 1983, found it especially difficult to become and remain a coherent force, because it had to incorporate two parties which had previously been rivals, and because it contained several strong personalities with formidable sets of followers. Our detailed account of the in-fighting under Hegde vividly demonstrates this last point. And yet, until recently, Janata Dal (comprised of the former Janata Party and some other parties) in Karnataka has managed to hold together as an institution of real substance. Disunity was responsible for its defeats in the state elections of 1989 and 1999. After each of these losses, it had appeared close to disintegration. But over time, its leaders coalesced again and rebuilt their organisation, with the result that the Janata Dal returned to power in 1994 and again performed surprisingly well in 2004. This capacity for revivals is remarkable when we compare it to the fates of political parties in other states which faced similar defeats and internal conflicts. It was only after 2004 that the Janata Dal in Karnataka degenerated into a family-run enterprise.

The Congress Party in the state has also managed to remain an institution of substance, even though at the national level it has become a family affair. Intrusions from New Delhi, especially the imposition of inept Chief Ministers and state party presidents, have often inflicted great damage. But the Congress in Karnataka has repeatedly bounced back. At one low point, one of us visited the party office in Bangalore to find it almost deserted, with no filing cabinets, a single telephone line, and minor officials burning the incoming mail, unopened.[11] But six months later, after an efficient new state party president had been appointed, filing cabinets had been procured and were being carefully filled, multiple telephone lines had been installed, and the office was humming with purposeful activity. Many such effective leaders with substantial popular bases have remained within the Congress Party to sustain it as an institution with sinew and reach.

If party structures in Karnataka have repeatedly been revived, the same can be said of the formal institutions of state. For mercifully brief periods, they have suffered severely at the hands of unbridled and maladroit Chief Ministers. The Gundu Rao period was one such episode, and at least one more followed under Bangarappa (1990–92). In each case, government institutions took a battering, but then more con-structive leaders from both the Janata and the Congress succeeded in regenerating them. This is remarkable, considering that in much of Asia and Africa, as well as in some north Indian states, when government institutions have eroded, it has been next to impossible to repair the damage.

How, then, are we to explain the resilience of political parties and state institutions in Karnataka? Much of the explanation can be found in the main themes explored in this book. The tradition of political accommodation and inclusion which predated Urs, but which was reinforced by the policies of his and Hegde's governments, has encouraged party leaders to share power with teams of lieutenants, rather than over-centralise in the manner of most senior politicians in South Asia.

This accommodative tradition has also persuaded leaders of all major parties in Karnataka to cultivate support from *all* social groups, and thus avoid narrow, intolerant appeals to limited sections of the society. The state has therefore escaped the destruction seen, for example, in Uttar Pradesh (UP) since the early 1990s. Here, three main parties — the BJP, the Samajwadi Party and the Bahujan Samaj Party (BSP) — from the early 1990s until 2007 reached out to different sections of society. To muster support from these narrow bases, each party has sought to inflame resentments between the groups which support them and others. Consequently, politics here has been overtaken

---

[11] James Manor paid this visit when Janardhan Poojary was serving as state party president, functioning, however, not from Bangalore but New Delhi.

by spite, of which we see little in Karnataka. Successive governments in UP have also uprooted the programmes of their predecessors and started again from scratch. This trend has made it impossible for this north Indian state to maintain the kind of policy continuity and consistent, supportive treatment of government agencies and institutions, which Karnataka has witnessed.

So the politics of accommodation in Karnataka, that is, the tendency of all major parties to build all-embracing social coalitions and thus seek support from the *same* social groups, has contributed mightily both to social harmony and to the health of state institutions. This political stability has been reinforced by another tradition of Karnataka's politics — anticipating emerging conflicts, and of acting to defuse them — which both Urs and Hegde carried forward. These approaches to politics have minimised conflict and discontent at the grassroots. They have helped to ensure that ordinary people have not felt the deep alienation that their counterparts in some other Indian states have experienced — alienation which has left them vulnerable to appeals from film stars and leaders who seek to polarise society between the haves and the have-nots, or between caste or religious groups. We regard this as constructive. Others may differ, but it should be apparent by now that in Karnataka, this has been the reality.

Was Karnataka Just Lucky?

It is important to stress that the political transformation discussed in this book would probably not have happened if Urs and Hegde had held power in reverse order. The political struggle that Urs had to wage with the Lingayats and Vokkaligas required a combative temperament, the skills of a political brawler and at key moments, a killer instinct. Urs possessed these qualities, but as several apparently minor incidents recounted in previous chapters indicate, Hegde did not. It is thus likely that if Hegde, rather than Urs, had emerged in 1972, he would eventually have been devoured by the dominant landed interests. By the same token, Urs lacked the political vision to recognise the promise of democratic decentralisation. In fact, he needed to centralise power in order to win the struggle that he faced. Hegde, on the other hand, had that vision, and was shrewd enough to seize upon the opportunity of decentralising power by utilising the services of Nazirsab, the real architect of the new Panchayati Raj system, who shared that vision and commitment. For

Karnataka, Urs and Hegde assumed power in the right sequence, and here, as so often, sequencing was decisively important.

In this and in several other ways, Karnataka was fortunate, but was it merely luck that was at work? We do not think so, and we are not arguing that the state was somehow blessed by higher powers either. Some analysts in the West do make such arguments about countries there. We read this in some accounts of the political histories of the United States and Britain, but in the current era of crass Anglo-American interventionism, perhaps we should consider a less objectionable example like, say, France. The historian Stanley Mellon (who is not French, but who exceeds many Frenchmen in his admiration for that country) seeks to convince us that France is indeed blessed, that it comes close to being the 'daughter of God'. Much of his writing carries one along convincingly, until the reader shakes himself and asks, 'Is this really plausible?'

It is not. Nor is it true of Karnataka. It should be clear from our account of Karnataka that the state was sometimes lucky in its leaders. But there was much more to their emergence than dumb luck. Two inheritances from the pre-independence period contributed to it. First, the agrarian order in Karnataka, especially in the southern districts of old Mysore, was extraordinarily equitable. This region had the lowest incidence of landlessness in British India. This fostered a social milieu in which the disadvantaged groups here faced less poverty and desperation than elsewhere in India. Partly because of this, and partly because the groups playing priestly roles[12] were not the same as those who owned the better land (and thus dominated the economy and village society), the dominance exercised by the land-owning Lingayats and Vokkaligas at the local level was less harsh than that which we find in other regions. Dominance and hierarchy were realities in rural Karnataka, but here these structures were more amenable to accommodations among social groups than their counterparts elsewhere.

Second, the maharajas of old Mysore, unlike princes in most other parts of India, had no connection to the powerful landed groups. They therefore felt compelled to develop a tradition of political accommodation which included bargains, understandings and a limited degree

---

[12] Brahmins in much of the state, and in Lingayat areas, the Jangama (priestly) *jati* or caste group within the Lingayat community.

of inclusion. At first, the locally dominant landed groups enjoyed most of the benefits accruing from this tradition, but when other groups emerged, even before, but especially after independence, this habit of at least limited inclusiveness gave openings to them as well. The landed groups who dominated state politics for the first 25 years after independence internalised this accommodative tendency, to some extent.

This was apparent as early as in 1937 when the Mysore Congress (comprised mostly of Brahmins) and another regional party (controlled by the dominant landed groups) negotiated a grand bargain and united in the struggle to achieve a democratic government in the state. It was further apparent in the mild, comparatively liberal posture that the princely government adopted towards the newly united Mysore Congress.[13] This accommodative tendency was made apparent yet again in the accommodations with a wide array of social groups forged by Chief Minister Hanumanthaiah, a forcefully urbane, open-minded Vokkaliga. His adaptation of the old tradition of limited accommodation was largely sustained by his successor, Nijalingappa, despite his more evident bias towards fellow Lingayats.

So even before Urs became Chief Minister in 1972, this tradition had been incorporated into the habits of statecraft in Karnataka. The bargains offered to disadvantaged groups were, even so, disappointing to them, and they appeared even more disappointing as these groups gained a fuller understanding of democracy over the years. Yet, these groups were

---

[13] The then Maharaja of Mysore, Krishnaraja Wadiyar IV, had secretly sent contributions to the Indian National Congress, and had actually taken to spinning, a Gandhian activity. He had also welcomed Gandhi as a state guest in the 1930s.

And when Congressmen undertook *satyagrahas* against the princely government, they received comparatively gentle treatment from the authorities. They were not brutalised by the police or subjected to severe persecution by the government, as were their counterparts in nearly all other princely states. In the climactic struggle for democratic government just after independence, Congressmen cleverly sought an accommodation with the Maharaja. They made loud claims about how he was an enlightened man, prevented from democratising by autocratic advisors. The reality was different, but by proceeding in this way, they enabled the Maharaja to concede to their demands without his having to feel humiliated in doing so. They then had him made the first Governor of the state, sealing the bargain. See Manor (1977c).

not crassly excluded, victimised and ground under, as they were in several other parts of India.

It is worth stressing that both Urs and Hegde, who broadened and deepened the tradition of accommodation, had learned their politics in the Congress Party, which had developed this tradition in a more limited form. And when Urs went looking for allies from disadvantaged groups to help him construct a much more broadly inclusive government, he was able to find them, thanks largely to the less inequitable economic and social order of Karnataka. It had enabled large numbers of people of lower status to obtain some education, and to play at least minor roles in public life. And when they did, the less extreme hierarchies in society, and the less extreme hierarchies in politics which they fostered, meant that they had not suffered the kind of severe ill-treatment experienced by their counterparts in many other Indian regions. They were thus less intimidated and less easy to intimidate. This was an immense help to Urs.

Nor was it an accident that Karnataka's (relatively speaking) equitable social milieu and accommodative tradition should have produced leaders like Hegde and, especially, Nazirsab who had the imagination to undertake a serious experiment with democratic decentralisation. In doing so, they were merely extending the state's tradition of accommodative politics to people at the grassroots, deepening democracy in the process. Evidently, much more than mere luck was at work in the processes that we discuss here.

What of the Future?

There are no guarantees that trends from the recent past will persist into the future. We have little confidence in future predictions, but changes are afoot in Karnataka which may eventually produce a different kind of politics in the state. Four are worth noting.

First, the BJP has gradually emerged as an important contender in Karnataka politics, and after the 2008 state election, it was finally able to form a government on its own. In Karnataka it has tended, most of the time, to pursue a strategy similar to that of the Congress and the Janata – seeking support from nearly all social groups. But it has sometimes adopted a narrower approach which, if emphasised, might fundamentally change the nature of political competition (and of state–society relations) here.

This narrower approach has been evident on two fronts. The BJP has tended to rely heavily on the support of Lingayats, the caste fellows of its leader in this state for the last 20 years. If this trend gathers strength, it might inspire social tensions and abrasive political conflict, both of which have remained manageably moderate in the past. Since taking over as Chief Minister after the 2008 state election, Yediyurappa has elevated Lingayat officials to many key posts in his government. But he is also unlikely to rely too heavily on his caste fellows, since even overwhelming support from the Lingayats will not suffice to produce election victories. The BJP has also sought, at times, to encourage antipathy between Hindus and the state's main religious minority, Muslims. Its attempts to create controversies in Hubli and in Chikmagalur district have largely failed so far.[14] But more concerted efforts might inflame religious passions which have largely remained in check so far. This approach appears unlikely to work, but the possibility cannot be lightly dismissed.

Second, since 1989, we have also observed changes in the efforts by non-Congress parties to turn anti-Congress sentiments at the grassroots to their advantage. Opposition to the Congress has always existed (to varying degrees in different periods) at the local level. But parties which have sought to challenge the Congress have succeeded only intermittently in translating this sentiment into the electoral strength that they need to capture power at the state level. Since 1989, anti-Congress voters have oscillated between the Janata Dal and the BJP, and at times have been split between them, to the disadvantage of both. This pattern may persist, or one rival to the Congress may become pre-eminent,[15] or still more parties may emerge and fragment anti-Congress sentiments further. Politics in Karnataka has become quite fluid and open (partly as

---

[14] The popular disinterest in aggressive Hindu nationalism was seen again in the state election of 2008 when speeches by the best-known exponent of it, Gujarat Chief Minister Narendra Modi, were greeted with embarrassingly small turnouts even in BJP strongholds.

[15] This may have happened in the state election of 2008. The Byzantine manoeuvres by Janata Dal leader Deve Gowda before polling day appear to have undermined confidence in the party. But it still gained over 19 per cent of the popular vote, and Deve Gowda's son, former Chief Minister H. D. Kumaraswamy, remains personally popular. So the Janata Dal might yet stage a comeback from this very low ebb, as it has done twice before.

a result of a third change discussed in the following paragraph), so that none of these scenarios can be ruled out. But whatever the outcome, it will have major implications for the character of the democratic process and state–society relations.

A third change has been happening at the village level in this predominantly rural state. The power of old caste hierarchies has waned quite substantially. This has made democracy more genuine, but it has also caused a loosening up of social relations at the grassroots which could change the character of politics. As the traditionally low-status groups have begun to feel less constrained by hierarchy and have thus asserted themselves, we have sometimes seen violence break out between them and the landed castes who once dominated village life, not least in the southern-most districts of the state where, ironically, inequities in land holdings (and thus in social relations) have long been less marked than in any other part of South Asia. These incidents have remained sporadic so far, but if they became more common and widespread, they would have serious political ramifications.

The 'loosening up' of social relations has also made it impossible for villagers to get things done on their own in ways that were once common. Because landed groups no longer dominate, elders can no longer persuade fellow villagers to act collectively to accomplish certain tasks. This has made villages more dependent on interventions by government actors and programmes to 'get things done'.[16] It has also created opportunities for local political entrepreneurs or 'fixers' to help to 'get things done' by reaching up to government actors at higher levels in the political system. Some of these intermediaries come from disadvantaged backgrounds. Such people have sometimes acquired greater popularity and prestige among villagers than leaders from the former dominant castes. They have also used their new-found influence to benefit people of low traditional status.[17] This makes local politics more equitable, but it also inspires resentment among the landed castes, increasing the likelihood of harsh conflict between the landed groups and those from disadvantaged backgrounds.

---

[16] This emerges vividly from Karanth, Ramaswamy and Hogger (2004).

[17] See Manor (2000) — also published in a longer version in Manor (2004) — and Inbanathan and Gopalappa (2002).

We see, then, that there are two new ways for villagers to access government resources from higher levels in order to 'get things done'. Political 'fixers' are one, and Panchayati Raj institutions are the other. If both prove disappointing — and the Janata Dal–BJP coalition government in the state has recently made this more likely by (probably temporarily) disempowering the panchayats — then discontents at the local level could grow. If they were to become acute, then it might even create opportunities for a different political combination, possibly one led by the BSP, to develop a potent alliance of Dalits and certain other groups. These things seem unlikely, but for the first time political trends in Karnataka suggest that they can (once again) not be ruled out.

Finally, as Bangalore and other urban centres boom, resentments in rural areas, where most voters live, have already begun to rise. Accusations of urban bias against Krishna's Congress government loomed large in the 2004 state election. If urban–rural tensions become more acute, they will test the accommodative skills of party leaders. And together with the other three changes, they could make broadly inclusive political bargains and rainbow coalitions more difficult to construct and sustain. Such bargains have been a major characteristic of Karnataka's recent political history, as this book has demonstrated. We suspect that the trend is strong enough to survive, but it is likely to become more difficult to achieve.

This book, however, is about the recent past, not the future. And that recent past in Karnataka has, in the main, been distinguished by constructive change in politics and state–society relations. It occurred amid petty squabbles, venality, miscalculations, and wilfully destructive actions. Politics everywhere is characterised by these ugly features, which have been extensively documented in our book. But we also need to consider the bigger picture, and when we do, we find extraordinary political imagination and skill being deployed in, for the most part, enlightened ways.

Bibliography

Brass, P. R. 1990. *The New Cambridge History of India: The Politics of India since Independence*. Cambridge: Cambridge University Press.

Census of India, 2001. 2001. *Census of India, 2001: Karnataka*. New Delhi: Government of India.

Crook, R. C. and J. Manor. 1998. *Democracy and Decentralisation in South Asia and West Africa: Participation, Accountability and Performance*. Cambridge: Cambridge University Press.

Frankel, F. and M. S. A. Rao (eds). 1989–1990. *Dominance and State Power in Modern India: Decline of a Social Order*, two vols. Delhi: Oxford University Press.

Inbanathan, A. and D. V. Gopalappa. 2002. 'Fixers, Patronage, "Fixing" and Local Governance in Karnataka', Working paper # 112, Bangalore: Institute for Social and Economic Change.

Jenkins, R. (ed.). 2005. *Regional Reflections: Comparing Politics across Indian States*. Delhi: Oxford University Press.

Karanth, G.K., V. Ramaswamy and R. Hogger. 2004. 'The Threshing Floor Disappears: Rural Livelihood Systems in India', in R. Baumgartner and R. Hogger (eds), *In Search of Sustainable Livelihood Systems: Managing Resources and Change*, pp. 265–74. New Delhi: Sage Publications.

Kochanek, S. A. 1976. 'Mrs Gandhi's Pyramid: The New Congress', in H.C. Hart (ed.), *Indira Gandhi's India: A Political System Reappraised*, pp. 93–124. Boulder: Westview Press.

Kothari, R. 1964. 'The Congress "System" in India', *Asian Survey*, 4(12): 1161–73.

Linz, J. J., A. Stepan and Y. Yadav. 2007. *Democracies in Multinational Societies: India and Other Polities*. Baltimore: John Hopkins University Press.

Manor, J. 1974. 'Kengal Hanumanthaiah in Mysore', *South Asia*, 4(1): 21–38.

———. 1977a. 'The Evolution of Political Arenas and Units of Social Organisation: The Lingayats and Vokkaligas of Princely Mysore', in M. N. Srinivas, S. Seshaiah and V. S. Parthasarthy (eds), *Dimensions of Social Change in India*, pp. 169–87. Bombay: Allied.

———. 1977b. 'The Lesser Leader Amid Political Transformation: The Congress in Mysore in 1941 and 1951', in W. H. Morris-Jones (ed.), *The Making of Politicians: Studies from Africa and Asia*, pp. 140–55. London: Athlone Press.

———. 1977c. *Political Change in an Indian State: Mysore, 1917–1955*. Canberra: Australian National University Press.

Manor, J. 1978. 'Where Congress Survived: Five States in the Indian General Election of 1977', *Asian Survey*, 18(8): 785–803.

———. 1980. 'Pragmatic Progressives in Regional Politics: The Case of Devaraj Urs', *Economic and Political Weekly*, 15 (Annual Number): 198–204.

———. 1981. 'Party Decay and Political Crisis in India', *The Washington Quarterly*, 4(3): 25–40.

———. 1982. 'The Electoral Process Amid Awakening and Decay: The Indian General Election of 1980', in P. Lyon and J. Manor (eds), *Transfer and Transformation: Political Institutions in the New Commonwealth*, pp. 87–116. Leicester: Leicester University Press.

———. 1984. 'Blurring the Lines between Parties and Social Bases: The Emergence of a Janata Government in Karnataka', *Economic and Political Weekly*, 21 August: 1623–32.

———. 1988. 'Seeking Greater Power and Constitutional Change: India's President and the Parliamentary Crisis of 1979', in D. A. Low (ed.), *Constitutional Heads and Political Crises: Commonwealth Episodes, 1945–1985*, pp. 126–41. London: Macmillan.

———. 1989. 'Karnataka: Caste, Class, Dominance and Politics in a Cohesive Society', in F. Frankel and M. S. A. Rao (eds), *Dominance and State Power in Modern India: Decline of a Social Order*, vol.1, pp. 322–61. Delhi: Oxford University Press.

———. 1993a. 'Panchayati Raj and Early Warnings of Disasters', *Economic and Political Weekly*, 22 May: 1019–20.

———. 1993b. *Power, Poverty and Poison: Disaster and Response in an Indian City*. New Delhi: Sage Publications.

———. 1994. 'Political Regeneration in India', in A. Nandy and D.L. Sheth (eds), *The Multiverse of Democracy: Essays in Honour of Rajni Kothari*, pp. 230–41. New Delhi: Sage Publications.

———. 1998. 'Southern Discomfort: The BJP in Karnataka', in T.B. Hansen and C. Jaffrelot (eds), *The BJP and the Compulsions of Indian Politics*, pp. 163–202. Delhi: Oxford University Press.

———. 1999. *The Political Economy of Democratic Decentralization*. Washington: The World Bank.

———. 2000. '"Towel over Armpit": Small-time Political "Fixers" in India's States', *Asian Survey*, 40(5): 816–35.

———. 2001. 'Centre–State Relations', in A. Kohli (ed.), *The Success of India's Democracy*, pp. 78–102. Cambridge: Cambridge University Press.

———. 2004. '"Towel over Armpit": Small-time Political "Fixers" in India's States', in A. Varshney (ed.), *India and the Politics or Developing Countries: Essays in Memory of Myron Weiner*, pp. 60–86. New Delhi: Sage Publications.

Manor, J. 2005. 'The Presidency', in D. Kapur and P. B. Mehta (eds), *Public Institutions in India: Performance and Design*, pp. 105–27. New Delhi: Oxford University Press.

McCormack, W. 1963. 'Lingayats as a Sect', *The Journal of the Royal Anthropological Institute*, 93(1): 59–71.

Melo, M. N. Ng'ethe and J. Manor. Forthcoming. *Against the Odds: Politicians and Institutions in the Struggle against Poverty.*

Morris-Jones, W. H. 1967. 'The Indian Congress Party: A Dilemma of Dominance', *Modern Asian Studies*, 1(2): 109–32.

Reddy, Chinnappa. 1990. *Report of the Karnataka Third Backward Classes Commission*, two vols. Bangalore: Government of Karnataka.

Srinivas, M. N. 1959. 'The Dominant Caste in Rampura', *American Anthropologist*, 61(1): 1–16.

Tandon, B. N. 2006. *PMO Diary II – The Emergency*. Delhi: Konark Publishers.

Weiner, M. 1967. *Party Building in a New Nation: The Indian National Congress.* Chicago: University of Chicago Press.

Index

For Product Safety Concerns and Information please contact our EU
representative GPSR@taylorandfrancis.com
Taylor & Francis Verlag GmbH, Kaufingerstraße 24, 80331 München, Germany

www.ingramcontent.com/pod-product-compliance
Lightning Source LLC
Chambersburg PA
CBHW070717280326
41926CB00087B/2394